P9-EGN-746

Praise for Disrupting Class

Clayton Christensen and colleagues describe how disruptive technologies will personalize and, as a result, revolutionize learning. Every education leader should read this book, set aside their next staff meeting to discuss it, and figure out how they can be part of the improvement wave to come.

— **Tom Vander Ark**, President, X PRIZE Foundation

In Disrupting Class, *Clay Christensen brings to K–12 education the powerful concept of "disruptive innovation" that has radically reshaped thinking about private sector innovation and business change. He considers the glancing impact that technology has had on classrooms, explains why this is so, and what it will take to reengineer our nation's schools for the 21st century.*

— **Frederick M. Hess**, Director of Education Policy Studies at the American Enterprise Institute and author of *Common Sense School Reform*

American school districts are pressed by policymakers demanding achievement, by students wanting relevant learning, by teachers looking for a professionally rewarding career, and by taxpayers hoping for some improvement in productivity. If they are to respond successfully to these challenges, the path Clayton Christensen maps out will be the way.

— **Ted Kolderie**, Senior Associate, Center for Policy Studies

Christensen, Horn, and Johnson argue that the next round of innovation in school reform will involve learning software. While schools have resisted integrating technology for instruction, today's students are embracing technology in their everyday lives. The question is whether the next innovation, truly individualized instruction, will occur inside or outside public education. This book offers promise to education reformers.

— **Kathleen McCartney**, Dean, Harvard Graduate School of Education

Clayton Christensen's advice has helped scores of major businesses. Here he applies to public education his theory about how organizations should respond to disruptive innovation . . . [and] shows boards and superintendents why they, too, need to "run two businesses in tandem," and explains how they can do that.

— **Ron Wolk**, Founder and former editor of *Education Week*

Disrupting Class *gets directly to the point of how $60 billion was spent over the last two decades putting computers and learning software in schools with no effect on student achievement . . . concisely explains how to create learning organizations needed for future generations.*

— **William G. Andrekopoulos**, Superintendent, Milwaukee Public Schools

As a former education policymaker and a continued advisor to education companies, I have felt frustrated by the seeming intractable challenges in transforming our public schools. This book tackles that frustration and proposes a road map and sound advice for how educators and policymakers can leverage innovation to achieve excellence in our schools.

— **Jane Swift**, Acting Governor of Massachusetts from 2001–2003

"A decade ago, Clayton Christensen wrote a masterpiece, The Innovator's Dilemma, *that transformed the way business looks at innovation. Now, he and two collaborators, Michael B. Horn and Curtis W. Johnson, have come up with another, focusing his ground-breaking theories of disruptive innovation on education."*

— **David Gergen**, U.S. Presidential Advisor

"Clayton Christensen's insights just might shake many of us in education out of our complacency and into a long needed disruptive *discourse about really fixing our schools. This will be a welcome change after decades in which powerful calls to action have resulted in only marginal improvements for our nation's school children."*

— **Vicki Phillips**, Director of Education, Gates Foundation

"Full of strategies that are both bold and doable, this brilliant and seminal book shows how we can utilize technology to customize learning. I recommend it most enthusiastically."

—**Adam Urbanski**, President, Rochester (NY) Teachers Association, and vice president, American Federation of Teachers

"Finally we have a book from the business community that gets it. A must read for anyone thinking and worrying about where education should be headed."

— **Paul Houston**, Executive Director, American Association of School Administrators

"After a barrage of business books that purport to 'fix' American education, at last a book that speaks thoughtfully and imaginatively about what genuinely individualized education can be like and how to bring it about."

— **Howard Gardner**, Author of *Five Minds for the Future*

DISRUPTING CLASS

How Disruptive Innovation Will
Change the Way the World Learns

CLAYTON M. CHRISTENSEN
MICHAEL B. HORN • CURTIS W. JOHNSON

New York   Chicago   San Francisco   Lisbon   London
Madrid   Mexico City   Milan   New Delhi
San Juan   Seoul   Singapore
Sydney   Toronto

The **McGraw-Hill** Companies

Copyright © 2011, 2008 by Clayton M. Christensen. All rights reserved. Printed in the United States of America. Except as permitted under the United States Copyright Act of 1976, no part of this publication may be reproduced or distributed in any form or by any means, or stored in a database or retrieval system, without the prior written permission of the publisher.

7 8 9 0   DOC/DOC   9 8 7 6

ISBN 978-0-07-174910-7
MHID 0-07-174910-1

McGraw-Hill books are available at special quantity discounts to use as premiums and sales promotions, or for use in corporate training programs. To contact a representative, please e-mail us at bulksales@mcgraw-hill.com.

Contents

Acknowledgments

"Isn't *Disrupting Class* an unsettling title for a book about the schooling process?" one of our friends recently asked. The title conveys multiple meanings, and that's why we chose it. The principal message is that *disruption*—a powerful body of theory that describes how people interact and react, how behavior is shaped, how organizational cultures form and influence decisions—can usefully frame why our schools have struggled to improve and how to solve these problems. We hope that our readers will come to see through what we present here that disruption is a necessary and overdue chapter for our public schools.

Further, we say disrupting *class* with some intent. For some, class will mean social class. To you we would say that, for too long and in far too many ways, our system of schooling has best served those who hail from homes where parents were themselves well schooled and who support their children with adequate resources and experiences. Class also is the venue in which most of our attempts at education take place. In many ways, what goes on in these classes profoundly affects social class, for good and for ill. Our nation has embarked on a commitment to educate *every* child. No nation has ever sought to do that. The societal stakes in improving our schools are high.

Managing innovation successfully has been the primary focus of my research and writing at Harvard. I'm a teacher, the husband and son of teachers, but I'm not an "expert" in education. I've *practiced* it for sure, but until we began writing this book, I hadn't *studied* education. Nearly a decade ago, however, representatives of a national network of school reformers called Education Evolving—men such as Ted Kolderie, Joe Graba, Ron Wolk, and Curtis Johnson, who had played pioneering roles in the chartered school movement—visited me with a proposal: "Clay, if you'd just stand next to the world of public education and examine it through the lenses of your research on innovation, we bet you could understand more deeply how to improve our schools." Kolderie's arguments about schools' institutional capacity for change and Graba's refrain that, "We simply cannot get all the schools we need by trying to fix the ones we have," compelled me to accept their invitation. I thank these pioneers, who have dedicated their lives to the improvement of our schools, for persuading me to join the movement.

The Harvard Business School is an extraordinary place for teachers to learn because in the case method of instruction, the teacher asks the questions and the students do the teaching. Some brilliant students—including Iris Chen, Trent Kaufman, Dan Dellenbach, Eleanor Laurans, Gunnar Counselman, Allison Sands, Josh Friedman, Emily Sawtell, and Ethan Bernstein—applied what they knew of innovation to the problems of public education and as a result taught their teacher masterfully. Sally Aaron, Will Clark, Scott Anthony, and Michael Horn selflessly postponed their business careers for an extra year after graduation to stay at HBS to work with me to peel off the layers of the onion one by one to discover the root causes of why, despite the talent and energy that so many administrators and teachers have thrown into the fight, our schools improve begrudgingly at best.

I never know how little I know about something until I try to write cogently about it. And I never know how complicated a problem is until I try to distill it and teach its essence to others in a simple (as opposed to simplistic) way. This project thereby quickly taught me that I knew very little about a very complex problem. As we've wrapped our arms around the problem piece by piece, however, patient and forgiving friends have invited us to speak at their seminars and conferences to test the validity and usefulness of what we'd been learning. Others volunteered to criticize drafts of the papers that culminated in this book.

These friends include Dennis Hunter (Applied Materials Inc.); Anoop Gupta and Stephen Coller (Microsoft); Dusty Heuston (Waterford Institute); Tom Vander Ark (X PRIZE Foundation); Gisele Huff (Jaquelin Hume Foundation); Steve Seleznow (Gates Foundation); Gregg Petersmeyer (America's Promise); Christopher Kellett and Thomas Payzant (Boston Public Schools); Justin Cohen and Susan Cheng (District of Columbia Public Schools); Peter Holland and Anne-Marie Mahoney (Belmont Public Schools); Leslie Feinzaig and Tim Huse (Innosight); Utah State Senator Howard Stephenson and Massachusetts Representative Will Brownsberger; Professors Don Deshler (University of Kansas), Paul Hill (University of Washington), and Øystein Fjelstad (Norwegian School of Management); Dean Kathleen McCartney, faculty members Chris Dede, Bob Schwartz, and Karen Mapp, and students such as Leland Anderson at the Harvard Graduate School of Education; Harvard Professor of Government Paul Peterson; Professors Dutch Leonard, Stacey Childress, and Allen Grossman (Harvard Business School); and friends Tracy Kim, Stig Leschly, Matthew Matera, and Marc Prensky all generously gave of their time, talent, and experience to help us improve and refine our ideas.

Accomplished author Sugi Ganeshananthan helped us bring our perspectives on public education together and to life by authoring the vignettes that introduce each chapter in this book. Lisa Stone and JaNeece Thacker, both experienced teachers, managed the administrative details of this project with aplomb. Danny Stern has helped us frame and position our findings for the diverse constituencies we hope this book will reach; Angelina Barlow's artistic eye helped shape the cover; and Mary Glenn and her editorial staff at McGraw-Hill masterfully refined what we had written. We are most grateful to these colleagues for their help.

I authored my first book, *The Innovator's Dilemma*, alone, primarily because the process of competing for tenure in academia almost mandates solitary confinement. I have recruited coauthors for each of the hundreds of articles and books I've subsequently written, however, because I desperately need colleagues who see things differently from the way I do. Researching and writing *Disrupting Class* with my coauthors, Michael Horn and Curtis Johnson, has been an unmitigated blessing to me. Michael is one of the best of thousands of brilliant students I've known through my classes at the Harvard Business School. He has contributed his expertise in writing and in government policy to this project in a humble, articulate, and rigorous way. Curtis Johnson, a former college president, has weathered the political wars of school reform and has been extraordinarily selfless and helpful in shaping the recommendations of this book to be actionable, not naive. I am grateful beyond words for the privilege it has been to work with these good men.

Finally, I give my deepest thanks to my family. My parents, Robert and Verda Mae, not only were wonderful teachers, but instilled in me a deep faith that the glory of God is intelligence and that truth has inestimable eternal value. This gave me a thirst for learning and a motivation to pursue knowledge boldly, without bias or fear, wherever I can find it. My wife, Christine, is the smartest person I have ever known. Thirty-two years ago she put her profession as a high school teacher of English literature on hold in order to become a professional mother to our five magnificent children—Matthew, Ann, Michael, Spencer, and Katie (who at age 16 prepared the index for this book). Christine has inspired them to love learning, to love each other, and to love doing what's right. She is a sterling, world-class teacher. One by one, each of the ideas in this book came home some evening in my head in muddled, half-baked form and returned to Harvard the next morning having been tested and refined through my conversations with Christine and my children. I dedicate this book to them with my deepest admiration, gratitude, and love.

Clayton M. Christensen
Harvard Business School
Boston, Massachusetts

■ ■ ■

I didn't go to Harvard Business School with the intention of writing a book. On the contrary, I attended so that I could move *away* from the world of writing. But at business school, I encountered the best teacher I've ever had in a class that transformed how I view the world. The teacher was Clayton Christensen, and the course was about his theories of disruptive innovation—theories that explain how the real world works in business and beyond. When the opportunity arose to coauthor a book with Clay on a topic as important as K–12 public education, the decision to return to the world of writing was an easy one. The two years that followed have taught and given me more than I could have imagined. I did not just write a book on education and continue to learn from an extraordinary teacher. I gained a mentor, I have had the opportunity to apply theories that make sense to an area of national need that is ripe for it, and I have grown from Clay's friendship and example. To him I owe eternal gratitude.

I also learned a tremendous amount from my other coauthor, Curtis Johnson, in these two years. His encouragement, knowledge, and work were vital to finishing this book.

Working with him was a privilege. Curtis's colleagues at Education Evolving were also instrumental in making this project possible, and I thank them for their insights and support.

I would be remiss in writing a book about public education if I did not give thanks to my public school teachers and fellow classmates at Wood Acres, Pyle, and Walt Whitman High School—special thanks to Ms. Brebbia, Mrs. Chism, Stuart Shifrin, Chris Allen, and Jan Bowman.

Beyond Clay, I have been lucky in life to have two caring mentors on whom I continue to rely—Charley Ellis and David Gergen. There has never been a time when they didn't have time for me. Charley, you were correct: Each of us has a book we're waiting to write.

I spent the first year of this project working for Clay as a Harvard research associate. Thank you to the staff, faculty, and students there, in particular, Stacey Childress and Tony Mayo, as well as my Gallatin RA crew—Chris Van Keuren, Terry Heymann, Tracy Manty, and Renee Kim—who kept work and life fun.

In the second year of writing this book, Jason Hwang and I cofounded Innosight Institute, a think tank, to apply the theories of disruptive innovation to solve social sector problems. Jason has become a great friend and a source of counsel. Thank you also to our friends at Innosight LLC for being a source of ideas, housing the institute, and feeding us every now and then.

Thank you to Clay's assistant, my friend Lisa Stone, for what she does for Clay and for the help she provided in making this book happen.

Thank you to Sugi Ganeshanathan, a close friend since middle school. Not only did she help us with the vignettes, but as a recently published book author, she also helped me know what to expect along the way.

There are countless other people and friends who were vital in this book. Among them, a special thank you to Gisele Huff, who has been a guiding light on this project.

I owe my biggest thanks to my loving family. I am fortunate to have all of them. Thank you to Grammy and Papa. The opportunities and unconditional love you provide have been integral to who I am today. Also, Andy, Barbara, Jeffrey, Susan, and Eric—thank you for always being there.

To my immediate family: I love you all. To my brothers: You are my best friends. Steven, you have grown from the baby brother whose smile filled me with sunshine to my taller peer whose same smile fills me with strength. Jonathan, I tried to be your "school teacher" when you were young, but you quickly surpassed me, and it is I who have had the privilege of learning from you. Mom and Dad, you are my source of inspiration, my heroes, and my role models. I dedicate this to you.

Michael B. Horn
Innosight Institute
Watertown, Massachusetts

∎∎∎

In consulting with people about what we were writing, I got an earful of welcome advice—and two recurring reservations. First, just mentioning that the book was rooted in *theory* raised eyebrows and red flags for some. Too thick and tedious, they said. But far from being the dry desert that only committed academics would walk through, Clay Christensen's theory, the product of a long and rigorous journey across multiple enterprises and industries, breathes real life into explaining why schools get only incrementally better and how the schooling process—learning—could leap forward in quality and results.

Second, people reminded me that public education is *different*, nothing like other industries. Of course it is different. Public schools are awash in legal constraints and operate in an inherently political system in which state policymakers, while bowing in many respects to local prerogatives, determine the standards, the fundamental rules, the resources, and the measures of evaluation. But, as we hope you will see, the theory holds—explaining today's conditions, outlining tomorrow's promise.

We respect the nation's push for standards and account-ability and the effort over the past decade to open up the supply side through chartering laws. But it is a mistake to confuse either the permission to create new schools or setting rigorous standards with learning. What matters is what happens in *class*, whether physical or virtual.

I am forever indebted to Clay Christensen for luring me into this project. Having once been a teacher and later the head of a policy research organization that gave birth to several Minnesota education reforms, this quest felt personal from the beginning, something I wanted to work on. But Clay made this experience a memorable intellectual journey. The most casual conversation could instantly turn into a seminar in which something that seemed simple became complex and then surprisingly comprehensible. And no one with a chance to observe him could fail to notice the attention he gives his students—outranked only by his unflagging devotion to his family and faith. He is the teacher, the colleague, the friend we all wish for and rarely find.

And then there was the colleague who made it all come together. Without Michael Horn's steady and dogged efforts to give order to the ideas through first drafts, adapt when the sequence of chapters made a radical shift, chase down all those references and details, and mediate the final words on each page from the editorial avalanches descending on him from the two of us—there would be no book. I am proud to have been able to work with him.

Clay has already mentioned the national network of Edu-cation Evolving. The work of founders Ted Kolderie and Joe Graba, along with director Jon Schroeder, had much to do with inspiring this book. Kolderie's 2004 book *Creating the Capacity for Change* (cited in chapter notes) about the insti-tutional capacity for change set the stage for understanding why things are the way they are in U.S. schools. Kim Ferris-

Berg regularly sent fresh insights about what today's students are thinking and saying, and Mark Van Ryzin shared his pioneering research on school typologies. Ron Wolk, the retired founding editor of *Education Week*, was a steady source of ideas, information, and encouragement. Robert Wedl added insights from his time as a commissioner of education. And Peter Hutchinson, an author and a consultant to a wide range of governments, offered a reality check reflecting on his years as a superintendent of schools in a large city.

My appreciation also extends to my Citistates Group partners, Neal Peirce and Farley Peters, who understood what working on this book would do to our regular schedule of work and made accommodations time after time.

The deepest thanks go without question to my family—to my wife Carol and the six children we share—who, in addition to understanding what researching and writing can do to a normal schedule, granted me the luxury of their unfailing and unconditional love and support.

Curtis W. Johnson
Citistates Group
Minneapolis, Minnesota

Introduction

We have high hopes for our schools. Although each of us might articulate these hopes differently, four seem common to many of us. We summarize these aspirations as:

1. Maximize human potential.
2. Facilitate a vibrant, participative democracy in which we have an informed electorate that is capable of not being "spun" by self-interested leaders.
3. Hone the skills, capabilities, and attitudes that will help our economy remain prosperous and economically competitive.
4. Nurture the understanding that people can see things differently—and that those differences merit respect rather than persecution.[1]

We're not doing very well in the journey toward these aspirations. Weakening churches and families must shoulder their share of the blame for our backsliding and wheel-

1

spinning. But most of us wish schools were playing a much more effective role in our efforts to move society toward goals like these.

Why do schools struggle to improve? Everyone has a theory. One is that *schools are underfunded.* If this is the problem, the answer must be more state appropriations, higher local property taxes, and additional fees from parents. Civil rights groups file lawsuits claiming that states that deny schools adequate funding are ignoring their constitutional obligations. And a 2006 Gallup poll suggests that the public favors higher compensation for teachers.

But is money the cause or the cure? The U.S. public education system spends more per student than all but a few other countries, and yet, on average, its students often perform at or below the level of those in other economically advanced countries. Over the past three decades, real spending per student has doubled without a commensurate gain in achievement. And across school districts, spending per student does not necessarily track performance. Just compare two schools in Kentucky: In 2004, Portland Elementary School in Jefferson County spent three times as much per pupil as did Carlisle County Elementary School. Yet Carlisle County, which has a similar demographic makeup to Portland,scored 26 percent better on the state accountability index.[2] This is not to say that money does not matter. But if money or the lack of it by itself explained why the struggles persist, we would not see the anomalies across nations, within Kentucky, or, indeed, across many other districts in the United States. Other forces must also be in play.

Perhaps there's a problem because there *aren't enough computers in the classroom.*[3] When the push to add computers in classrooms started in the mid-1980s, this now-common tool of work and play was just beginning to penetrate every sector of society. Many people predicted that computers would revolutionize the world, and they viewed not having computers in schools as an injustice.

Similar to spending overall, spending on computers in schools has increased dramatically. By 1995, the average public school in the United States had 72 computers available to support instruction. By 2003, this average had nearly doubled to 136. And whereas in 1998 there was an average of 12 students for every computer with Internet access, by 2003, that number was down to nearly 4. If the addition of computers to classrooms were a cure, there would be evidence of it by now. There is not. Test scores have barely budged. There must be a better explanation than more computers and technology.

Another camp *blames the students and their parents*. Educators often complain about students who are uninterested and not ready to learn or parents who do not monitor homework or show up for conferences. This argument resonates with the public. They see kids on street corners with their hats in a backwards pose and their trousers dragging and droopy. Indeed, just to exacerbate the problem facing schools, the number of students from minority backgrounds, who have historically performed least well in U.S. schools, has skyrocketed in recent years, from just over 20 percent in the 1970s to around 35 percent today. And the population of those who do not speak English at home, a population that has also underperformed historically, has also climbed, from just under 10 percent before 1980 to around 20 percent today.[4]

These factors certainly make a school's job harder. But there are anomalies to this generalized explanation that suggest that this is not the root cause of schools' struggles either. Many schools where these "least promising" children dominate the enrollment have comparable results to schools with more affluent populations. Take the example of Montgomery County Public Schools in Maryland, which has divided its schools into two categories: red-zone schools, which are those highly affected by poverty, and green-zone schools, which are not. Ever since the district identified the red-zone schools and began treating them differently from their green-zone counterparts, performance by minority students in the red-zone schools has soared to the point where it now approaches that of the predominately white students in green-zone schools.[5] Furthermore, the entering quality of students tells us nothing about how the schools themselves are operating once the students are in the classroom. There has to be a better explanation than simply blaming the students.

Could it be that the *U.S. teaching model is simply broken compared to other models in other countries?* Picture a school in which in every classroom, the teacher stands at the front of the room and lectures all day at the students. The students never speak, and even if they do not understand a concept, they never ask for help. The teacher just keeps lecturing. Exams test rote memorization. Now contrast this with a class in which the teaching methods are more varied and the environment more energetic. Yes, the teacher lectures, but students frequently raise their hands to participate in discussions. Other times students do work while the teacher walks around and offers a helping hand. And at still other times, students work on fun projects in groups.

Which school is better? Most say the latter one is. What is interesting, however, is that the former school is representative of the traditional classroom model in much of Asia, while the latter more typifies the U.S. style.[6] Based on this, we would expect the students from Asian classrooms to perform more poorly than those in the United States. But, on average, the Asian students actually score far higher on math assessments than the U.S. students do. Paradoxically, many of these Asian schools have been adopting many of the U.S. schools' practices. So there must be a better explanation than a broken teaching model.

Then the *teachers unions must be the problem.* Many make the argument that unions force school districts to put a higher priority on the needs of the professionals working in the system than on the students' needs. If we could free the schools from the unions' stranglehold, the logic goes, the schools would better serve their students.

Like all explanations, this may be true to a degree, but as the definitive explanation, it does not hold up. The Montgomery County Public Schools district, for example, has a strong teachers union, whereas the Charleston County, South Carolina, district has no teachers union. And yet, students in Montgomery County Public Schools outperform those from Charleston.[7] Indeed, some chartered schools in the United States, which are free from the constraints of teachers unions, perform no better—and sometimes perform even worse—than the unionized schools.* So solving the union problem may not solve the schools' problem.

So if too little money, too few computers, uninterested or unprepared students (and parents), a broken teaching paradigm, and strong unions individually are not the root cause of the U.S. public schools' struggles, might it be that *they all are conspiring collectively to constrain* the United States? Of course. But all these issues are at work in other nations' schools as well—and yet the evidence is that many of them obtain better results than we do in the United States.

As the evidence discredits the common explanations for the educational struggles one by one, another accounting has more recently emerged: *The way we measure schools' performance is fundamentally flawed.* This, of course, is also true. Even the best measures are an approximation of the underlying reality— for every country's schools.[8]

But consider this observation, which goes beyond the hotly contested validity of test scores. One of the authors of this book,

---

* In this book we use the term *chartered schools* rather than the commonly used *charter schools*. We are referring to the same phenomenon, but we use the different language in reaction to the fallacy of the common expression, which expresses as a compound noun what is an adjective and a noun. Calling a school a *charter school* implies a typology that does not exist. The notion of charter refers only to the manner in which a new school was created. Indeed, schools that were created through charters today reflect a rather full range of typologies—some are quite traditional in their practices, whereas others are organized around student projects or are virtual schools with no physical structure. So although it will strike some as odd, we prefer the word "chartered" because it is a more accurate characterization of the shift in public policy that began in the early 1990s.

Clayton Christensen, has frequented Silicon Valley's corridors and cubicles for much of his professional life. Thirty years ago, people born and educated in the United States largely occupied those workspaces. Today, a stunning proportion of the people in these offices and cubicles are Israeli, Indian, and Chinese. Those educated in U.S. schools are losing share—and it's not because the United States is uniquely unable to measure true academic achievement. The United States has kept its technological edge in the world not because its public schools are sending the best potential technologists to U.S. colleges. The United States is clinging to its advantage because it has continued to be a magnet for the best talent in the world. But this, too, has begun to change.[9]

If the common explanations do not explain the problem, what is the reason for the educational woes?

❖ THE CAUSES OF EDUCATIONAL MALAISE

The purpose of this book is to dig beneath the sorts of surface explanations summarized above to expose more fundamental root causes for why schools struggle to improve. Upon that basic foundation, we then construct a set of recommendations to resolve those problems. Our methods for reaching these conclusions are unique. Most books on the topic of improving schools have reached their conclusions by studying schools. In contrast, our field of scholarship is innovation. Our approach in researching and writing this book has been to stand *outside* the public education industry and put our innovation research on almost like a set of lenses to examine the industry's problems from this different perspective. The ability of these lenses to shed new light on complicated problems has been proven in contexts ranging from national defense to semiconductors, from health care to retailing, and from automobiles to financial services to telecommunications. We hope that this novel approach to the problems of public education will prove to yield comparably innovative insights.

So let's diagnose the fundamental problem. If other countries have these same factors at work in their schools as we do in the United States, why is it that so many of their students out-perform U.S. students?

Motivation is the catalyzing ingredient for every successful innovation. The same is true for learning. We all know that becoming a great athlete or a great pianist requires an extraor-dinary amount of consistent work. The hours of time required to train the brain to fire the synapses in the correct ways and thus hone the necessary muscle memory and thinking required is no different from that needed to learn to read and process information or think through math and science problems. Motivating customers to do something is a problem that every organization faces. It is not unique to education.

Motivation can be extrinsic or intrinsic. *Extrinsic motivation* is that which comes from outside the task. For example, a person might learn to do something not because she found the task itself stimulating or interesting, but because learning it would give her access to something else she wants. *Intrinsic motivation* is when the work itself stimulates and compels an individual to stay with the task because the task by itself is inherently fun and enjoyable. In this situation, were there no outside pressures, an intrinsically motivated person might still very well decide to tackle this work.[10]

When there is high extrinsic motivation for someone to learn something, schools' jobs are easier. They do not have to teach material in an intrinsically motivating way because simply offering the material is enough. Students will choose to master it because of the extrinsic pressure. When there is no extrinsic motivation, however, things become trickier. Schools need to create intrinsically engaging methods for learning.

Consider this example. When Japanese companies were developing their world-class manufacturing clout and passing U.S. companies in the 1970s and 1980s, a common expla-nation was that four times as many Japanese college students were studying math, science, and engineering than were U.S. students—despite the fact that Japan had only 40 percent of the population of the United States. These scientists and engineers, many concluded, were responsible for Japan's economic ascendancy, which was widely seen as a threat to the U.S. economy.[11]

As Japan reached prosperity, an interesting thing happened, however. The percentage of students that graduated with science and engineering degrees declined. Why did this happen? The answer has little to do with the schools themselves, which did not change significantly. Prosperity was the culprit. When Japan was emerging from the ashes of World War II, there was a clear extrinsic motivation that encouraged students to study subjects like science and engineering that would help lift them out of poverty and reward them with a generous wage. As the country and its families prospered, however, the external pressure diminished. Some people who are wired to enjoy science and engineering in the way schools traditionally teach it—and therefore are intrinsically motivated—or those who have other extrinsic motivations in play still study them. But many no longer need to endure studying subjects that are not fun for them. The same downward trend is now beginning in Singapore and Korea. As their economies have prospered, a smaller portion of their students are studying math and engineering because the extrinsic motivation has disappeared—and there is precious little intrinsic motivation, given the way these subjects are taught.

Let's take one more example. As we said earlier, one of the authors of this book, Clayton Christensen, knows many of the "founders" of Silicon Valley well. These men and women are world-class engineers, mathematicians, and scientists. Few of the children of these titans, however, have studied these subjects. Instead, they've chosen fields in the humanities and social sciences. With prosperity in the family, one extrinsic motivation to study these subjects is gone. As the U.S. president John Adams famously wrote:

I must study politics and war that my sons may have liberty to study mathematics and philosophy. My sons ought to study mathematics and philosophy, geography, natural history, naval architecture, navigation, commerce, and agriculture in order to give their children a right to study painting, poetry, music, architecture, statuary, tapestry, and porcelain.

Adams was on to something. As a developing country develops an industrial-based economy, studying science, math, and engineering offers big rewards that ensure students an escape from poverty. When the same country achieves stability and prosperity, students have more freedom to study subjects that they find fun and intrinsically motivating.

Oddly, therefore, prosperity can be an enemy to the motivation needed to study topics that are not taught in intrinsically motivating ways.[12] This is a key reason why technological advantage shifted first to Japan and is now shifting to China and India. Because of a variety of cultural, economic, and societal factors, the United States' schools start from a disadvantage compared to many of their international counterparts, where there is far more extrinsic motivation present in society. We also note that in many developing countries, studying hard and mastering science and engineering in school does not necessarily result in prosperity—at least not yet. In those countries, there isn't much of an extrinsic reason to endure school either.[13]

Prosperity isn't the only factor, of course. As we explain in Chapter 7, the primary job or fundamental driver among every student is to feel successful, and all students are motivated to do that. Schools as currently constructed do not nail this job, however, for many students, including many lower-income students in prosperous societies, in part because there are complicated cultural and familial influences at work as well. The famous Coleman report (1966) made this argument. It showed that family background was the factor of greatest importance in determining how a student performed in school in the United States. A conclusion is that schools cannot be expected to carry society toward the objectives we list at the outset of the chapter. Nonetheless, schools must be a significant, positive force in this direction, and if they are tailored to nail students' jobs, they can certainly improve.[14]

Schooling can and should be an intrinsically motivating experience. The questions are why this often has not been the case, and how to resolve these problems. Explaining why and how is the purpose of this book.

❖ SOURCES OF SCHOOLS' STRUGGLES

The following chapters summarize what we have seen by standing outside the public education industry and examining it through the lenses of the theories of disruptive innovation. These theories have emerged from two decades of research. These are theories whose applicability is not limited to specific industries or to for-profit enterprises only. As you'll see in the following chapters, they shed considerable light on the challenge of making learning intrinsically motivating for each student. From this diagnosis of the root causes, a promising path emerges that offers a way forward for educators from around the world to ensure that each individual student learns.

Although the examples in this book are largely from the United States, we believe that the lessons apply to contexts around the world. In fact, some of our recommendations already are beginning to be implemented in many developing countries.

Many of the theories on innovation have emerged from our own research, but we are also indebted to many other scholars and practitioners for much of what follows. Here is a chapter-by-chapter preview of the book:

Chapter 1: Every student learns in a different way. This idea—that students have different learning needs—is one of the cornerstones of this book. A key step toward making school intrinsically motivating is to customize education to match the way each child best learns. As we explain in this first chapter, schools' interdependent architectures force them to standardize the way they teach and test. Standardization clashes with the need for customization in learning. To introduce customization, schools need to move away from the monolithic instruction of batches of students toward a modular, student-centric approach using software as an important delivery vehicle.

Chapter 2: What gives us confidence that schools are able to make the shift to a student-centric approach? A primer on the theory of disruptive innovation reveals that schools in the United States have in fact constantly improved. Society just keeps moving the goalposts on schools by changing the definition of quality and asking schools to take on new jobs. Even in these new landscapes, where most successful organizations fail, schools have adapted remarkably well.

If you aren't familiar with the theory of disruptive innovation, Chapter 2 will prove helpful to your understanding the rest of the book. Disruption is a positive force. It is the process by which an innovation transforms a market whose services or products are complicated and expensive into one where simplicity, convenience, accessibility, and affordability characterize the industry.

Chapter 3: Given the present interdependent curricular architecture of most schools, what might allow them to migrate to a more modular, student-centric approach? Technology presents a promising path. We broadly define technology as the processes by which an organization transforms inputs of labor, capital, materials, and information into products and services of greater value. Hence, all firms, including schools, employ a range of technologies. Some of these are *student-centric technologies* that can mediate the clash caused by the need to standardize the way schools teach and test versus the need to customize how students learn. In its most common manifestation, student-centric technology comprises a computer with software, which can tailor itself to a student's specific type of intelligence or learning style. An individual tutor would be another type of student-centric technology. *Monolithic technology*, in contrast, employs a single instructional style for all students. A teacher lecturing a classroom of students, all of whom use the same textbook, is the most common monolithic technology in education. But computers whose software tries to teach all students in the same way would also be a monolithic technology.

The question is: why haven't schools been able to march down this path? After all, they have spent upwards of $60 billion over the last two decades placing computers in schools. The answer is that schools have done what all organizations are inclined to do when instituting a new technology. They have "crammed" the new technologies into their existing structure, rather than allowing the disruptive technology to take root in a new model and allow that to grow and change how they operate.

Chapter 4: How then can schools successfully implement computer-based learning? The key is to let it compete against nonconsumption at the outset, where the alternative to taking a class from the computer is nothing at all. We explain what this means in this chapter, as well as offer examples of how schools are already doing this and how they might do it even more successfully.

Chapter 5: Disruption is a two-stage process. We show in Chapter 4 that schools are already implementing computer-based learning. But to move to full student-centric learning, we will need to incubate many of these technologies outside the K–12 public education system. Disruption and student-centric technology must first solve important problems outside the traditional classroom before they transform learning in schools. In so doing, they will, over time, likely fashion an entirely new commercial system in education. We give some educated guesses in this chapter at what this might look like.

Chapter 6: The first five chapters form an interdependent argument about how to migrate from monolithic methods of instruction to student-centric technologies in the K–12 years—something we believe is crucial to enable children to realize their highest potential. There is an overwhelming body of evidence, however, that starting at age 5 in kindergarten is much too late. Indeed, our experiences in the first 18 months of life largely shape our intellectual capacities. And much of the self-confidence that buoys us up or bogs us down through the rest of our lives is essentially in place by age 5. Addressing these issues is itself a book-length project, but as the movement to expand to universal pre-K grows, it's something important to address. In Chapter 6, we take a 10,000-foot view of these challenges and evaluate the possible efficacy of certain solutions that have been proposed.

Chapter 7: The challenge of student motivation is a pervasive and increasingly problematic barrier to improving students' learning. As we mentioned earlier, motivating one's customers is a problem every organization faces. In this chapter, we reframe this problem by asking what jobs are students trying to do in their lives—and the insights may surprise you. Answering this question shows us that students are actually highly motivated—but also that schools are competing for students' time against many other opportunities that aren't related to education and, in many cases, are falling short.

Chapter 8: Here we explain why the standard research approach in collegiate schools of education has not provided clear guidance to educators. This chapter suggests a way forward for education research in the field to improve predictability in education.

Chapter 9: Why do solutions that transform one organization prove impossible to implement in another? Rarely is the root cause that employees in one institution are eager to improve and solve problems, whereas those in the other passively embrace mediocrity. Most often it relates to the willingness or ability of the managers in the different organizations to create organizational structures that enable new solutions to be formulated and implemented successfully. In this chapter, we apply theories from our research to offer a managerial tool kit to school leaders and policymakers as an aid in implementing these changes and specifically talk about the need for autonomy, separation, and the use of power tools in setting up new schools—like chartered and pilot schools—and structures to solve pressing problems in education.

The road to realizing our highest hopes for our schools is not an easy one. But with breakthroughs occurring every day in understanding how children learn and how they build intellectual capacity, there is a great opportunity to make strides in the years ahead, provided we do so with an understanding of the root causes of why schools have struggled so much. If we embark upon the promising path we outline in this book, we can make schooling intrinsically motivating and help our children maximize their individual potential to realize their most daring dreams.

To start us down this path, we begin with a fictional story set in a struggling high school in California. This opening vignette introduces us to the central characters in a story that runs through the book at the beginning of each chapter.

NOTES

1. We thank our friend Dennis Hunter for helping us articulate these widely shared goals. Over the past few years of researching this book, many people have expressed to us high hopes for our schools. Our list here is certainly not collectively exhaustive or a scientific approach to capturing these aspirations, but it represents an attempt by us to capture the spirit and intent for what many of us hope our schools will help those in the next generation attain.

2. Like Portland, over 50 percent of Carlisle's students are on free/reduced lunch.

3. Although most educators have moved beyond making this argument after seeing its limitations, many politicians and pundits still put forth this point, and many polls capture the feeling from the public that investment in computers is vital for a school. Indeed, as we suggest in this book, computers can play an important part in helping our schools improve, but it matters far more how they are used and implemented than just the mere addition of them.

4. "Elementary/Secondary Education: Table 5-1," *Participation in Education*, National Center for Education Statistics, http://nces.ed.gov/programs/

coe/2007/section1/table.asp?tableID=667. "Elementary/Secondary Education: Table 6-1," *Participation in Education*, National Center for Education Statistics, http://nces.ed.gov/programs/coe/2007/section1/table.asp?tableID=668.

5. For example, the percentage of African American and Hispanic kindergartners in the red zone reading at or above the end-of-year reading benchmark now nearly matches that of white students in the green zone, up from a significant gap just five years ago. Montgomery County Public Schools presentation, Harvard Public Education Leadership Conference, June 20, 2007.

6. Michael Alison Chandler, "Asian Educators Looking to Loudoun for an Edge," *The Washington Post*, March 19, 2001, p. B01. Also from Clayton M. Christensen's firsthand observations.

7. We understand that private school enrollment ratios factor in here. They are quite high in Charleston among white students, although this plays into the "bad-student argument." Still, the anomalies show that the existence of teachers unions cannot be argued as the crucial pivot point for the success of schools.

8. To some extent all countries face the same problems the United States does. First, no country has agreed upon the magic all-encompassing "purpose of education"; while the United States frets over low test scores, the Japanese wonder if their rote learning teaching style stifles creativity. Maybe U.S. students' willingness to question authority and ask "why" is a positive that tests just do not capture. Second, no nation has been able to satisfactorily educate each and every one of its citizens.

9. An article in *The Economist* adds weight to this observation. "America's high-tech industries are powered by foreign brains," it notes. "Almost a third of Silicon Valley start-ups since 1995 were founded by Indians or Chinese. They also power great U.S. universities, particularly the science departments. About 40 percent of people earning Ph.D.s in computer science and engineering are foreign-born." But as we note, America's attraction to foreign-born talent is waning. *The Economist*'s article talks about how U.S. immigration laws create long waiting times for talented workers to enter the country and, consequently, turn them off. Furthermore, other countries— "including Australia, Canada, Britain, Germany, and even France"— are clamoring for this talent. "At the same time the Indian and Chinese economies are booming. . . . Indians and Chinese were once willing to put up with any humiliation for a chance of a career in the United States. Now they have more and more choices back home." "American Idiocracy: Why the Immigration System Needs Urgent Fixing," *The Economist*, March 24–30, 2007, p. 40.

10. To capture what social scientists call the "discretionary effort" of students, people are giving more attention to the sources of motivation. Mihaly Csikszentmihalyi, a psychology professor at Claremont Graduate University and

a leading proponent of positive psychology, is best known for writing about the "flow." In an interview with *Wired* magazine for its September 2006 issue, Csikszentmihalyi described "flow" as "being completely involved in an activity for its own sake. The ego falls away. Time flies. Every action, movement, and thought follows inevitably from the previous one, like playing jazz. Your whole being is involved, and you're using your skills to the utmost." This concept is another way of thinking about intrinsic motivation. See "Go With the Flow," *Wired*, September 2006, issue 4.09.

11. C. M. Christensen, T. Craig, and S. Hart, "The Great Disruption," *Foreign Affairs*, vol. 80, March/April 2001, pp. 80–95.

12. In a report, parents and students note that they don't see the relevance of these higher-level topics and skills for their own lives. Public Agenda, which produced the report, noted that this mirrored national results. Interestingly, parents and students were more motivated to push for these subjects if it would benefit them in the college application process. See Alison Kadlec and Will Friedman with Amber Ott, *Important, but Not for Me: Parents and Students in Kansas and Missouri Talk about Math, Science, and Technology Education*, Public Agenda, 2007. Summarized in Meris Stansbury, "Parents, Kids Don't See Need for Math, Science Skills," *eSchool News*, September 21, 2007.

There are more cards stacked against producing more U.S. scientists, according to several reports. A *Chronicle of Higher Education* article cites evidence that the "long periods of training, a shortage of academic jobs, and intense competition for research grants" cause many of America's brightest students to bypass careers in science. More and more Ph.D.s enter into temporary postdoctoral positions, as opposed to full-time jobs, and therefore their job security and economic futures are uncertain. Many undergraduates see the problem early and opt out of the sciences while they're still in college. Others jump ship for other opportunities in commercial fields. Richard Monastersky, "The Real Science Crisis: Bleak Prospects for Young Researchers," *The Chronicle of Higher Education*, September 21, 2007.

As another article says, "Many qualified Americans shun science because, far more than the drum beaters let on, science can be a risky, unrewarding career choice. When it comes to agricultural picking and stooping, our foreign reliance is easily understood even without a rudimentary grasp of economics: The pay and working conditions are so miserable that only impoverished foreigners see the chance of a step up. . . . The reliance on foreigners to fill U.S. science classrooms and staff labs and science and engineering faculties is similarly clear." He goes on to detail the career choice for someone thinking about law school with its $100,000 salary in three years or a Ph.D. with its pay of $40,000—maybe—in five to seven years. "For the many young foreign students from developing countries who seek promising careers, science in America is extremely attractive compared to the choices back home." Dan Greenberg, "No Mystery Why Americans Shun Science Careers," *The Chronicle of Higher Education*, December 17, 2007.

13. In a study in Usenge, Kenya, researchers tested children's ability to adapt to their indigenous environment. What they found was that students had great knowledge of how to survive in their climate—how to recognize and overcome parasitic illnesses, for example. Children's scores on tests to measure this were inversely correlated with tests that measured more academic knowledge, such as that taught in schools. They did well in the former and poorly in the latter. In Robert Sternberg's words, "From the standpoint of an academic test, the rural Kenyan children would not look very bright. But in fact, they have learned knowledge that was important in their own cultural context. . . . To these children in rural Kenya, however, the intelligence needed for survival and success in life, in general, may not be the same as the intelligence needed for success in school, and the former may be more important to them than the latter." In other words, the children would learn what they had an outside motivation and need to learn because it was more relevant to their immediate lives. Robert J. Sternberg, "Who Are the Bright Children? The Cultural Context of Being and Acting Intelligent," *Educational Researcher*, vol. 36, no. 3, 2007, pp. 149–150.

14. There is a long-running debate on this. For one side of it, see Richard Rothstein's *Class and Schools*, which makes the argument that schools can't fix these problems alone. The country needs policy changes in health care, improvements in early childhood care/education, and so on. A book by Abigail and Stephan Thernstrom titled, *No Excuses: Closing the Racial Gap in Learning*, takes the other side. It hypothesizes that there are some schools, like the Knowledge Is Power Program (KIPP) and others, that do not have any excuses—in other words, they don't blame health care or poor parenting—and they do what Rothstein says is impossible and turn really poor students into high achievers. Rothstein addresses this concept specifically in his book with a multifaceted response. First, he says that a few anomalies do not prove anything. He presents research on the KIPP children, who are supposedly the worst-performing and poorest children in the surrounding public schools. He polls teachers from surrounding schools, however, and finds that they are, in fact, sending the children with the highest potential. This and the fact that KIPP forces parents to be involved—just the very fact that they have to apply and sign a contract indicates that they are more invested than the average parent—means that to Rothstein, this is not a fair sample. He also cites that KIPP is a middle school, and there is no evidence that its students attend college or succeed in the long run at greater rates. He also cites AVID (Advancement Via Individual Determination) and

says that you cannot use it as an example that the Thernstrom argument is possible because children are interviewed and those with the highest potential, despite poor grades, are taken in. See Richard Rothstein, *Class and Schools: Using Social, Economic, and Educational Reform to Close the Black-White Achievement Gap* (New York: Teachers College, Columbia University, 2004). Abigail Thernstrom and Stephan Thernstrom, *No Excuses: Closing the Racial Gap in Learning* (New York: Simon & Schuster, 2003).

Randall Circle High School

Robert James is one of some 2,000 students at Randall Circle High School in southern California. Today, when the school bell rings at 7:15 a.m. to indicate the 10-minute warning for the start of class, the skinny white junior is dawdling in the parking lot. Talking to soccer buddies, he tries to avoid the thought of the chemistry class that awaits him. He kicks at some loose gravel. He'd rather just get to practice. Rob used to be a punctual kid, and he used to like science, but these days, the thought of Mr. Alvera's chemistry class makes him want to run away from the school's bright blue doors.

In fact, it's not just Rob. Most of the soccer players dawdle in the sunshine. Still, conscience pulls him toward the entrance when he spots the stern-faced new principal, Dr. Stephanie Allston, aiming a look in their direction. Rob slouches in past the administrator and dodges eye contact beneath the brim of his Boston Red Sox hat. He's pretty sure that Mr. Alvera is on the verge of reporting him to the administration for his poor performance, and he doesn't know what to do about it. His engineer dad just might flip out if he hears about it. He wonders if he can get his friend and neighbor Maria to work with him during study hall again. She's twice as helpful as Mr. Alvera anyway, although she seems to be late this morning, too.

Rob thinks Stephanie Allston is watching him, but the grey-suited woman leaning against the blue paint has what she considers bigger problems: she's the new hired gun at a school teetering on the edge of failure, thanks to poor results on state exams. Known for her success at a nearby middle school, she's not worried about Rob being in over his head. Allston's worried that she's in over her own head. She cringes when she thinks about her first encounter with Carlos Alvera, the chemistry teacher who told her, "I teach it. I don't have the resources to do much more, but that's worked for 25 years." If only every student were like Academics Bowl champ Maria Solomon. The petite black junior grins at Allston as she rushes inside just in time for class, her red backpack bouncing under her ponytail of braids. The bell trills, and Allston smiles back at her. Minus Maria, she's got 2,000 problems waiting inside for her. And to think she could have been a lawyer.

Chapter 1

Why Schools Struggle to Teach Differently When Each Student Learns Differently

Maria slides into her seat two seconds before the bell rings and curses her alarm clock. She's already behind. Class starts practically before the bell rings because Mr. Alvera likes to cram the period full with as much information as possible. Maria glances over the handout waiting on her desk—it's a bullet-point recap of last night's reading, which she digested easily. She shoots a glance over at Rob and mimes the gesture of taking off his hat. Catching her eye, Rob complies before Mr. Alvera has a chance to say anything.

Rob tugs a hand through his mussed dark red hair and pulls out a notebook as the chemistry teacher explains the formula for the thermodynamic behavior of a gas. He tries to focus on the scrawled chalk that says "$pV = nRT$"—and diligently copies it into his notebook, as though that will change the fact that he doesn't get it. Mr. Alvera has spent some extra time trying to help him out, but there's limited time for that, and Mr. Alvera only seemed able to explain the same concepts in the same ways—just slower and louder. If Rob's grades keep slipping, Mr. Alvera is required to report him. And if that happens before tomorrow night's soccer game, he suspects he'll be riding the bench. But he's got soccer down: he actually feels worse about the fact that after spending last night poring over the textbook, he still doesn't get the concept.

Across the aisle, Maria sits up and raises her hand to ask a question. "Using $pV = nRT$, how would I find the density of a gas at standard temperature and pressure?"

Beside her, Rob's soccer teammate, second-stringer Doug Kim, looks like he's taking notes. Rob's heart sinks. Doug plays forward, too. Rob never used to think of himself as stupid, but these days, he suspects, most people at Randall Circle High School think of him as a dumb jock.

Rob's slumped shoulders in the third row of the classroom do not escape Alvera's notice, but Alvera has little time during the class period to dwell on one kid. His experience as a teacher has taught him to triage: some students get it, and others don't. In a school this big, what can he do? He's already met with Rob several times after class and given it his best shot. In his own school days, he'd been a miserable English student. Even now, Alvera is not a confident writer; yesterday, he'd had another teacher read over his draft of the memo to Stephanie Allston about Rob's class performance. He didn't want to give the new principal a bad impression. And he's not looking forward to talking to Allston about the school's star soccer forward. But Alvera can't afford to pay too much special attention to Rob; he likes the kid and admires his willingness to work hard, but Alvera's got 120 students in his five classes. All he can do is teach the theory as best he can and move on within the time they have. Alvera allows himself a fleeting moment of regret. Despite hours of extra assistance, he can't get through to Rob. But he knows that Rob isn't dumb.

And Rob knows he isn't dumb. He heads home that afternoon after soccer practice pleasantly sweaty from running sprints in the hot fall afternoon. Unusually, though, the exercise hasn't made him any less frustrated. Maria had been busy during study hall, and Mr. Alvera had another meeting already scheduled after school. Now Rob's going to have to face down a problem set with no idea how to tackle it.

Rob is still sitting at the kitchen table, head propped in hands, when his father arrives home from work. Rob doesn't even look up at the sound of the door opening and closing. Flipping through the pages of his textbook to check the answer to a practice problem, he groans.

"What are you working on?" his dad asks. He sets his briefcase down and starts going through a stack of mail.

Rob looks up at his father. Keep getting the problems wrong, or ask his dad? "I don't understand this thermodynamic gas stuff," he says after a long pause, "and Maria wasn't around to help."

"Let me see," his father says, and Robert shoves the textbook over to his father, who seems surprisingly undisturbed.

"OK, Rob, this isn't so bad," his father says. "Tell you what. Go down to that store that sells the balloons with helium and bring a few back here."

The tightness in Rob's chest eases. Soccer game tomorrow night! By the time he has dashed to the corner store and back with a set of balloons, the evening has started to cool, but it's still in the 90s. His father is waiting for him in the garage.

"Now take one of the balloons and put it in the car and close the door," his father suggests. Frowning, Rob does as his dad says, and the two loiter in the waning light until a bang makes Rob jump. His father laughs.

"It's the balloon! OK, now, I want you to think about the effect of temperature on pressure," his father says, "and think about how that expands volume beyond the breaking point of the balloon's rubber . . ."

Rob grins. He's starting to get it.

■■■

Rob struggled in chemistry class because his brain is not wired like his teacher's or Maria's. It's not that Rob is not smart. He mastered the chemistry concept when the teaching was customized to the way he learns. So why can't schools customize their teaching? As we'll show, schools have a very interdependent architecture, which mandates standardization. So how do we get customized learning for each student? Modularity allows for customization, so the solution is to move to a modular architecture in schools. Only then can Rob have a learning solution customized to how he learns.

Most of us intuitively know that we all learn differently from one another—through different methods, with different hooks, and at different paces. We remember not being able to pick up a concept at the same time someone else grasped it instinctively. And we remember that occasionally a teacher or parent or another student would explain it in a different way, and it clicked. Or perhaps it just took more time. Other times we figured things out faster than our classmates. We grew bored when the class repeatedly drilled a concept for those who struggled to get it. And most of us had friends who excelled in certain classes but struggled in others. Our experience is that we learn differently.

In the last three decades, increasing numbers of cognitive psychologists and neuroscientists have acknowledged this, too. Researchers have produced a multitude of schemes to explain the straightforward idea that people learn differently from one another. This research has bubbled up under different rubrics. Although there is considerable certainty that people in fact learn differently, considerable uncertainty persists about what those differences are. At the moment, the only sure thing is no one has yet defined these differences so unambiguously that there is consensus on what the differences specifically are. Food fights periodically erupt in academia about what the salient differences are. As our understanding of the brain improves, we will better understand how it processes information—how neurotransmitters fire across synapses, which parts of the brain do what, how these develop, and so on—so we can better understand how different people learn. As neuroscientists help us to understand these underlying causal mechanisms, we will then be able to understand some of the mysteries of how human beings learn and what role our environment and experiences have on that ability. For now, however, the uncertainty persists.

In this book, we consciously avoid the controversies about whose definition of these differences is correct by making a simple assertion—people learn in *different ways*. Some of this difference is coded in our brains when we are born; other differences emerge based on what we experience in life, especially in our earliest years.

We use one of the more well known of these rubrics to illustrate what we mean by these differences, and although you might not agree with the schematic we chose, that's not the point. In the pages that follow, we employ language about people possessing different intelligences, but thinking about this as people having different aptitudes or preferences or any number of other schematics is fine as well. We merely introduce this theory of different intelligences so that readers can visualize how students might learn in different ways, whether the *domain* or *field* is math or music, languages or science.[1]

❖ RETHINKING INTELLIGENCE AND HOW WE LEARN

Research from some academic psychologists has set the stage for an escape into a new understanding of intelligence. In the past, scholars reduced intelligence to a number, considered it unitary, and gave it a name—intelligence quotient, or IQ. They then proceeded to compare people within age groups by this measure. But some research indicates that intelligence is much broader than this, although there are still disagreements. Many scholars, however, use the word "intelligence" to denote competence in a variety of areas. The result is a proliferation of definitions of intelligence.[2]

Harvard psychologist Howard Gardner is the pioneer in this multiple intelligences field. Gardner first posited the idea of many types of intelligence in the early 1980s as he introduced his "theory of multiple intelligences."[3] A cursory examination of Gardner's definition of intelligence and his categorization scheme shows how people can have different strengths and how the learning experience can be tailored to those differences. Here's how Gardner defines intelligence:

- The ability to solve problems that one encounters in real life.
- The ability to generate new problems to solve.

- The ability to make something or offer a service that is valued within one's culture.[4]

That definition escapes the narrow clutches of an IQ score. In studying intellectual capacity, Gardner established criteria to aid him in deciding whether a talent that could be observed was actually a distinct intelligence and therefore whether it merited its own spot in his categorization scheme. His criteria are that "each intelligence must have a developmental feature, be observable in special populations such as prodigies or 'savants,' provide some evidence of localization in the brain, and support a symbolic or notational system."[5] From this, Gardner originally came up with seven distinct intelligences. He has since added an eighth to that list and given consideration to a couple more.

Gardner's eight intelligences, with brief definitions and an example of someone who exemplifies each one, are:

- *Linguistic:* Ability to think in words and to use language to express complex meanings: Walt Whitman.
- *Logical-mathematical:* Ability to calculate, quantify, consider propositions and hypotheses, and perform complex mathematical operations: Albert Einstein.
- *Spatial:* Ability to think in three-dimensional ways; perceive external and internal imagery; re-create, transform, or modify images; navigate oneself and objects through space; and produce or decode graphic information: Frank Lloyd Wright.
- *Bodily-kinesthetic:* Ability to manipulate objects and fine-tune physical skills: Michael Jordan.
- *Musical:* Ability to distinguish and create pitch, melody, rhythm, and tone: Wolfgang Amadeus Mozart.
- *Interpersonal:* Ability to understand and interact effectively with others: Mother Teresa.
- *Intrapersonal:* Ability to construct an accurate self-perception and to use this knowledge in planning and directing one's life: Sigmund Freud.

- *Naturalist:* Ability to observe patterns in nature, identify and classify objects, and understand natural and human-made systems: Rachel Carson.[6]

How does this relate to teaching and learning? When an educational approach is well aligned with one's stronger intelligences or aptitudes, understanding can come more easily and with greater enthusiasm. Put differently, the learning can be intrinsically motivating. For example, in the above story, Rob struggled to grasp the material when the teacher taught it in a logical-mathematical form. Almost surely this form of intelligence is not one of his strengths. His classmate, Maria, has a high logical-mathematical intelligence, so she grasped it immediately. But when his father demonstrated the same concept to Rob in a different, spatial way that aligned with how Rob learns, he not only understood, but found it interesting.[7]

Gardner and others have researched ways to teach various content materials so that they are in line with each of these intelligences. In the book *Teaching and Learning through Multiple Intelligences*, the authors Linda Campbell, Bruce Campbell, and Dee Dickinson demonstrate this by telling a story about a girl who was several grade levels behind in school. The more she struggled, the more she hated school—and her self-esteem plummeted. When she entered the sixth grade, she had a teacher who observed how gracefully she moved, which prompted the teacher to wonder if she might learn through movement. Without being an expert in intelligence typologies, that teacher could see that this student had the gift of great bodily-kinesthetic intelligence. The student generally refused to read, write, or practice spelling. But following her hunch, the teacher suggested to the girl that she "create a movement alphabet using her body to form each of the twenty-six letters." The next day, the girl ran into the classroom before school started with something to show her teacher. She danced each letter of the alphabet and then sequenced all twenty-six into a unified performance. She then spelled her first name and last name through dancing. That night she practiced all her spelling words through dancing—and performed the dance for her classmates the next day. Soon she began writing more and more words. First she would dance them; then she wrote them down. Her writing scores increased, as did her self-confidence. A few months later she no longer needed to dance out words to spell them; learning through her strength in bodily-kinesthetic intelligence had opened a world of reading and writing to her forever. These skills are important no matter what path she pursues in life.[8]

Gardner's research shows that although most people have some capacity in each of the eight intelligences, most people excel in only two or three of them. His research, which implies the need for learning opportunities that line up with individual strengths, also cautions against pigeonholing people and not developing all their intelligences.

In addition, these differences in intelligences are only one dimension of cognitive ability. Within each type of intelligence, there might be different *learning preferences*. Some students need to write a concept down before they understand it, play it out, talk it through, and so on. Although there is dispute over this idea, just to make the point clear, a person who learns best visually in one type of intelligence—by seeing images or reading text—may not necessarily do well visually when using another type of intelligence. Finally, nested within these, there is another dimension of difference with which no one disagrees. People learn at different *paces*—slow, medium, fast, and all the variations within.

Given that we all learn in different ways, one might assume that we would teach in different ways, too. But think back to your experience in school. Because schools place students in groups, when a class was ready to move on to a new concept, all students moved on, regardless of how many had mastered the previous concept (even though it might have been a prerequisite for understanding what came next). When it was time to take Algebra 2, even if we had not yet mastered all the requisites in Algebra 1, we took Algebra 2. Some people moved on even if they did not pass the prerequisite class. Conversely, it did not matter if some percentage of students could cover the World History curriculum in a quarter; everyone was stuck in the class for a full year. And when our fourth-grade teacher taught long division in the manner that corresponded to how she best learned it and understood it, maybe it clicked for us and maybe not; whether we understood it right away and became bored with the repeated explanations or sank deeper into bewilderment, unable to grasp the logic, we sat in the class for the duration.[9]

Why do schools work this way? If we agree that we learn differently and that students need customized pathways and paces to learn, why do schools standardize the way they teach and the way they test?

❖ INTERDEPENDENCE AND MODULARITY

To explain this conflict between schools standardizing the way they teach in the face of students needing customization for the way they learn, we first need to step back and understand the concepts of interdependence and modularity from the world of product design.

All products and services have an architecture, or design, that determines what its parts are and how they must interact with one another.[10] The place where any two parts fit together is called an *interface*. Interfaces exist within a product, as well as between groups of people or between departments within an organization that must interact with one another.

A product's design is interdependent if the way one component is designed and made depends on the way other components are designed and made—and vice versa. When there is an unpredictable interdependency across an interface between components—that is, we can't know ahead of time how we must build a certain part until we have built both parts together—then the same organization must develop *both* of the components if it hopes to develop *either* component.

These architectures are almost always proprietary because each organization will develop its own interdependent design to optimize performance in a different way.

By contrast, in a modular product design, there are no unpredictable interdependencies in the design of the product's components or stages of the value chain. Modular components fit and work together in well-understood, crisply codified ways. A modular architecture specifies the fit and function of all elements so completely that it does not matter who makes the components or subsystems as long as they meet the defined specifications. Modular components can be developed in independent work groups or by different organizations working at arm's length.

To illustrate, consider the "architecture" of an electric light. A light bulb and a lamp have an interface between the light bulb stem and the light bulb socket. This is a modular interface. Engineers have lots of freedom to improve the design *inside* the light bulb, as long as they build the stem so that it can fit the established light bulb socket specifications. Notice how easily the new compact fluorescent bulbs fit into our old lamps. The same company does not need to design and make the light bulb, the lamp, the wall sockets, and the electricity generation and distribution systems. Because standard interfaces exist, different companies can provide products for each piece of the system.

When there is an interdependent interface, by contrast, integration across that interface is essential. For example, when Henry Ford built his high-volume Model T assembly line in Dearborn, Michigan, he learned a painful truth. When his workers pressed a flat sheet of steel into a die to form it into the shape of an auto-body part, the steel did not conform itself precisely to the die's shape (which is the metalworker's equivalent of a mold). Instead, the steel sprang back somewhat after it was fully pressed into the die. Ford's die makers could cut the dies slightly deeper to account for this spring-back. But if the batch of steel that was delivered from Ford's supplier on Monday sprang back 2 percent, whereas Tuesday's batch of steel sprang back 6 percent, then the size of the parts would vary by as much as 4 percentage points from one day to the next—and the pieces of the car just wouldn't fit together. Working independently, the steel suppliers couldn't solve this problem because they weren't stamping the steel in Ford's environment. And Ford couldn't solve it because he wasn't making the steel. So Ford integrated. He built a massive steel complex on the River Rouge west of Detroit so that as his engineers worked to control the metallurgical properties of the steel, they could interdependently change the way the dies and stamping machines were designed and used.

When someone changes one piece in a product that has an interdependent architecture, necessity requires complementary changes in other pieces. Customizing a product or service, as a result, becomes complicated and expensive. Many of these interdependencies are not predictable, so all pieces must be designed interactively. Customizing a product whose architecture is interdependent requires a complete redesign of the entire product or service every time.

On the other hand, modular architectures optimize flexibility, which allows for easy customization. Because people can change pieces without redesigning everything else, real customization for different needs is relatively easy. A modular architecture enables an organization to serve these needs. Modularity also opens the system to enable competition for performance improvement and cost reduction of each module.

The level of interdependence found in a product is a function of the underlying technology's maturity. In the early days of most new products and services, the components need to be tightly woven together to maximize the functionality from an immature technology that is not yet good enough to satisfy customer needs. Customers are willing to tolerate the product standardization that component interdependence mandates because customization is prohibitively expensive. They are generally willing to conform their expectations and their behavior to accommodate use of the standard product. Differences in usage patterns—and therefore customers' individual needs—are not obvious during this stage of an industry's evolution.

As an illustration, Apple led the charge in the 1980s at the outset of the personal computer revolution by controlling essentially the whole computer—from the hardware and operating system to the software applications. The architecture of this system was proprietary and interdependent. The unfortunate downside, however, was that customization was prohibitively expensive for Apple.

As products and their markets mature, technology grows more sophisticated, as do customers. They begin to understand their unique needs and to insist on customized products. Technological maturity makes customization possible. Product and service architectures become more modular in this environment. In the early days of personal computers, a modular offering was not possible. But the technology matured, which made the Dell approach to satisfying different customer needs a realistic option. Peeling the cover off a Dell reveals that Dell does not manufacture any of the components. A different company makes each. This allows Dell to invite its customers to specify the features and functions they want and then to assemble and deliver a customized computer within 48 hours.

The personal computer operating system is currently going through the same evolution. Microsoft's Windows operating system is interdependent. Changing just ten lines of code could necessitate rewriting millions of others. It would cost millions of dollars to customize Windows exactly to your needs. The economics of interdependence mandate standardization, and we live with it. Most of us are unaware of how our lives might improve if we had easily configurable operating systems at our disposal; it's just a luxury that had never been feasible. Once Unix technology had matured sufficiently, however, an open-source operating system such as Linux became feasible. Linux's architecture is modular and standardized and therefore can be customized—witness how the open-source programming community continually updates and enhances it, kernel by kernel.

❖ THE SCHOOLING DILEMMA: STANDARDIZING TEACHING VERSUS CUSTOMIZING LEARNING

How does this relate to U.S. public schools? Think about schooling's architecture. The dominant model today is highly interdependent. It is laced with four types of interdependencies. Some of these interdependencies are *temporal*: you can't study this in ninth grade if you didn't cover that in seventh. There are *lateral* interdependencies, too. You can't teach certain foreign languages in other more efficient ways because you'd have to change the way English grammar is taught; and changing the way grammar is taught would mandate changes elsewhere in the English curriculum. There are also *physical* interdependencies. There is strong evidence, for example, that project-based learning is a highly motivating way for many students to synthesize what they are learning as well as to identify gaps in their knowledge that need to be filled. But many schools can't adopt widespread project-based learning because the layout of their buildings simply can't accommodate it. And finally, there are *hierarchical* inter-dependencies. These range from well-intentioned mandates, which are often contradictory, from local, state, and federal policymakers that influence what happens in schools to union-negotiated work rules that become ensconced in contracts and policies at the state and local levels. Curriculum and textbook decisions made at school district headquarters also circumscribe the ability of teachers to innovate, especially across the curriculum. Although an innovative teacher might see a way to teach algebra in the context of chemistry, it would be nearly impossible to do it because the structure of what can be taught in the classroom depends on how the district headquarters carves up and defines the curriculum; and changes in the curriculum would also require changes in standardized tests and admissions standards. Even more problematic, this kind of change in practice would require changes in the way prospective science and math teachers are trained and certified.

Because there are so many points of interdependence within the public school system, there are powerful economic forces in place to standardize both instruction and assessment despite what we know to be true—students learn in different ways. The problem is that customization within interdependent systems is expensive. We explore how hierarchical interdependency restricts customization in much greater depth in Chapter 5 when we introduce the concept of a "commercial system," but here's one telling example to illustrate the point. In the 1960s and 1970s, society began requiring schools to customize offerings for students deemed to have special needs. By the 1970s, 10 percent of all children were covered by federally funded programs for children with special needs.[11] Students who qualify for these designations typically require individual approaches, codified in an individualized education plan (IEP). In another special case, educators place immigrant students from non-English-speaking families into custom-designed English language learner (ELL) programs. Customization is almost surely an important advantage for both these categories of students, but it is also terribly expensive. For example, in Rhode Island, it costs $22,893 a year on average to educate a special-education student, whereas it costs $9,269 for a regular education student.[12] Spending increases for special education students have outpaced spending for regular education by a considerable margin over the last 40 years, to the point where special education now accounts for over a fifth of the spending in many districts.[13]

As a consequence, there is a constant struggle over who is eligible for "special" consideration, and, because those costs soak up so many resources (lower staff ratios, special spaces, tailored instructional approaches), schools increasingly standardize for everyone else.[14] But here is the dilemma: because students have different types of intelligence, learning styles, paces, and starting points, *all students* have special learning needs.[15] It is not just students whom we label as having disabilities. Or, to put it as singer-songwriter Danny Deardorff did, we are all "differently abled."[16] The students who succeed in schools do so largely because their intelligence happens to match the dominant paradigm in use in a particular classroom—or somehow they have found ways to adapt to it.[17]

❖ CAN WE CUSTOMIZE ECONOMICALLY WITHIN THE PRESENT FACTORY MODEL SCHOOLS?

In the one-room schools that characterized public education during most of the 1800s, teaching was customized by necessity, at least by pace and level. Because the room was filled with children of different ages and abilities, teachers spent most of their day going from student to student, giving personalized instruction and assignments, and following up in individually tailored ways. But as classrooms filled in the late 1800s, this method of teaching changed as larger enrollments forced schools to standardize. Americans tolerated it; progressive thinkers from earlier generations encouraged it. Just as in the early stages of other industries' histories, society's expectations and behaviors actually conformed to the standardization; Americans no longer expected customized learning. Much of the support behind this standardization—categorizing students by age into grades and then teaching batches of them with batches of material—was inspired by the efficient factory system that had emerged in industrial America. By instituting grades and having a teacher focus on just one set of students of the same academic proficiency, the theory went, teachers could teach "the same subjects, in the same way, and at the same pace" to all children in the classroom.[18]

The question now facing schools is this: Can the system of schooling designed to process groups of students in standardized ways in a monolithic instructional mode be adapted to handle differences in the way individual brains are wired for learning?[19]

Some school districts have made efforts to personalize learning, and many schools have attempted to use Gardner's framework to teach to multiple intelligences within a classroom. But because of the high level of interdependence in a classroom, this is not an easy thing to do successfully on a large scale. Montgomery County Public Schools in Maryland, for example, has begun instituting forms of personalized learning to take into account varied learning needs. Through real-time assessments, such as those offered by Wireless Generation,[20] a company that provides mobile educational assessment solutions, teachers gain insight into where students actually are in their learning so that they can then tailor instruction to each student.

The Maryland effort is a noble one. But teaching to multiple intelligences in a monolithic model is fraught with problems. Although most students have some capacity in each of the eight intelligences, most truly excel in only two or three of the intelligences. Teachers, of course, are no different and excel in a discrete number of styles. Like all of us, they therefore tend to teach in ways compatible with their strengths.

What happens then in the typical classroom is a kind of "reverse magnetic attraction." Every magnet, you may remember, has a positive and a negative pole. Like poles repel each other, and opposite poles attract. In the typical classroom, those "like poles"—similar types of intelligence—attract, rather than repel, each other.

This reverse magnetic attraction creates a vicious cycle. The teachers in classrooms are products of the monolithic batch-processing system that characterizes public education today. In that system, students who naturally enjoy the teaching approach they encounter in a given class are more likely to excel. For example, the subject material in a high school language arts class relates in obvious ways to linguistic intelligence. Students with that intelligence type naturally comprise most of the ones who excel in language arts. They're the ones who choose to major in that subject in college and then choose teaching careers in that field. Specific subject matter tends to be linked to specific intelligences through the way textbooks are written—by experts who are strong in that specific intelligence type. As a result, what has emerged in every domain are "intellectual cliques," composed of curriculum developers, teachers, and the best students in that subject area. Their brains are all wired consistently with one another. Just as members of a social clique often are unaware of the degree to which they easily understand and communicate with one another to the exclusion of those outside the group, members of these intellectual cliques are often unaware of the extent to which their shared patterns of thinking exclude those with strengths in other kinds of intelligences.

Students who are not endowed with strong linguistic intelligence are therefore predictably frustrated in an English class. Teachers are similarly trapped by their own strengths. In any given classroom; there are students who do not have strong linguistic intelligence and are therefore effectively excluded from excelling in this subject. And the pattern repeats itself from generation to generation. The same happens in each of the academic disciplines. For example, teachers who teach math tend to have high logical-mathematical intelligence, and therefore the students who excel in their classes also tend to have this type of intelligence. Many other students are excluded.

Gardner and others who agree with him work to train teachers and schools to teach to multiple intelligences. This effort is more manageable at the elementary school level, with its activity-center, exploratory learning model. But in most U.S. schools, especially at the middle and high school level, even a heroic effort by a teacher to pay attention to multiple intelligence patterns is, because of the way the system is arranged around the monolithic architecture, almost guaranteed to fail. When that teacher caters to one type of intelligence, some students will tune in, but others will tune out.

In summary, the current educational system—the way it trains teachers, the way it groups students, the way the curriculum is designed, and the way the school buildings are laid out—is designed for standardization. If the United States is serious about leaving no child behind, it cannot teach its students with standardized methods. Today's system was designed at a time when standardization was seen as a virtue. It is an intricately interdependent system. Only an administrator suffering from virulent masochism would attempt to teach each student in the way his or her brain is wired to learn within this monolithic batch system. Schools need a new system.

❖ THE POTENTIAL FOR CUSTOMIZED LEARNING IN STUDENT-CENTRIC CLASSROOMS

If the goal is to educate every student—asking schools to ensure that all students have the skills and capabilities to escape the chains of poverty and have an all-American shot at realizing their dreams—we must find a way to move toward what, in this book, we call a "student-centric" model. We use the word "toward" intentionally here because this is not, at least immediately, a binary choice. A monolithic batch process with all of its interdependencies is at one end of a spectrum, and a student-centric model that is completely modular is at the other. For a very long time there will be some issues, skills, and subjects that the traditional model will handle best. But one by one, the instructional jobs that teachers now shoulder are destined, as we will show, to migrate toward a student-centric model.

How might schools start down this promising path? Computer-based learning, which is a step on the road toward student-centric technology, offers a way. As we explain in subsequent chapters, computer-based learning is emerging as a disruptive force and a promising opportunity. The proper use of technology as a platform for learning offers a chance to modularize the system and thereby customize learning. Student-centric learning is the escape hatch from the temporal, lateral, physical, and hierarchical cells of standardization. The hardware exists. The software is emerging. Student-centric learning opens the door for students to learn in ways that match their intelligence types in the places and at the paces they prefer by combining content in customized sequences. As modularity and customization reach a tipping point, there is another opportunity for change: As we explain later, teachers can serve as professional learning coaches and content architects to help individual students progress—and they can be a guide on the side, not a sage on the stage.

Is this a pipe dream? How can schools, which are public institutions driven by political decisions and seemingly insulated from market demands, make the shift to a student-centric classroom? In the following chapter, we show that historically schools have in fact done a remarkable job of shifting to meet the public's demands. Explaining the disruption theory and a brief history of schooling in the United States shows that schools actually have consistently improved over time. Although it won't be easy, we think they can make this shift to a student-centric classroom, too, if they take the right steps forward.

NOTES

1. The Ball Foundation puts forth a different rubric from the primary one we use in this book, for example. It has done significant work exploring people's different aptitudes and what this means for their learning. From a Web site about the Ball Foundation's Ball Aptitude Battery: "An individual's aptitudes are a primary factor in identifying the types of skills one can expect to learn most quickly and easily. This in turn is a predictor of the types of tasks that an individual is likely to enjoy. So an individual who understands their own aptitude profile can be more confident that their time and energy is invested in education that is going to offer the greatest rewards." "The Ball Aptitude Battery," Career Vision Web site, http://www.careervision.org/About/ BallAptitudeBattery.htm (accessed April 1, 2008). There are many other theories and schematics in use to think about the differences in how people learn as well, including talents; motivations, interests, or passions; learning styles (although there is considerable evidence that the popular categorization schemes in use here are not valid); and so forth. There is also lots of ongoing work applying this research in education, including that of Scientific Learning, which is based on the work of neuroscientist Paula Tallal, and All Kinds of Minds, which is based on the research work of pediatrician Mel Levine. For a good overview of all of this work, we also recommend

Mary-Dean Barringer, Craig Pohlman, and Michelle Robinson's book *Schools for All Kinds of Minds: Boosting Student Success by Embracing Learning Variation* (San Francisco: Jossey-Bass, 2010).

2. Many researchers have proposed different categories or types of intelligence. Among the categories are Peter Salovey and John Mayer's emotional intelligence. See P. Salovey and J. D. Mayer, "Emotional Intelligence," *Imagination, Cognition, and Personality*, vol. 9, no. 3, 1990, pp. 9, 185–211.

Daniel Goleman's latest book is about social intelligence, another category of intelligence. See Daniel Goleman, *Social Intelligence: The New Science of Human Relationships* (New York: Bantam, 2006).

Robert Sternberg has developed a multiple intelligences theory that pinpoints three intelligence types—analytical, creative, and practical—based on his own definition of intelligence, which is culturally dependent and broader than the traditional measure. R. J. Sternberg, *Beyond IQ: A Triarchic Theory of Human Intelligence* (New York: Cambridge University Press, 1985).

In a different line of work, Sally Shaywitz has broken new ground in understanding how one set of people, those with dyslexia, learn differently from others. Shaywitz's research details how dyslexics' brains actually function differently from others through the use of correlations in MRIs of the brain. See Sally Shaywitz, *Overcoming Dyslexia: A New and Complete Science-Based Program for Reading Problems at Any Level* (New York: Random House, 2003).

3. Howard Gardner, *Multiple Intelligences* (New York: Basic Books, 2006), p. 6.

We also recommend reading a delightful book in which Gardner responds to critiques of his work. See Jeffrey A. Schaler, ed., *Howard Gardner Under Fire: The Rebel Psychologist Faces His Critics* (Chicago: Open Court, 2006).

4. Linda Campbell, Bruce Campbell, and Dee Dickinson, *Teaching and Learning through Multiple Intelligences* (Boston: Pearson, 2004), p. xx.

5. Campbell et al., p. xix.

6. Campbell et al., p. xxi.

7. Jack Frymier, who has spent his life in public education as a teacher, administrator, professor, and researcher, provides more insight into why this would be more intrinsically motivating. Because motivation is an individual matter and children differ from one another, it stands to reason that different things motivate different children. No effort at instilling intrinsic motivation will succeed unless it works with these differences. See Jack Frymier, "If Kids Don't Want to Learn You Probably Can't Make 'Em: Discussion with Jack Frymier," notes by Ted Kolderie (October 28, 1999), http://www.education evolving.org/content_view_all.asp.

8. Campbell et al., pp. 63–64.

9. Gardner's research supports this. Schools and standardized tests tend to emphasize linguistic and logical-mathematical intelligence and ignore the other kinds of intelligences. And most teachers tend to rely on one or two intelligences to the exclusion of the others. Campbell et al., pp. xx, xxiii.

In a *Time* magazine story on high school dropouts, the article cited that of the 30-plus percent of high school students who did not finish school, 88 percent of those dropping out had passing grades when they left. Dropouts frequently report boredom as the reason for leaving. Nathan Thornburgh, "Dropout Nation," *Time*, April 9, 2006, http://www.time.com/time/print out/0,8816,1181646,00.html.

10. We sometimes use the word "product" exclusively, but in this context, it serves as a synonym for "service." The concepts of interdependence and modularity and their implications apply equally to both products and services; we use the word "product" most of the time to simplify the text.

11. David Tyack and Larry Cuban, *Tinkering Toward Utopia: A Century of Public School Reform* (Cambridge, Massachusetts: Harvard University Press, 1995), p. 25.

12. Jennifer D. Jordan, "Special-Needs Students Apart," *Providence Journal*, February 8, 2007, http://www.projo.com/education/content/special_education21_01-21-07_P83O6B6.15f1fb4.html.

13. Stacey Childress and Stig Leschly, "Note on U.S. Public Education Finance (B): Expenditures," HBS Case Note, November 2, 2006, pp. 2, 11. Also see Eric A. Hanushek and Steven G. Rivkin, "Understanding the Twentieth-Century Growth in U.S. School Spending," *Journal of Human Resources*, vol. 32, no. 1, Winter 1997, pp. 46–53 for a further breakdown of the increase in special education costs relative to overall spending. The authors use an estimate from Stephen Chaikind, Louis C. Danielson, and Marsha L. Brauen, "What Do We Know about the Costs of Special Education? A Selected Review," *Journal of Special Education*, vol. 26, no. 4, pp. 344–370 that a special education student costs roughly 2.3 times what a regular education student costs.

14. An article in *Threshold* paints a picture of how teachers who aim to customize for struggling students give less attention to others in the class. "Personalization in the Schools: A Threshold Forum," *Threshold*, Winter 2007, p. 13.

15. An article in *Threshold* brings this point to life with some in-depth and concrete examples. See Dianne L. Ferguson, "Teaching Each and Every One: Three Strategies to Help Teachers Follow the Curriculum While Targeting Effective Learning for Every Student," *Threshold*, Winter 2007, p. 7.

16. Campbell et al., p. 127.

17. There actually is some modularity and customization in public schools. In the youngest grades, during parts of the day, students often can stay at various learning centers as long as they choose, before moving to other centers. In high school, students have considerable choice in the classes they take. These options allow them to customize what they learn. But they have little freedom to choose how they will learn it—and that is the challenge.

18. Tyack and Cuban, p. 89.

Also, as ethnographer Herb Childress has written, U.S. high schools are "additive" factories in which multiple certified specialists screw on their component and pass the child along to another; some screw on algebra, others world history, others Hemingway. He infers that high school is devoted to a set of processes above all else. We delve into this idea more in Chapter 5 when we explain the concept of the value-chain business. Herb Childress, *Landscapes of Betrayal, Landscapes of Joy: Curtisville in the Lives of Its Teenagers* (New York: SUNY Press, 2000).

19. Success for All is an example of a "batch processing" system that has tried to customize. It is a reading program that groups kids by ability. It has a tight feedback loop where it frequently assesses and regroups its students as it attempts to teach students at their level. It doesn't target different learning preferences, however. It is a slight improvement over the lockstep system and it points in the direction of mass customization. But it is still stuck in the monolithic paradigm of schooling.

20. Among its assessments, Wireless Generation offers teachers an improved way to conduct early reading assessments. Teachers have a handheld device that they use when administering a reading assessment. When the session is over, the teacher has captured a rich set of data about the student in a far easier manner than was previously possible. Teachers can then sync the handheld to a Web site to view and analyze reports on the student as well as the whole class. They can then use this information to tailor instruction to the students' needs—and Wireless Generation's product offers guidance here, too.

Chapter 2

Making the Shift:
Schools Meet Society's Jobs

Fresh from a meeting with his new boss, Carlos Alvera turns his sputtering car out of the school parking lot exit and looks to his left, where cars stream by him. The directions to the state teachers' convention weren't too clear, but this year, for once, he's determined to go. Stephanie Allston makes him nervous. State standards make him nervous. He goes right and makes another turn to go toward the interstate and the university, the home of this year's meeting. At least when he asked, Allston agreed to make Alvera one of the Randall delegates.

In previous years, he'd turned down many chances to go to the state teachers' convention. But this year, many things have changed. Any day now, the powers that be may declare his school a failure. And Allston's presence signals change: the newcomer seems hell-bent on doing things differently, even if Alvera isn't sure what good it would do.

Randall High has been around for longer than Alvera's 25 years of service. But as an urban high school, it is now in the bull's-eye of the California Standardized Testing and Reporting (STAR) program. And it's not looking good, despite the fact that Randall High has adequate facilities, a qualified faculty, a varied curriculum, and strong arts and athletics programs. How did Randall High, Alvera's second home, end up looking so bad?

At the convention at Middleburg University, Alvera passes the time by making small talk with the other teachers. The teachers gab about tests, principals, unions, and standards. It is with a rising sense of alarm that he notes the frequent use of the word "achievement." It's not that he's opposed to success, but when, Alvera muses, did society start expecting schools to ensure achievement and not merely access to education?

He pulls back into the Randall parking lot at the end of the day, ready to coach the Chemistry Bowl team as usual. It's the same thing he's done every Wednesday for years—but as he walks into the building, he realizes that although his job might be the same, his job description sure seems different. He hefts the conference tote bag onto his shoulder and notes its heaviness. He hasn't had a chance to go through all the material yet, but he hopes like crazy that there's something useful in the 10 pounds of paper they handed out.

■■■

Alvera is right. Randall Circle High School used to be viewed as a great school as it built up a vast array of programs to serve its large, diverse student population over many years. In our research on innovation, improving the products and services that organizations are providing at a pace that satisfies customers actually is rarely a problem. Most companies want to keep improving what they do—and generally they are quite good at doing just that. The public school system is no different. As we will show, contrary to widespread perception, on average, public schools have a steady record of improving on the metrics by which they are judged, just like the other organizations we've studied.

What our studies of innovation show, however, is that a specific type of innovation, which we call *disruption*, almost *always* trips up well-managed, improving companies. Disruption is difficult because the definitions and trajectories of improvement change. What were valuable improvements before the disruption now are less relevant. And dimensions of the product that had been unimportant become highly valued.

For a host of reasons we describe next, dealing with disruptive redirections in the trajectory of improvement has defied the abilities of even the most capable executives in the world's best companies.

In the past 25 years, as Alvera had begun to realize, two significant disruptions of this sort have swept through the U.S. public schools, marked by the Nation at Risk report and the No Child Left Behind Act. Assigning schools new jobs for which they were not built—and therefore are not necessarily doing—has meant that schools don't look as good in light of the new requirements. But given how difficult it is to negotiate these disruptive currents, as we show in the pages that follow, the schools have done remarkably well—which provides some hope that they may be able to switch to a student-centric learning mode, too, through a disruptive implementation of computer-based learning.

❖ THE DISRUPTIVE INNOVATION THEORY

The *disruptive innovation theory* explains why organizations struggle with certain kinds of innovation and how organizations can predictably succeed in innovation. Its basic constructs are depicted in Figure 2.1, which charts the performance of a service or product over time. Look first at the graph in the back plane of the three-dimensional diagram. It suggests that there are two types of improvement trajectories in every market. The solid line describes the pace of improvement that companies deliver to their customers by introducing new and improved products and services. The dotted lines represent the rate of performance improvement that customers can utilize. As these intersecting lines suggest, customers' needs in a given market application tend to be relatively stable over time. But companies typically improve their products at a much faster pace than customers need, so that products, which at one point were not good enough, ultimately pack in more features and functions than customers can use. As an illustration, every year

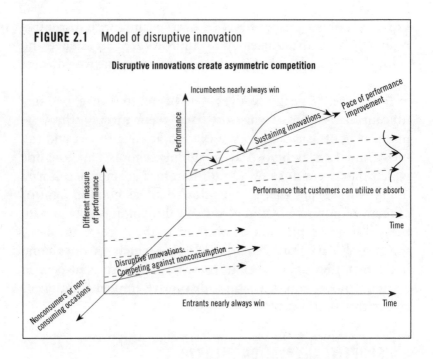

FIGURE 2.1 Model of disruptive innovation

Disruptive innovations create asymmetric competition

Incumbents nearly always win

Performance

Sustaining innovations

Pace of performance improvement

Different measure of performance

Performance that customers can utilize or absorb

Time

Disruptive innovations: Competing against nonconsumption

Nonconsumers or non-consuming occasions

Entrants nearly always win

Time

car companies give us new and improved engines, but most of us can't use all of the engine power they give us because speed limits and traffic jams get in the way.

We call innovations that drive companies up the solid line *sustaining innovations*. As suggested at the back of Figure 2.1, some are dramatic breakthroughs whereas others are routine; but the competitive purpose of these innovations is to sustain the performance improvement trajectory in the established market. Airplanes that fly farther, computers that process faster, cellular phone batteries that last longer, and televisions with clearer images are all sustaining innovations. In our research, we have found that in almost every case, the companies that win the battles of sustaining innovation are already the industry leaders. And it seems not to matter how technologically challenging the innovation is. As long as it helps the leaders make better products that they can sell for better profits to their best customers, they figure out a way to get it done.

The technologies in the original "plane of competition" at the back of Figure 2.1 are typically complicated and expensive. As a result, the only people who can own and use the products are those who have a lot of money and a lot of skill. In the computer industry, for example, mainframe computers arose in the back plane. Companies such as IBM manufactured these gargantuan machines from the 1950s to the 1970s, and their customers paid millions of dollars to buy them. When people needed to compute, they took a big stack of punched cards to the corporate mainframe center and gave it to the computer expert, who ran the job for them. The mainframe companies focused their innovative energies on making bigger and better mainframes. They were good and successful at what they did. The same was true in automobiles, telecommunications, printing, commercial and investment banking, beef processing, photography, steel making, and many, many other industries.

All that would seem to make for a boring and orderly world. But from time to time, things get shaken up when a different type of innovation emerges in an industry—a *disruptive innovation*. A disruptive innovation is *not* a breakthrough improvement. Instead of sustaining the traditional improvement trajectory in the established plane of competition, it *disrupts* that trajectory by bringing to the market a product or service that actually is not as good as what companies historically had been selling. Because it is not as good, the existing customers in the back plane in Figure 2.1 cannot use it. But by making the product affordable and simple to use, the disruptive innovation benefits people who had been unable to consume the back-plane product—people we call "nonconsumers." Disruptive innovations take root in simple, undemanding applications in what, as depicted in the front of Figure 2.1, is a new plane of competition—where the very definition of what constitutes quality, and therefore what improvement means, is *different* from what quality and improvement meant in the back plane. The impact of this change in the definition of quality is that the disruptive products in the new plane are not attractive to the customers of products in the original plane. They don't want and can't use them. Because companies need to meet the needs of their customers, the companies that made the products in the original plane of competition have a difficult time engaging simultaneously in the new, disruptive plane as well.

The personal computer is a classic example of a disruptive innovation. Prior to its introduction, the least expensive computer was the minicomputer, the name of which came from the fact that it was much smaller than mainframe computers, which had filled an entire room. But minicomputers cost well over $200,000, and required an engineering degree to operate them. The leading minicomputer company was Digital Equipment Corporation (DEC), which, during the 1970s and 1980s, was one of the most admired companies in the world economy. But it missed and was ultimately destroyed by the personal computer. Why?

Apple, one of the pioneers in personal computing, originally sold its model IIe computer as a toy to children. Children had been nonconsumers of computers before, so they did not care that the product was not as good as the existing mainframe and minicomputers. None of DEC's customers could even use a personal computer for the first 10 years it was on the market because it wasn't good enough for the problems they needed to solve. That meant that the more carefully DEC listened to its best customers, the less signal it got that the personal computer mattered, because in fact it didn't—to those customers.

We've replicated in Figure 2.2 the chart from Figure 2.1, and we have added to it what the numbers for new products looked like to DEC's management. Note that in the original, back plane of competition, DEC could generate $112,500 (45% × $250,000) in gross margin dollars each time it sold a minicomputer. The $800 in gross margin dollars that could be earned from selling a personal computer paled in comparison to this profit engine in the mainstream of DEC—or to the $300,000 in margin dollars per machine (60% × $500,000) that it stood to make if it made even bigger and better mainframe computers.

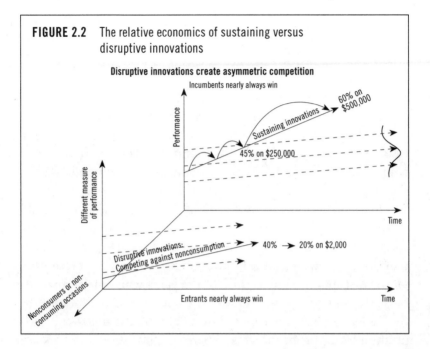

FIGURE 2.2   The relative economics of sustaining versus disruptive innovations

Disruption rarely arrives as an abrupt shift in reality; for a decade, the personal computer did not affect DEC's growth or profits. During the early years after a disruptive innovation has taken root in simple applications in the new plane, users still must take their complicated problems to the expensive experts in the back plane.

But little by little the disruption improves. Just as the original players in a market innovate with predictability no matter how challenging the innovation, the same is true in this new market. The new companies introduce what for them are sustaining innovations along this new trajectory; as long as an innovation helps a company make better products that it can sell for better profits, the company figures out a way to get it done.[1] And at some point, users can take tasks that formerly could be done only in the back plane and do them in the affordable, accessible front plane. Apple and the other personal computer companies were no different.

Within a few years, powered by improvements in microprocessor technology, the smaller personal computers were capable of doing work that previously required mainframes or minicomputers. This made computing widespread and cheaper, and it created a huge new market. It left almost everyone— except the mainframe and minicomputer companies—better off. Disruption almost always kills such companies, as they lose their customers. Again, DEC and the other minicomputer companies were no different; virtually all of them collapsed in the late 1980s.

The question people always ask is, "How in the world could these companies not see the train wreck coming?" They certainly do not lack resources like money or technological expertise. What they do lack, however, is the motivation to focus sufficient resources on the disruption. Why is this? In the years when the companies must commit to the innovation, disruptions are unattractive to the leaders because their best customers can't use them, and they promise lower profit margins. Therefore, investment dollars are always more likely to go toward next-generation sustaining innovations instead of toward disruptive ones. DEC's managers were not stupid; they were in fact very logical as they improved their company in the way it was built to operate.

This asymmetric motivation is precisely how and why disruptive innovations typically cause a dramatic change in the landscape of an industry. The Kodak camera, Bell telephone, Sony transistor radio, Ford Model T (and more recently Toyota automobile), Xerox photocopier, Southwest Airlines affordable flight, Cisco router, Fidelity mutual fund, Google advertising, and hundreds of other innovations all did—or are doing—the same thing.[2]

As a general rule, the vertical axis on the disruption diagram measures the type of improvement for which customers will pay more. One factor that makes it so hard for the incumbent leader to pursue a disruptive innovation is that the way product performance is defined in the disruptive market is antithetical to the sorts of improvements that are required to succeed in the original market. Making a better personal computer, for example, entailed making it smaller, cheaper, and easier to use. Making a better minicomputer generally entailed making it bigger and more powerful. The fact that the sustaining trajectory in the original plane of competition takes a company in a direction that is opposed to the direction of disruption makes life all the more difficult for the incumbent leaders.

❖ APPLYING DISRUPTION THEORY TO PUBLIC SCHOOLS: DEFINING PERFORMANCE

In the private sector, the metric on the vertical axis of the disruption diagram is the type of improvement that merits premium pricing. But in the public sector, where we can also draw these diagrams, the political or societal importance of programs determines the metric on the vertical axis. Public agencies consistently move up-market, away from initiatives that are less politically important and toward those that are more important.

Public schools are, of course, public institutions. Some programs are intensely important in the communities that schools serve, whereas others are less important. We explain in the paragraphs below that *schools actually have been improving—* moving up the vertical axis of their industry just like the companies in all the industries we have studied. In a manner analogous to disruption in the private sector, society has moved the goalposts on schools and imposed upon them new measures of performance. What is unique about public schools is that laws and regulations make them a virtual monopoly, which makes it difficult and sometimes impossible for new business models to compete on the new measures. Society has asked schools to pursue the new metric of improvement from within the existing organization, which was designed to improve along the old performance metric. In essence, the public schools have been required to do the equivalent of rebuilding an airplane in mid-flight—something almost no private enterprise has been able to do. On average, however, schools have done just that—adjust and then improve on each new measure. But doing so has not been easy.

To obtain a fuller understanding of how society has tasked schools with pursuing new disruptive performance measures—in essence assigning them new, primary jobs to be done—we'll briefly step back into the history of public schools. In the description that follows, we frame the story in the context of the disruptive innovation model. Because it is a summary, we necessarily resort to generalizations that will mask important details and exceptions. But our aim is simply to provide some general context to understand how society and schools evolved over time.

Job 1: Preserve the Democracy and Inculcate Democratic Values

At the country's founding, most children did not attend school. Universal public education was not on the national agenda. The topic of education or schools is not even mentioned in the U.S. Constitution.[3]

There were some early thinkers, however, on the role schools should play in U.S. society. Among these were Thomas Jefferson and Noah Webster, for whom preserving the newly created democracy was a paramount goal and a constant worry. They saw schools as a way to meet the goal. Basic education needed to be universal, they reasoned, so that all citizens could participate in the democracy. Schools needed to teach what we think of today as "the basics"—reading, writing, and arithmetic. They also needed to instill sound morals in students, as well as civics lessons on how the republic functioned—which they could do by teaching Greek, Roman, European, and American history. And schools needed to serve as the melting pot for children from different backgrounds by teaching them social norms and assimilating them into a common American culture. These thinkers hoped that, by doing this, schools could help all citizens become functioning, self-governing members of the republic. Beyond preparing this base, schools also were expected to further prepare an elite group—selected on merit from this entire pool of students, not just those from the upper class—to lead the country wisely in elected office. This would allow the democracy to survive and thrive. Jefferson proposed a three-tiered school system to accomplish this.[4]

Jefferson's system was not enacted, however, because Virginians did not want to pay the necessary taxes. But this changed by the 1830s and 1840s. Horace Mann and the leaders of the common school movement led the charge to formalize schooling. Various states responded by funding a system that bore strong similarities to Jefferson's vision. Mann and many others implemented it. Elementary education expanded rapidly as elected officials, school leaders, and teachers performed admirably. Despite the introduction of grade levels in schooling in Quincy, Massachusetts, in the mid-1800s, most of the early schools were one-room schoolhouses. And only an elite group of students continued their education beyond grade school, all of which paved the way for a relatively seamless transition to the new job that society hired schools to do in the twentieth century.[5]

Job 2: Provide Something for Every Student

In the 1890s and early 1900s, competition with a fast-rising industrial Germany constituted a minicrisis; Americans responded in the early twentieth century by handing schools a new job: prepare *everyone* for vocations. The goal was to produce a sound workforce for jobs ranging from administrative functions to technically demanding manufacturing positions so that America could compete with Germany. The old job of preparing the next generation to lead and participate in democracy did not go away; society simply asked schools to perform both jobs.[6]

To do this new job, the school systems needed to extend high school to everyone. And to do this, they had to expand a high school's offerings and services to fit the needs of all sorts of students going into all sorts of careers. The depth and breadth of courses and the percentages enrolling in and progressing through high school became the new performance measures on the vertical axis that were used to assess how well schools were doing the new job.

Typically, in a private industry disruption, a new company would emerge to produce the disruptive product that would address this new job, and the old dominant player would wither away after some time. As a public institution with a monopoly in this field, however, schools did not wither away. Because most people were not even attending high school, there were many nonconsumers out there and not many high schools to serve them. In fact, by 1900 there were still over 200,000 one-room schoolhouses in the nation, and only 50 percent of the 5- to 19-year olds were enrolled in school.[7] It was therefore relatively easy for schools to mold themselves to meet the new demand—as well as to continue to excel at the first job by expanding and improving elementary education.

Over the next generation, public schools did just this, as they changed dramatically and revolutionized U.S. education. In 1905, only a third of children who enrolled in grade 1 made it to high school, roughly a third of those graduated from high school, and even fewer went to college. By 1930, in contrast, over 75 percent of students were entering high school, and almost 45 percent graduated.[8]

A spike in the numbers attending high school meant a change in the kinds of people who went to high school. The students now came from different backgrounds, had different goals, and therefore possessed differing interests. In response, the high school curriculum expanded and shifted. Previously, public high schools had offered a narrow curriculum, which focused on the "academic" subjects then needed to progress to college, such as Latin and Greek. For the new students attending high school, however, going to college often was not the goal, so high schools swept Latin to the side. These new "comprehensive" high schools intended to educate all of their students for whatever each needed, so they began offering music and art for enrichment, which previously were not seen as relevant. And they added vocational classes like shop work and stenography, which made students marketable immediately upon graduation. By 1950, and even much earlier in some places, most comprehensive high schools offered a slate of courses that bore a strong resemblance to the heart of today's high school curriculum—math courses through trigonometry; sciences with the familiar biology, chemistry, and physics; social studies courses featuring world and U.S. history; and a few years of foreign languages, generally French and Spanish.[9]

Schools implemented additional services as well. They added physical education and recreation, as well as instruction in health. Summer school, school lunch programs, counselors, and medical and dental care also arrived on many school campuses. Extracurricular activities expanded, too, from student government to sports to clubs.[10]

The 1950s delivered two shocks to public schools, one direct and the other indirect. Neither was disruptive, however; both resulted in the need for more sustaining innovations from schools—more equality of access and more offerings to still better prepare all students for the workforce. In 1954, the Supreme Court delivered its *Brown v. Board of Education* decision, which ordered the desegregation of schools. The decision laid bare the inequities between blacks and whites, but it did even more. Not only were blacks not taking part in the explosion in educational opportunities, but neither were females, the poor, the working-class immigrants, the disabled, or the rural residents. Schools began fixing this problem over the next decades as they further opened their doors and expanded their offerings.[11] And in 1957, an event thousands of miles outside the United States also shocked the nation's schools. When the Soviet Union beat the United States in launching the first satellite, *Sputnik*, into space, many panicked. A 1958 cover story in *Life* magazine proclaimed a "Crisis in Education."[12] The implication was clear: The Soviets had beaten the Americans because of the superiority of their schools. Never mind whether this was true. The jolt spawned an outcry for more rigorous science and math courses—and schools again met the demand over the next decade with new offerings and lab equipment.

Schools, in other words, did a good job moving up the sustaining trajectory of performance improvement, as improvement was defined at that time.

The 1960s and 1970s saw the emergence of a generation of parents who had not been raised in the Great Depression, but rather in an environment of relative prosperity. Their definition of good parenting, as a consequence, expanded to encompass providing enriching experiences for their children. In response to this desired expansion, the schools began to improve in this way as well. Advanced Placement (AP) courses, college-level classes offered in high school, expanded beyond the basic topics like biology to include subjects like art and music theory.[13] Japanese language courses appeared in more schools. Rather than funding just one school band and one school choir, schools introduced orchestra; the symphonic, marching, and jazz varieties of the band; and different choral groups as well. Schools expanded their art offerings to include different art forms—from painting and drawing to photography and art appreciation. Sports for boys broadened from the core football, baseball, basketball, and track teams to include tennis, golf, soccer, and lacrosse. Schools began offering interschool sports for girls, too.

By the 1970s, the public school landscape did not look anything like what it had at the beginning of the century. Schools were larger. Although the number of high schools in the nation had remained roughly constant since 1930 at 24,000, the number of high school graduates exploded. Whereas in the early twentieth century the typical high school had roughly 100 students enrolled, now the average high school enrollment approached 1,000. From the 8 percent of students who graduated from high school in 1900, by 1960 that number was 69 percent. Both school size and graduating numbers continued a slow climb. Larger schools with more students generated capacity for a greater diversity of courses and services. In 1890, there were only nine different course offerings across the whole of U.S. high schools; by 1973, high schools offered 2,100 classes under different headings. Within schools, there were four distinct tracks for students—college, commercial, vocational, and general—each with its own set of courses and requirements. By 1973, more and more elementary schools had added the kindergarten year, and 60 percent of children were enrolled. Real per pupil expenditures rose rapidly, of course, to pay for the expanded services.[14]

While not all public schools were equal—certainly some urban and rural schools did not match the breadth and depth of those in suburban areas—virtually all improved through the 1970s in accordance with the trajectory of improvement that was prevalent at that time. The schools considered the best were those that offered the most opportunities (Figure 2.3). Schools became complex and expensive as they offered a historically unmatched array of offerings.

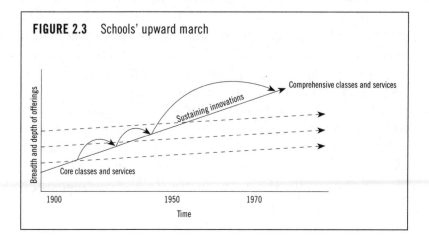

FIGURE 2.3   Schools' upward march

Job 3: Keep America Competitive

If public schools were improving so steadily, then how did we get to today's environment, where there is constant worry and complaint? In essence, society moved the goal posts. In the language of disruption, society changed the definition of improvement on the vertical axis. The nation asked its schools to take on the new job of keeping the United States competitive. Although seemingly similar to the previous job, it was actually quite different.

Beginning in the late 1960s, a host of Japanese companies began disrupting their U.S. counterparts. GDP growth plummeted as Canon disrupted Xerox, Japanese car companies disrupted Detroit's automakers, and Sony disrupted RCA, to name a few. The United States questioned its competitiveness. By 1980, it began to feel the bite of disruption as company after company downsized. Just as it had in the late 1950s, the nation turned to its schools for answers. This time, however, Americans noticed something different: in comparison to other countries, U.S. students were not performing as well as measured by certain standardized tests. Some defended the American schools with the logic that even though not every child was succeeding, the United States had a larger proportion of children enrolled in school than most other nations. By using the achievements of students taken from all strata of society, the argument went, American schools were given a lower average grade than schools in countries that focused largely on only educationally oriented children. The argument did not carry much weight; the College Board, which administers the SAT, revealed in the mid-1970s that average SAT scores had been declining since 1963. This observation sparked society to change schools' job again: The axis on which schools were judged became improvement in average test scores. A nice feature of this redefinition of improvement, not coincidentally, was the ease with which this metric facilitated comparison between the U.S. schools and those of other countries.[15]

Against this backdrop, the public's confidence in its nation's schools declined. Polls on public attitudes in the 1940s and 1950s suggested that the public believed schools were already good and also improving. But by the 1970s, this had changed. In 1974, people graded their schools a B–, and by 1981, this had fallen to a C–. More found them worse than they used to be and no longer saw them as improving.[16] This trend tracked the larger loss of faith in most public institutions at this time, but, as noted above, there were other elements stirring.

As so often happens, government lagged behind the public's anxiety by a few years. First it produced reports, then legislation. In 1981, the U.S. secretary of education created the National Commission on Excellence in Education, which, in 1983, produced the landmark report, "A Nation at Risk."[17] The report did take note of schools' unparalleled breadth of courses, services, and access. But it was less sure this was a good thing. For example, in one section, it said: "Secondary school curricula have been homogenized, diluted, and diffused to the point that they no longer have a central purpose. In effect, we have a cafeteria style curriculum in which the appetizers and desserts can easily be mistaken for the main courses."[18] Students had too many choices, it said; they were not completing the important classes. What had been a virtue was suddenly a vice. We moved the goal posts.

The report was sure of something else. Its first lines read, "Our Nation is at risk. Our once unchallenged preeminence in commerce, industry, science, and technological innovation is being overtaken by competitors throughout the world." For the first time, the United States was losing its international economic competitiveness to the Japanese and Europeans, and its schools needed to help it get it back. As evidence, the report gave several accounts of U.S. students' subpar performance on output measures, such as test scores, because it suggested that quantifiable outputs mattered more than inputs.[19] It asserted that measuring what resources were put into schools wasn't nearly as valid a metric of performance as what was coming out of them. And, thank goodness, there was a standardized way to measure that.

This certainty about the needed direction of change spread quickly across the country. No longer could students choose most of their classes or focus on the vocational or general or academic track depending on their interests or talents. Virtually everyone had to focus on the core academic classes and take the same tests. Japan's disruption of America's manufacturing industries increased the pressure for all students to attend college, which further ratcheted up the need to focus on the core subjects and tests because postsecondary schools increasingly required them. This was a radically different demand of schools.[20] Parents increasingly compared one community's schools with those of neighboring communities based upon their students' average test scores.[21] Public policy changes at the state level soon cemented the new metric. More standardized tests were implemented, and students, teachers, and schools were held accountable for test-score performance.[22]

With the shift to a new performance measure (depicted in Figure 2.4), what would we expect to see in any other industry? We would expect a coterie of start-up companies to emerge, with different business models structured to deliver the new value proposition. Personal computer makers like Compaq and Dell would arise to overthrow Digital Equipment Corporation. Wal-Mart and Target would supplant department stores. Apple, not the major recording companies, would change the way we consumed music.

People did not create new disruptive business models in public education, however. Why not? Almost all disruptions take root among nonconsumers. In education, there was little opportunity to do that. Public education is set up as a public utility, and state laws mandate attendance for virtually everyone. There was no large, untapped pool of nonconsumers that new school models could target.[23]

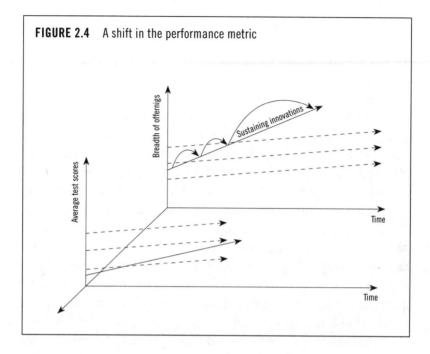

FIGURE 2.4   A shift in the performance metric

But because the United States has been unwilling or unable to facilitate the entrance of new organizations with new business models to disrupt the old, public school districts have had to negotiate this disruptive redefinition of performance entirely within their existing schools. In our studies of disruptive innovation in the private sector, we are not aware of a single instance in which a for-profit company was able to implement successfully the disruptive innovation within its core business in the "back plane" of Figure 2.1. The few that survived disruption did so by creating, under the corporate umbrella, a new business unit, with a new business model attuned to the disruptive value proposition. Asking the public schools to negotiate these disruptions from within their mainstream organizations is tantamount to giving them a demonstrably impossible task. And yet, they've done reasonably well.

The change has been wrenching, yet when one examines the National Assessment of Educational Progress (NAEP) scores for math and reading since the early 1980s, the numbers have trended upwards (see Figure 2.5).

These score increases are not as modest as they might seem. First, math scores rose more than reading scores most likely because people focused more here. While "A Nation at Risk" and subsequent publications on the topic did talk about illiteracy, America's future competitiveness in technology and innovation—math and science-related subjects—was referenced in the report's opening lines and was the impetus for change. Second, schools had an established and widespread base of test scores across the population on which they were trying to improve (again, contrast this with the first shift, where there was no base). And the school population itself has changed markedly. The number of students in U.S. public schools has risen in the last 20 years, and the composition of those students has tilted more and more toward those groups who historically have done least well in school. Many of the new students come from immigrant, non-English-speaking families, and their scores are included in the reported averages.[24] Not only that, but in the past, these students would not have all followed an academic track in school; now they have significantly less choice. Because of the nature of this widening base, consistent small increases in test scores are actually quite significant.

Job 4: Eliminate Poverty

The No Child Left Behind Act not only federally cemented average test scores as the primary metric for performance improvement, but also arguably once again shifted the goalposts. No longer can public schools simply raise the *average* test scores in their schools; instead, public schools must see to it that *every* child in *every* demographic improves his or her test scores. Now the performance measure for schools is the percentage of students who are proficient in core subjects. The essential motivation for asking schools to make sure that

FIGURE 2.5*   With new emphasis, test scores increase

Average NAEP mathematics scale score by age†

	1982	1986	1990	1992	1994	1996	1999	2004
9-year-olds	219	222	230	230	231	231	232	241
13-year-olds	269	269	270	273	274	274	276	281
17-year-olds	298	302	305	307	306	307	308	307

Average NAEP reading scale score by age‡

	1980	1984	1988	1990	1992	1994	1996	1999	2004
9-year-olds	215	211	212	209	211	211	212	212	219
13-year-olds	258	257	257	257	260	258	258	259	259
17-year-olds	285	289	290	290	290	288	288	288	285

*Digest of Education Statistic Tables and Figures, 2005. Tables 118 and 108.

†"Excludes persons not enrolled in school and those who were unable to be tested due to limited proficiency in English or due to a disability. Includes public and private schools. A score of 150 implies the knowledge of some basic addition and subtraction facts, and most can add 2-digit numbers without regrouping. They recognize simple situations in which addition and subtraction apply. A score of 200 implies considerable understanding of 2-digit numbers and knowledge of some basic multiplication and division facts. A score of 250 implies an initial understanding of the four basic operations. They can also compare information from graphs and charts, and are developing an ability to analyze simple logical relations. A score of 300 implies an ability to compute decimals, simple fractions, and percents. They can identify geometric figures, measure lengths and angles, and calculate areas of rectangles. They are developing the skills to operate with signed numbers, exponents, and square roots. A score of 350 implies an ability to apply a range of reasoning skills to solve multistep problems. They can solve routine problems involving fractions and percents, recognize properties of basic geometric figures, and work with exponents and square roots. Scale ranges from 0 to 500. Totals include other racial/ethnic groups not shown separately. Some data have been revised from previously published figures. Standard errors appear in parentheses." U.S. Department of Education, National Center for Education Statistics, National Assessment of Educational Progress (NAEP), NAEP 2004 Trends in Academic Progress; and unpublished tabulations, NAEP Data Explorer (http://nces. ed.gov/nationsreportcard/nde/), retrieved July 2005. (This table was prepared July 2005.)

‡"The NAEP scores have been evaluated at certain performance levels. Scale ranges from 0 to 500. Students at reading score level 150 are able to follow brief written directions and carry out simple. discrete reading tasks. Students at reading score level 200 are able to understand, combine ideas, and make inferences based on short uncomplicated passages about specific or sequentially related information. Students at reading score level 250 are able to search for specific information, interrelate ideas, and make generalizations about literature, science, and social studies materials. Students at reading score level 300 are able to find, understand, summarize, and explain relatively complicated literary and informational material. Includes public and private schools. Excludes persons not enrolled in school and those who were unable to be tested due to limited proficiency in English or due to a disability. Some data have been revised from previously published figures. Standard errors appear in parentheses." U.S. Department of Education, National Center for Education Statistics, National Assessment of Educational Progress (NAEP), NAEP 2004 Trends in Academic Progress; and unpublished tabulations, NAEP Data Explorer (http://nces.ed.gov/nationsreportcard/nde/), retrieved January 2006. (This table was prepared February 2006.)

all students are proficient in reading, math, and science is to eliminate poverty. This new demand again is not terribly removed from the purpose of school; in theory, teachers taught so that people would learn. But again, in its output focus

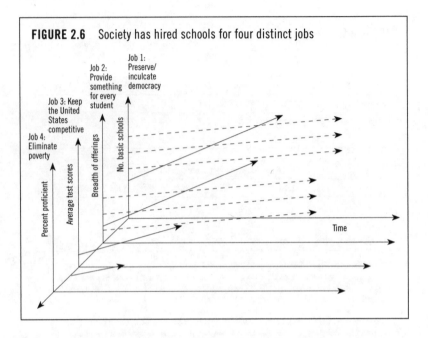

FIGURE 2.6 Society has hired schools for four distinct jobs

and singular purpose, it is quite different. Society has hired schools to perform four distinct jobs (see Figure 2.6). Once again, the change has been wrenching and the outcry loud. But compared to how private sector companies have done when confronted with disruptions like these, schools have actually done remarkably well.[25]

❖ IT'S NOT THE TEACHERS AND ADMINISTRATORS

So we return to our earlier question: Can schools move to a student-centric classroom through the adoption of computer-based learning? One reason we might believe it is not possible centers on another common gripe about why schools struggle—their teachers and administrators aren't sufficiently motivated to improve. Yet, just as the other common explanations summarized in our introductory chapter do not hold up under scrutiny as being *the reason* for schools' struggles, we hope the above analysis shows that most school administrators and most individual teachers are strongly motivated to improve. In the face of enormous hurdles and despite changing demands on schools, teachers and administrators have constantly improved public schools in the United States and navigated the disruptions imposed upon them. The latter is something almost no manager in private industry has been able to do. Although migrating to the promising path that a student-centric classroom presents will not be easy, we do not question the abilities and motivation of administrators and teachers as individual professionals.

To do it, they will need the right tools and strategy to understand how to introduce innovations to have impact because, as we show in the next chapter, although people have spent billions of dollars putting computers into U.S. schools, it has resulted in little change in how students learn. And most products that the fragmented and marginally profitable educational software industry has produced attempt to teach students in the same ways that subjects have been taught in the classroom. As a result, they have catered to the intelligence type that has been historically privileged in each subject.

But the fact that past investments have failed to produce the hoped for results does not doom future efforts. We believe that the disruptive innovation theory we have recounted in this chapter provides the framework for school leaders, administrators, politicians, teachers, parents, and students to migrate to a student-centric classroom. We explain how in the following chapters.

NOTES

1. This raises an important observation: Disruption is a relative term. What is disruptive to one company is sustaining to another. So while the personal computer disrupted minicomputers, the innovations within personal computing were sustaining to Apple. Also, just because a technology might by

itself appear to be disruptive, if it is employed in a way that is a sustaining improvement for the incumbent players (allows the incumbents to make more money in the way they are built to make money), the incumbents will be motivated to fight back. Incumbents win these battles of sustaining innovation with predictable regularity.

2. Clayton M. Christensen and Michael E. Raynor, *The Innovator's Solution* (Boston: Harvard Business School Press, 2003), pp. 31–72.

3. In a lecture at Yale for its tercentennial democratic vistas class, then Yale College Dean Richard H. Brodhead gave a lecture in which he makes this very point. See Richard Brodhead, "Democracy and Education," www.yale .edu/terc/democracy/media/mar27.htm, p. 3 of the lecture transcript.

   John Lienhard makes a related point. As he says, "Being self-taught had once been the norm more than the exception . . . A great part of America's unschooled 19th-century population was remarkably well read. One need only listen to readings of the letters of Civil War soldiers to appreciate how well America had tuned its ear to the rhythm of language; to the style and content of books." John Lienhard, *How Invention Begins: Echoes of Old Voices in the Rise of New Machines* (New York: Oxford, 2006), p. 198.

4. In particular, Brodhead notes Webster's 1787 essay, "Of the Education of Youth in America" and Thomas Jefferson's proposed legislation in Virginia, a "Bill for the More General Diffusion of Knowledge." Brodhead, pp. 2–8.

   Joel Spring offers an extensive discussion of Webster's role in public education, including the groundwork he laid in the early 1800s for Horace Mann and the common school movement with his work in the Massachusetts legislature. Webster's nationalist concern is paramount. See Joel Spring, *The American School: 1642–1993*, 3rd ed. (New York: McGraw-Hill, 1994), pp. 33–36.

   Larry Cuban, *Oversold and Underused: Computers in the Classroom* (Cambridge, Massachusetts: Harvard University Press, 2001), pp. 7–8.

   David Tyack and Larry Cuban, *Tinkering Toward Utopia: A Century of Public School Reform* (Cambridge, Massachusetts: Harvard University Press, 1995), p. 59.

5. The actual implementation was of course nothing as formal as Jefferson envisioned, but the basic structural tenets were quite similar, even if the sorting system was not nearly as concrete as he wanted and therefore still gave the advantage to those with money. Still, Alexis de Tocqueville did mention in his work on America, *Democracy in America*, that U.S. public schools were there for everyone, regardless of wealth. This was as early as 1832. See Brodhead, pp. 4–8.

   For a discussion of the expansion of elementary education in the nineteenth century, see Tyack and Cuban, p. 86.

6. For a discussion of the German challenge, see Tyack and Cuban, p. 49, and Cuban, p. 9.

Cuban also observes that this new job had roots in the old one, as Mann made the point that education had an economic purpose, but for him that economic purpose was not its own end, but was instead a means to bolster democracy and support public schooling. See Cuban, p. 8.

Brodhead also discusses Mann's economic argument from his annual reports as secretary of the Massachusetts State Board of Education from 1837 to 1848. The economic argument is in the 1848 report. See Brodhead, pp. 7–8.

7. Tyack and Cuban, pp. 21, 86, and Spring, pp. 116–117.
8. James Bryant Conant, *The Revolutionary Transformation of the American High School* (Cambridge, Massachusetts: Harvard University Press, 1959), p. 3.
9. Conant, *Revolutionary Transformation*, pp. 3–4, and see James Bryant Conant, *The American High School Today: A First Report to Interested Citizens* (New York: McGraw-Hill, 1959).
10. Tyack and Cuban, p. 20.
11. Tyack and Cuban, pp. 22–26.
12. "Crisis in Education, Part I: Schoolboys Point Up a U.S. Weakness," *Life*, March 24, 1958, pp. 27–35.
13. "Advanced Placement Program," Wikipedia, http://en.wikipedia.org/wiki/Advanced_Placement_Program (accessed on February 20, 2007).
14. Tyack and Cuban, pp. 21, 40, 48, and 66.
    The graduation rate of students graduating on time was up to 74 percent in the 2003–2004 school year. See "Elementary/Secondary Persistence and Progress," *Student Effort and Educational Progress*, National Center for Education Statistics, http://nces.ed.gov/programs/coe/2007/section3/table.asp?tableID=701.
15. Jay Matthews, "Just Whose Idea Was All This Testing? Fueled by Technology, Nation's Attempt to Create a Level Playing Field Has Had a Rocky History," *The Washington Post*, November 14, 2006, p. A06.
16. Tyack and Cuban, p. 13.
17. "A Nation at Risk," U.S. Department of Education, April 1983, www.ed.gov/pubs/NatAtRisk/intro.html.
18. "A Nation at Risk," www.ed.gov/pubs/NatAtRisk/findings.html.
19. Tyack and Cuban show how much the focus was really on inputs in schools by those seeking to make them better, not on outputs. They write: "Educators lobbied state governments to require local schools to meet minimum requirements in order to receive state aid. These included the quality and safety of buildings, the qualifications of teachers, the length of the school term, congruence with the state course of study, and even the size of flags and pictures on the walls. University professors developed 'score cards'— appealing to a sense of competition—to evaluate schools. These featured precise specifications about playground space and apparatus, pupils' desks, globes and musical equipment, hygiene and sanitation, and even 'community

spirit.' Thirty-four state departments of education managed to 'standardize' more than 40,000 schools by 1925 in accord with legislation, regulations of the state board, or rulings of the state superintendents. Private accreditation agencies also insisted on great institutional uniformity, especially at the secondary level, all in the name of progress." See Tyack and Cuban, p. 20.

Testing at this point was used as an input as well. So-called intelligence tests, precursors of the SAT and other standardized tests, were used to track students into differentiated courses of study, not to measure how well people were learning or how well teachers were teaching. See Tyack and Cuban, p. 58.

20. There is a wide-ranging debate over the importance of college as a goal for all students, just as there is a debate over standards in terms of standards for what knowledge and skills for which students. For example, Paul Barton wrote in a report for the Educational Testing Service in 2006 that, "Reformers don't seem to understand what skills and abilities the labor market values because employers' views—documented in many surveys—have not been reflected in the high school reform debate." Barton's research suggests that 69 percent of employers put the highest priority on the so-called soft skills: showing up on time with motivation to work (p. 13). Also important are adequate reading and writing skills. Grades ranked low on the list. Barton also points to the U.S. Bureau of Labor Statistics projections for the period 2001 to 2012, which suggest that of the 44 more prevalent occupations available, half of the openings would require only short-term on-the-job training and only 14 would require a higher education degree. Employers look for maturity, but no high school curriculum can make young people older. See *High School Reform and Work: Facing Labor Market Realities*, ETS Policy Information Report (Princeton, New Jersey: Educational Testing Service, June 2006).

One can infer a counterpoint to the above argument from a much-cited book by Frank Levy of MIT and Richard Murnane of Harvard University. In it they ask, what do computers do better than humans, and what do humans do better than computers? Their answer to the latter question is expert thinking and complex communications, which would seem to imply the importance, if not an imperative, for substantial postsecondary education. See Frank Levy and Richard J. Murnane, *The New Division of Labor: How Computers Are Creating the Next Job Market* (Princeton, New Jersey: Princeton University Press, 2004).

Still another perspective comes from Larry Rosenstock, the principal and CEO of High Tech High School in San Diego. He told us in October 2006, "You know, every successful enterprise has to have a central metric. . . . I've thought a lot about what that should be for a high school. My best answer: it's the percentage of your students who get into a college program that fits and stick with it." From Larry Rosenstock remarks to a visiting delegation to High Tech High School in San Diego, notes by Curtis W. Johnson (October 17, 2006).

The Gates Foundation seems to have agreed, as it has made its principal goal to see that 80 percent of low-income and minority students will graduate from high school college-ready by the year 2020.

21. Even today this persists. Real estate values are affected by people's perceptions of the neighborhood schools—better local schools make the housing more desirable and thus more expensive. According to studies looking at this connection, the perception of whether a school is good is mostly shaped by its average test scores. Jay Mathews wrote about it in *The Washington Post*, "Finding Good Schools," March 13, 2007, www.washingtonpost.com/wp-dyn/content/article/2007/03/13/AR2007031300491.html.

22. One piece, by Marshall Smith and Jennifer O'Day, is widely seen as the intellectual foundation for what became the standards movement of the 1990s and beyond. Marshall S. Smith and Jennifer O'Day, "Systemic School Reform," *The Politics of Curriculum and Testing: The 1990 Yearbook of the Politics of Education Association*, eds. Susan Fuhrman and Betty Malen (New York: Falmer Press, 1991), pp. 233–267.

23. But, you might ask, what about chartered schools? Since 1991, 40 states and Congress acting as the legislature for the District of Columbia have enacted laws that have allowed entities other than districts to start and run a public school. Despite this sea change that has seen the birth of many new school models, chartered schools have not proven to be disruptive. Were they so, according to the model of disruption discussed earlier, district public schools would want to ignore these chartered schools and would be pleased when they enrolled their students. But except for instances where district schools aren't serving students—as with dropouts or pre-kindergarten students—this has not been the case. An example is the Maya Angelou Public Charter School in Washington, D.C., which is taking over Oak Hill's prison school for incarcerated youth. In most states, if districts ignore unaffiliated chartered schools and give them students, they lose the per-pupil funding. In cities where significant numbers of students move, the district schools lose jobs. The asymmetric motivation to ignore chartered schools does not exist, and so districts and unions are motivated to oppose chartering in whatever shape—and do. We return to chartered schools in Chapter 9 to explain their role in innovating in education.

24. "Elementary/Secondary Education: Table 5-1," *Participation in Education*, National Center for Education Statistics, http://nces.ed.gov/programs/coe/2007/section1/table.asp?tableID=667. "Elementary/Secondary Education: Table 6-1," *Participation in Education*, National Center for Education Statistics, http://nces.ed.gov/programs/coe/2007/section1/table.asp?table ID =668.

25. Although there is lots of contradictory evidence on whether this is the case right now, some early signs indicate that schools will adjust. One major independent study was released in June 2007 that suggested that test scores were up since No Child Left Behind went into effect. See Amit R. Paley, "Scores Up Since 'No Child' Was Signed," *Washington Post*, June 6, 2007, p. A01.

A significant book that had not been published at the time we were writing *Disrupting Class* notes that a strongly deleterious impact of the No Child Left Behind legislation is that schools, more than ever, are "teaching to the test," rather than teaching critical skills. We recommend this book. See Tony Wagner, *The Global Achievement Gap* (New York: Basic Books, 2008).

Chapter 3

Crammed Classroom Computers

Maria and her friends rise in the stands to cheer as Rob knocks the ball behind the opposing team's goaltender.

"Goaaaaaaaallllllllllllllllll!" they yell as they clap and hug each other. The team is destined for at least another boys' soccer county championship as long as Rob can remain academically eligible, and, lately, Maria's been pretty optimistic about that.

After the game, Rob and Maria walk home together. They have another chemistry assignment tonight, but Rob is confident about this one: all they have to do is use Microsoft Excel to make a graph of some data. Then, for extra credit, they can write short papers about chemists by using the Internet for research. Then they will present the papers in small groups.

"Cake," Rob says to Maria, still jubilant with victory. She agrees, and they part at the corner of his street and hers.

Later that evening, she is finishing up the extra-credit portion of the assignment when her mother comes into the study where Maria does her homework.

"Whatcha doin', kiddo?" her mother asks.

"Biography of Marie Curie," Maria says absently as she types her citations.

"Really? I did that for Mr. Alvera when I had him," her mother says. "Your grandmother called Uncle Dan, and I grabbed the encyclopedia. We felt so smart."

Maria looks up at that, but her mother has already gone into the kitchen. It figures that even though she was practically born playing computer games, she's still doing the same assignments her mother did 20-some-odd years ago, when Mr. Alvera was a rookie teacher. Maybe college will be better?

■ ■ ■

Despite the widespread presence of computers, Maria's school experience isn't too much different from her mother's experience a little over two decades earlier. Whereas her mother did the research through reference books, Maria now does it online; and whereas her mother typed out her project on a typewriter, Maria types it using a word processor. Why haven't computers brought about a transformation in schools the way they have in other areas of life?

In 1996, President Bill Clinton announced a transformative vision for computing in schools. He called for: (1) modern computers and learning devices available to all students, (2) classrooms connected to one another and the outside world, (3) making educational software an integral part of the curriculum and as engaging as the best video game, and (4) having teachers ready to use and teach with technology.[1]

Personal computers have been around for three decades. Schools are well populated with them—largely fulfilling the first two of President Clinton's mandates. But the second two are as distant as ever. Classrooms look largely the same as they did before the personal computer revolution, and the teaching and learning processes are similar to what they were in the days before computers. As we say in the Introduction, the billions that schools have spent on computers have had little effect on how teachers teach and students learn—save possibly to increase costs and draw resources away from other school priorities. They haven't brought schools much closer to realizing the promising path of building students' intrinsic motivation through student-centric learning.

The reason for this disappointing result is that the way schools have employed computers has been perfectly predictable, perfectly logical—and, if transforming learning is the goal, perfectly wrong. As we show in this chapter, schools have crammed them into classrooms to sustain and marginally improve the way they already teach and run their schools, just as most organizations do when they attempt to implement innovations, including computers. Using computers this way will never allow schools to migrate to a student-centric classroom. If school administrators will change course, however, and first implement computer-based learning in places and for courses where there are no teachers to teach, then computer-based learning will, step by step, disrupt the *instructional* job that teachers are doing in a positive way, by helping students learn in ways that their brains are wired to learn *and* by allowing teachers to give students much more individual attention.

❖ DEPLOYING DISRUPTIVE INNOVATIONS AGAINST NONCONSUMPTION

Recall from the last chapter how Apple disrupted Digital Equipment Corporation (DEC) and the minicomputer companies. When Apple introduced its personal computer, it created a completely new market for computing by selling its model Apple IIe as a *toy* for *children*. Apple didn't attack the existing markets where minicomputers already were being used, nor did it frame its main competition as being DEC. Because it targeted applications where in the past computers had been too expensive and complicated to be used, Apple didn't need to make better computers than DEC to delight its customers. All it had to do was make a product that was better than the customers' other alternative, which was no computer at all.

Had Apple tried to cram its personal computer into the existing market by framing it as a sustaining innovation in the original plane of competition, DEC would have crushed Apple and its personal computer, whose performance was not even close to that of DEC's machines. Any effort to emulate DEC's minicomputer capability at the outset within the desktop computer architecture would have cost billions of dollars over many years, and even then it would have been unlikely to take root. To succeed, disruptive technologies must be applied in applications where the alternative is nothing. Indeed, selecting these applications is far more important for the successful implementation of the technology than is the technology itself.

❖ TECHNOLOGY IMPLEMENTATION AND THE LEGISLATIVE PROCESS

In every organization there are forces that shape and morph every new innovative proposal so that it fits the existing organization's own business model, rather than fitting the market it was intended to serve. One way to understand these forces is to visualize how the legislative process works. A congresswoman sees a pressing societal problem and envisions an innovative solution. She drafts the enabling legislation and introduces the bill. Within a few weeks, the labor unions inform her that unless she modifies the legislation to address their concerns, they'll block it. She changes her bill to win their support. A short time later, the Chamber of Commerce announces its opposition to the bill unless it is modified in certain ways, so she amends her proposal to address their concerns. Then she learns that a powerful senator from Texas won't support it unless she adds special considerations favorable to Texas, and so on. To win the support needed for Congress to enact the proposed legislation into law, the congresswoman shapes the bill to fit the interests of those with powerful votes; as a result, what comes out at the end of the legislative process looks *very* different from what went into it.

The same forces are at work in every company. Companies shape every innovative idea to fit the interests of the groups in the company that must support the proposal in order for it to receive funding. Innovative ideas never pop out of the innovators' heads as full-fledged business plans. Rather, they are fragments of a plan. As the innovator tries to sell the idea to the powerful entities in the company, he runs into a set of hurdles that are frightfully comparable to those the congresswoman encountered. He realizes that the sales force won't support his idea unless he adapts the innovation to appeal to the customers with whom the sales force already has relationships. Then he learns that unless he changes his estimates for pricing and gross margins, the finance department will veto the idea; and the head of engineering warns that unless he agrees to reuse certain components from earlier product designs, the engineering department will oppose it; and so on. To win the support of all the powerful entities within the organization whose endorsement is critical to getting the innovation funded, the innovative idea morphs into a concept that fits the business model of the organization, rather than the market for which the innovator originally envisioned it.

In the language of disruption, here is what this means: unless top managers actively manage this process, their organization will shape every disruptive innovation into a *sustaining* innovation—one that fits the processes, values, and economic model of the existing business—because organizations *cannot* naturally disrupt themselves. This is a core reason why incumbent firms are at a disadvantage relative to entrant companies when disruptive innovations emerge. And it explains why computers haven't changed schools.

Histories of Nypro, an injection molding firm; Merrill Lynch, an investment management company; and RCA, an electronics firm, illustrate this problem and show how a manager can solve it. We've picked illustrations from such diverse industries to show how pervasive the challenge of deploying disruptive technologies to compete against nonconsumption is. Schools, in other words, are not unique in how they have implemented computer-based learning.

Nypro's Novaplast Machine

Nypro, Inc., is one of the world's top precision-injection molders of plastics. The business model that leads to Nypro's success focuses on producing parts for its customers' products in volumes numbering in the millions, to tolerances as precise as plus or minus 2 microns. Nypro's plants span the globe. Each operates as a profit center. Through multiple mechanisms, Nypro's CEO, Gordon Lankton, has created a system of ranking the plants' financial performances against each other. This motivates plant managers to adopt any process innovation that helps them achieve the best financial performance among Nypro's plants.

In the mid-1990s, Lankton saw fundamental changes coming in his market. He saw it shifting away from customers needing millions of units per product and moving toward customers demanding a broader variety of parts with much shorter run lengths and much faster turnaround. To respond to this shift, Lankton initiated development of a small, radically disruptive molding machine dubbed the "Novaplast." The Novaplast could mold parts to the same degree of precision as the huge, inflexible machines Nypro historically had used. But engineers could set up the Novaplast to run new parts in a few minutes instead of a few hours. And the molds it used were much simpler and cheaper to make because molding pressures were low. These innovations were critical to help Nypro compete in the emerging market for fast, customized variety.

Consistent with his established practice of allowing his plant managers autonomy to adopt those innovations that they thought would help them compete more profitably in their markets, Lankton offered each plant the opportunity to lease, rather than buy, Novaplast machines from corporate headquarters. Most of his plant managers agreed to lease the machine because the technology was exciting and seemed disruptive. To Lankton's dismay, however, all but two of the plants returned their Novaplast machines to corporate headquarters as soon as the terms of the lease allowed it. The reason? The plant managers uniformly responded that there was no market for fast, customized variety.

Only two plants kept their Novaplast machines. Both, it turned out, were producing thin-walled plastic liners that fit inside the casings of AA batteries that one of Nypro's biggest customers made. This liner had to be manufactured to *very* tight tolerances in high volumes. For a host of reasons, the part ran better on the Novaplast machine than on the company's traditional machines.

What was going on? The votes in Nypro's "legislative" process were clear. Novaplast didn't fit the business model of the plants, so the plant managers rejected it. Nypro's plants were wedded to a process whose economics mandated production of huge volumes of a few products. This was critical to keeping overhead costs low. Likewise, the salespeople for each plant made much higher sales commissions on high-volume products. Low-volume products were simply antithetical to Nypro's plants' formula for making money. Novaplast was, in other words, a disruptive innovation relative to the business model of these plants—and an organization cannot disrupt itself. It cannot implement an innovation that does not make economic or cultural sense to itself. The plants that were able to put Novaplast to productive use implemented it as a sustaining technology. It helped them produce a standard high-volume part even more profitably than before.

For Nypro to address the market Lankton had seen (which history now confirms he saw with farsighted acuity), he would have had to implement Novaplast in factories whose process economics were tuned to the market for fast, customized variety. And this plant would have required a sales force whose compensation system rewarded, rather than penalized, the pursuit of such business. While Nypro's existing plants could not have done this, had Lankton set up a new, independent plant complete with its own sales force, Nypro could have implemented the Novaplast disruptively.

Merrill Lynch, Charles Schwab, and Online Brokerage

In the late 1990s, firms such as E*TRADE and Ameritrade began disrupting the stock brokerage market with online trading. In the language of our research, these firms led a new-market disruption that enabled a much larger population of people to manage their own diversified portfolio of stocks. Two of the incumbent firms, Charles Schwab and Merrill Lynch, announced their intention to counter the disruptive attack by initiating online trading as well.

Schwab created a separate business unit to conduct online trading and made a masterful transition to the computer-centric investment management world—ultimately phasing out its original broker-based business unit. How? To make money at heavily discounted prices per trade, the new unit operated at much higher trading volumes and significantly lower costs than those characterizing the traditional business.

Merrill Lynch also implemented an online trading system for its clients. But rather than creating a distinct business unit whose economics were appropriate for the opportunity, it instead chose to attempt to build an online trading business within its core broker-centric business. The result? Like the Novaplast machine in Nypro's two plants, Merrill Lynch implemented its online system in a way that helps its well-compensated brokers get better information faster so that they can do a better job serving the needs of their high-net-worth clients. The system had the same disruptive potential as did the E*TRADE, Ameritrade, and Schwab systems. But because Merrill Lynch's core business unit implemented it, Merrill used it in a way that sustained the current business. The technology didn't transform anything—and we could expect nothing else. An organization simply cannot disrupt itself. But as the Schwab example shows, a manager who sits one level up from the organization she wants to disrupt can set up a new organization with different resources, processes, and priorities and successfully disrupt the old, internal organization. Merrill Lynch could have done the same, just as Lankton and Nypro could have.

The Impact of Transistors on RCA and Sony

In almost every case, when disruptive innovations emerge, the industry leaders *see* the disruptive change coming. The personal computer was not news to DEC; Nypro's Lankton saw the burgeoning market for fast, customized variety; and Merrill Lynch could see online trading. But their instinct was to utilize their existing business infrastructure and sell the disruptive products to their existing customers. We call this phenomenon "cramming." The reason why the established industry leaders instinctively cram disruptive technologies into the established market is that they need to serve their existing customers. Furthermore, these are big companies, with big needs to grow even bigger. Disruptive markets are by definition small at the outset because disruptive products compete against nonconsumption. Within established companies, the firm's "legislative" system, or resource allocation process, shapes every proposal to serve the existing customers better and thereby generate substantial growth—even if the proposal is more suitable for a disruptive approach.

Cramming what should be a disruptive innovation into an existing marketplace is fraught with expense and disappointment because new disruptive technologies never perform as well as does the established approach in its own market. When companies cram disruptions into head-on competition against the existing approach, it costs extraordinary sums as the leaders work incessantly to improve the technology. At the same time, entrant firms are exploiting the technology in new markets where the alternative is nothing at all. To see how and why this happens, we recount a third case history, in which we chronicle the way Sony disrupted the Radio Corporation of America (RCA).

In 1947, scientists at AT&T's Bell Laboratories invented the transistor, the technological building block of what became known as *solid-state electronics*. Transistors were disruptive relative to vacuum tubes, the established technology at the time, because while they enabled smaller, less power-hungry devices, transistors could not handle the power that the electronic products of that age—tabletop radios, floor-standing televisions, and early digital computers—required. All the vacuum tube companies like RCA saw the transistor coming and licensed it. They then framed solid-state electronics as a technological challenge because the transistor could not handle the power required to build big televisions and radios. Adjusted for today's dollars, they spent upwards of $1 billion in research and development trying to make the transistor work in the market as it existed at that time.

While RCA's engineers were in their labs working to improve the technology, the first commercial application of the transistor appeared in 1952. It was a little hearing aid, where the transistor's lower power consumption was highly valued. A few years later, in 1955, Sony introduced the first battery-powered, pocket transistor radio. In comparison with the big RCA tabletop radios, the Sony pocket radio was tinny and static-laced. But Sony chose to sell its transistor radio to nonconsumers—teenagers who could not afford a big tabletop radio. It allowed teenagers to listen to music out of earshot of their parents because it was portable. And although the reception and fidelity weren't great, it was far better than their alternative, which was no radio at all. The pocket radio was a big hit for Sony.

While it made a profit on this simple beachhead application, Sony continued to improve the technology. In 1959, Sony introduced its first portable television using the transistor. Again, Sony's TV won a welcome market reception because it competed against nonconsumption. Sony's transistor enabled a whole new population of people, whose bank accounts and apartments had been too small, to afford a TV. By the late 1960s, solid-state electronics had improved to the point where the transistor could handle the power required to make larger products, and, just as happened to DEC a few decades later, all the vacuum-tube companies, including RCA, vaporized.

This is a punishing but predictable tale. The only way RCA's customers could have used transistors was if solid-state electronics were more cost- and performance-effective in the markets that RCA served. In the 1950s and early 1960s, this was a *very* difficult technological hurdle for RCA to surmount. But because Sony deployed the transistor against noncon- sumption, all it had to do was make a product that was better than nothing. And that presented a *far* less ambitious techno- logical hurdle at the outset.

❖ CRAMMING COMPUTERS IN SCHOOLS

So what do these three cases of attempting to cram disruptive technologies into mainstream markets have to do with how public schools have dealt with computers? The parallels are everywhere. Just as RCA saw the transistor coming, educators have seen computers reinvent many other professions. As a result, they have invested *heavily* in computers. In 1981, there was one computer for every 125 students in schools. By 1991 there was one for every 18; and in 2000, there was one for every five students. Many schools now have a laptop for every child; and if a $100 laptop becomes a reality, they will likely be everywhere. Over the last couple of decades, schools have spent well over $60 billion on equipping classrooms with computers.[2]

Despite these investments, students report using the com- puters sparsely in their schools. Fifth graders report using com- puters 24 minutes a week in class and in computer labs. Eighth graders report using computers an average of 38 minutes a week. Because many high schools have begun offering courses in how to use computers and in vocational classes that relate strongly to computers, older students use them more than those in the younger grades. But even then, schools use computers as a tool and a topic, not as a primary instructional mechanism that helps students learn in ways that are customized to their type of intelligence.[3]

Larry Cuban, who has conducted highly regarded studies on this topic, reports that in early-grade elementary school classrooms, computers serve to sustain the traditional early childhood school model. Computers have become just another activity center for children that they can opt to use in the course of the day. At the computer, they can play such games as "Franklin Learns Math" or "Math Rabbit." Although these games are popular with the children, they do not supplant traditional teaching; instead, teachers use them to supplement and reinforce the existing teaching model. As such, computers add cost while failing to revolutionize the classroom experience.[4]

In middle and high school core academic classes in particular, students report that computers have had little to no impact on the way they learn. Teachers still deliver the instruction. Students use computers primarily for word processing, to search the Internet for research papers, and to play games. A small number of middle school teachers—under 20 percent— reported using computers for drill-and-practice software or for math games and the like. High school teachers report having made good use of computers to make better lesson plans and to communicate more with parents through e-mail and blogs. But again, as Cuban concluded, "In the end, both supporters and critics of school technology (including researchers) have claimed that powerful software and hardware often get used in limited ways to simply maintain rather than transform prevailing instructional practices."[5]

Some argue that even where education technology *has* been used, the results have been no better than teacher-based instruction.[6] One might conclude from this that the software just isn't good enough yet, which then implies that if school leaders, software companies, and educators just keep working on the technology with a few billion dollars more, the impact will materialize.

We don't think so. To see why, consider the case of Jaime Escalante. Escalante began teaching math at Los Angeles' Garfield High School in the late 1970s. In a school where drugs, gangs, and violence were daily realities, against all conventional wisdom Escalante offered Advanced Placement (AP) Calculus to a few students in 1982. At the end of the year, all these students passed the AP exam. The Educational Testing Service (ETS), which administers the AP exams, thought they must have cheated. It was simply implausible that 100 percent of the students from the class in Garfield High would pass AP Calculus. The students retook the exam and passed again. It was a testament to the students, but also to Escalante and his ability to teach and motivate. By 1991, when Escalante left the school, 570 Garfield High students were taking AP exams.

Escalante was an exceptional teacher. Why not capture Escalante's instructional magic on film and make it available to schools anywhere? Sure, it's not the same as having Escalante there himself (nor are we arguing that this would offer the potential of customizing an education through the power of computer-based learning), but if he is that good, why narrow his impact to one classroom in one school? People have in fact done this with great teachers of Escalante's caliber. But these sorts of films have had little impact because they were simply crammed into classrooms as a tool on top of the traditional teaching methods.[7] Not surprisingly, never has a calculus teacher announced to the class, "Kids, today is a great day. We have these films of a teacher in Los Angeles, and you just need a technician to run the projector. You don't need me any more."

The sum of these assessments is that traditional instructional practices have changed little despite the introduction of computers and other modern technologies. A class does not look all that different from the way it did a couple of decades earlier, with the exception that banks of computers line the walls of many classrooms. Lecturing, group discussions, small-group assignments and projects, and the occasional video or overhead are still the norms. Computers have not increased student-centered learning and project-based teaching practices. The implementation of computers has not caused any measurable improvements in achievement scores.[8] And, most important for the purposes of this book, computers have made almost no dent in the most important challenge that they have the potential to crack: allowing students to learn in ways that correspond with how their brains are wired to learn, thereby migrating to a student-centric learning environment.

Understanding how schools have spent so much money on computers, only to achieve so little gain, isn't so hard. Schools have crammed the computers into the existing teaching and classroom models. Teachers have implemented computers in the most commonsense way—to sustain their existing practices and pedagogies rather than to displace them.

So how could schools implement computer-based learning in ways that transform teaching and learning? We illustrate how by first recounting the phonograph's commercialization— and then its ultimate disruption of live music.

❖ HOW TO IMPLEMENT COMPUTER-BASED LEARNING: LESSONS FROM RACHMANINOFF

Through the 1870s, people had few options for listening to music. They either had to provide the music themselves or arrange for a local musician to play. People were of course limited by their particular repertoire and skill. Rarely could you hear the music you wanted to hear where and when you wanted to hear it—and most of the time you couldn't hear music at all.

Thomas Edison began to change all this when he invented the phonograph in 1877. Suddenly you could hear music in places other than those where it originated. And you could now hear more than just the local instrumentalists. As people recorded the great musicians like Rachmaninoff, you could hear the best musicians' brilliance right in your living room. But imagine what would have happened if RCA Victor, which pioneered the ability to record music with Edison's technology, had made a recording of Rachmaninoff playing his second piano concerto and then sold tickets to a concert in Carnegie Hall where people could listen to Rachmaninoff—but instead of the real person playing the music with a live orchestra, the concert's promoters had rolled a Victrola phonograph onto the stage and played the recording into a microphone. The same people who would have been delighted with the quality of the recording when they were listening at home in Poughkeepsie, New York—where it was infinitely better than nothing—would have been deeply disappointed when the recording was pitted in head-on competition against the real people in the real place.

Fortunately for the recording industry, RCA Victor didn't attempt the Carnegie Hall stunt. It instead sold its phonographs and recordings to people who couldn't go to Carnegie Hall, and its customers could play them whenever and wherever they wanted to hear music. It took about a century for the technology to become good enough that listening to the recording was nearly as good as hearing the music live. Today, nearly everyone, from the casual music listener to music connoisseurs, hear the majority of their music through recordings, not live.

Imagine the outcome if the early recording industry had marketed its products to be played after the intermission during live symphony concerts to allow the performers to go home early. Or what if it had decided that it couldn't com- mercialize Edison's technology at all and kept working on it in laboratories until it was quality-competitive with the best live musicians? The industry would have spent billions and achieved little. Success with disruptive innovations always originates at the simplest end of the market, typically com- peting against nonconsumption. Then, from that base, the technology gets better and better until, ultimately, it performs well enough that it supplants the prior approach.

If the recordings of Rachmaninoff found a welcome market by *not* competing directly with the live musician himself, why should people pit the recordings of teachers like Escalante in direct competition with teachers? Just as no one would pay to go to Carnegie Hall to listen to a phonograph recording, we should not expect teachers today to use a recording of Escalante to teach when they can use their own skills. The technology will become successful only if it is allowed to compete against nonconsumption, where it surely would be better than nothing. Then bit by bit it could improve and change the way learning takes place in schools.

It's not just the recording industry and the Sony pocket radio. Virtually *every* successful disruptive innovation took root similarly—competing against nonconsumption—so that people were delighted to have a product, even if its capacities were limited. Cisco's router, with its 4-second latency delay, couldn't be used to switch voice calls at the outset. So it was used to transmit data over the Internet. But today, Cisco products route phone calls over the Internet through VoIP (Voice over Internet Protocol) with aplomb. IBM and Kodak attacked Xerox's high-speed photocopiers head-on in the 1980s, got bloodied, and withdrew. But Canon attacked nonconsumption first by deploying small tabletop copiers in locations and in small companies where a high-speed Xerox machine wasn't economical. Once in that market, Canon improved its copiers one step at a time until most companies no longer needed costly Xerox machines in their high-speed photocopy centers. Google and craigslist are disrupting advertisements in newspapers in the same manner. And on and on.

In the next chapter, we discuss how school districts can actively deploy computer-based learning in schools in a disruptive, rather than cramming, mode. By migrating instruction delivery to custom-configured vehicles that are able to meet individual students' needs, schools can realize the dream of transforming the classroom from a monolithic one into a student-centric one where all students can learn in the ways their individual minds are wired to learn.

NOTES

1. U.S. Department of Education, *Getting America's Students Ready for the Twenty-First Century: Meeting the Technology Literacy Challenge* (Washington, DC: June 1996), quoted in Larry Cuban, *Oversold and Underused: Computers*

in the Classroom (Cambridge, Massachusetts: Harvard University Press, 2001), p. 16.

2. These numbers come from a variety of sources in which the authors did their own calculations. In particular, see Evan Hansen, "Public Schools: Why Johnny Can't Blog," CNET News.com, November 12, 2003, http://news.com.com/2009-1023-5103805.html. The article cites statistics from Quality Education Data. See Cuban, p. 17. And see *America's Digital Schools* (The Greaves Group and The Hayes Connection, 2006).

3. Cuban, pp. 72 and 90.

   A Department of Education report gives further evidence of how education technology is used mostly to support instruction and as a tool rather than to deliver the instruction itself. *Effectiveness of Reading and Mathematics Software Products: Findings from First Student Cohort*, report to Congress, U.S. Department of Education (National Center for Education Evaluation and Regional Assistance, March 2007), p. xiv.

4. Cuban, pp. 52–67. Also, because of their activity-center structure, K–4 classes tend to be more student-centric, so the lack of transformation is arguably not as big a deal as perhaps it is in the later grades. It is also important to develop many different intelligences and learning styles for children at this younger age, according to Howard Gardner and others.

5. Cuban, pp. 72–73, 90–91, 95, and 133–134. Even though Cuban's studies were published in 2001, not much has changed in the seven years since. Our own observations traveling to schools around the country confirm his observations, as do interviews and a specific case study of the Arlington, Massachusetts, school district that Josh Friedman conducted for a Harvard Business School independent study report for Clayton Christensen in the 2007 winter semester.

6. *Effectiveness of Reading and Mathematics Software*, p. xiii.

7. Cuban has also done research on how other technologies have been implemented in the past. In the 1950s, instructional television was hailed as the answer to a looming teacher shortage; but by and large this, as well as instructional films, first developed in the early part of the twentieth century, has sustained existing practices and been used to give teachers breaks, for example, rather than to overturn how instruction was delivered in schools. Cuban, pp. 137–138.

   In an example of videotaped lectures having an impact, BAR/BRI, the standard for bar exam studying, creates videos of professors to accomplish this teaching purpose for students studying for the bar exam. For example, a group of students can study for the New York Bar Exam in Toronto and receive the best instruction possible. They assemble daily and pop in a BAR/BRI video that has a different professor lecturing on a different bar exam topic each day.

8. Cuban, pp. 90–91, 95, 133–134, and 178.

A *New York Times* story followed up on a U.S. Department of Education report about the effectiveness of computer-based learning with a story on the Liverpool, New York, school district giving up on laptops. In the article, it references Mark Warschauer, an education professor at the University of California at Irvine and author of *Laptops and Literacy: Learning in the Wireless Classroom* (New York: Teachers College Press, 2006). Warschauer also found no correlation between the use of laptops and test scores, but he also said, "Where laptops and Internet use make a difference are in innovation, creativity, autonomy and independent research." Winnie Hu, "Seeing No Progress, Some Schools Drop Laptops," *New York Times*, May 4, 2007, http://www.nytimes.com/2007/05/04/education/04laptop.html.

Chapter 4

Disruptively Deploying Computers

The next day, as Maria files into the guidance counselor's office to register for next semester, she really, really hopes that college will be better than this. Prompted by interests in religion and international security, she's been reading about the growing importance of Arabic and its popularity as a subject of study in the United States. Dr. Allston had told her that there was an outside chance that there would be a class at Randall next term, but now, flipping through the offerings in the guidance office's booklet, Maria sees that she won't have the option. She frowns at the booklet when it's her turn to talk to the counselor. Instead of registering for class, she makes an appointment to meet with Allston to see if she can get the principal's special permission to attend an Arabic class at the local university.

But the appointment is unnecessary. Allston wanders in the doorway of the guidance office.

"This young lady just made an appointment to see you," says Rachel Hudson, the guidance counselor.

"There's no Arabic," Maria says in response to the principal's raised brow. "I thought I could go to Randall University."

Oddly, Allston's face lights up. "There wasn't enough demand," she says. "But we came up with another way for you to do it. Why don't you just come into my office?"

Maria pads down the hall toward the principal's office. She's already grumpy at the idea of a commute to the local university, but she wants to study Arabic now—not two years from now. The principal gestures at a chair in front of her desk, and Maria plops down. Allston, still standing, rifles through a pile of mail on her desk.

"Aha," she beams. "Here."

She hands an envelope to Maria.

"This is the pilot program of a state-accredited Arabic class, offered only online. You can take it with all the other kids in the county who are interested in Arabic. Just go down the hall to the computer lab in the library, go to the Web site referenced in the packet, and follow the directions."

"Wow, that simple?" asks Maria, amazed.

"Yep, that simple," Allston says. "Your own pace, your own schedule. The program, with the help of the online teacher, will even customize for how fast you learn. A live teacher would have been great, but you're the only one here who wants to take the course. There are two kids at Spencer Circle, and three at Matthew Key—together, you're enough for the district to try this. I'm hoping to offer Japanese next year, if those of you taking Arabic do well."

Maria offers a hasty thanks, and then she's on her way to the library.

■ ■ ■

Up until this point in time, student-centric technology in the form of computers hasn't had much impact on mainstream public education. But as is the case with all successful disruptions, if you know where to look—competing against nonconsumption—computer-based learning is methodically gaining ground as students, educators, and families find it to be better than the alternative—having nothing at all. Despite skepticism and pessimism from many that the lack of an open market means that schools would not implement this computer-based technology in disruptive fashion, things are changing. Public education enrollments in online classes like the one for which Maria signed up are exhibiting the classic signs of disruption as they have skyrocketed from 45,000 in 2000 to roughly 1 million today.

How has this happened? At first glance, there is little non-consumption in U.S. schooling, and one therefore might expect to see the disruption occurring only in developing countries where education is not universal; after all, children are required to attend school in the United States. On the contrary, looking at the class level within U.S. schools reveals many areas of non-consumption where computer-based solutions can take root. Some of the opportunities where the alternative is nothing at all include Advanced Placement (AP) and other specialized or advanced courses; small, rural, and urban schools that are unable to offer breadth; "credit recovery" for students who must retake courses in order to graduate; home-schooled students and those who can't keep up with the schedule of regular school; high-school dropouts; students needing special tutoring; and pre-kindergartners.[1] Computer-based learning has already planted itself in these foothold markets. It is gaining "market share" at a predictable pace. Like all disruptions, it first appears as a blip on the radar, and then, seemingly out of nowhere, the mainstream rapidly adopts it.

If the history of these types of innovations can serve as a guide, the disruptive transition from teacher-led to software-delivered instruction is likely to proceed in two stages. We call the first of these stages *computer-based*, or *online, learning*. In this stage, the software will be proprietary and relatively expensive to develop. It will also still be relatively monolithic with respect to students' preferred methods of learning in that the instructional methods in this software will largely mirror the dominant type of learning method in each subject. Computer-based learning is not as completely monolithic as the teacher-delivered mode is, however. Online learning today accommodates different paces of learning, and some allows students to choose different pathways to learning the material.

The second phase of this disruption we term *student-centric technology*, in which software has been developed that can help students learn each subject in a manner that is consistent with their learning needs. Whereas computer-based learning is disruptive relative to the monolithic mode of teacher-led instruction, student-centric technology is disruptive relative to personal tutors. Tutors today are largely limited to the wealthy; and for those privileged few, good tutors come as close as possible to helping students learn each subject in ways that match the way their brains are wired to learn. Like all disruptions, student-centric technology will make it affordable, convenient, and simple for many more students to learn in ways that are customized for them.

❖ NEW-MARKET DISRUPTIONS TAKE ROOT

Let's explore just a few of the most significant areas of nonconsumption in which these online courses are taking root. One of these is AP classes—college-level courses offered to high school students. There is vast nonconsumption of AP courses in most high schools. Thirty-three percent of schools nationwide offered no AP classes in 2002–2003.[2] Those that provide AP courses offer only a fraction of the 34 courses for which AP exams are available because there is inadequate demand and resources to hire more AP teachers. More generally, many schools are unable to offer courses for gifted students or the appropriate enrichment classes for special-needs children. Students who want or need to take these courses currently have no option in many schools.

Some schools have more difficulty offering this sort of breadth than do others. For example, bigger schools have more teachers, resources, and students, which result in more supply and demand for a wide range of courses; smaller schools have less of all three, which means they have more problems offering this breadth. Rural schools tend to be smaller, so this disproportionately affects them. And even those rural schools that are larger and have more funding available for more teachers often find that they cannot recruit qualified faculty to the needed locations. Under No Child Left Behind's regulations requiring districts to have only "highly qualified" teachers for each subject, compliance may further limit the offerings. For example, in a small town, a teacher who is trained in physics, but who formerly taught biology and chemistry as well, may no longer be allowed to teach anything except physics. The school might have to cut the other two classes entirely, even if they are state-required courses, because finding or hiring a new teacher or two is not easy to do or to afford.[3] Smaller schools are therefore often the perfect places for online learning to take root.

Urban secondary schools, especially in low-income areas, are a third ideal market for computer-based learning. Some of these schools are as resource-constrained as the rural schools are, and many struggle to find highly qualified teachers who are committed to working in such challenging environments. As society has raised the stakes on testing in the core subjects, as we discuss later, schools have responded by allotting proportionately more resources and attention to these tested subjects. A casualty of this resource allocation has been many of the "nice-to-have" courses—in the humanities, languages, arts, economics, statistics, and so on. Diminishing supply of such courses means growing nonconsumption in these areas. In an odd way, this is actually good news. Online learning is a welcome solution when the alternative is to forgo learning the subject altogether.

Homebound and home-schooled students are another ideal market application for online learning. Homebound students are those who cannot go to school for a variety of reasons, from those who have been suspended, to severely ill students, to students who cannot attend school for the full day because of other commitments. The home-schooled population presents a similar ideal market, and it is growing rapidly. According to the U.S. Department of Education, in the spring of 1999 there were 850,000 home-schooled students in the United States. Some home-schooling research groups estimate that the number of home-schooled students now has surpassed 2 million.[4] In the past, both home-schooling advocates and critics have expressed concern that the range of subjects and the depth of learning available to these students were limited by their parents' own knowledge. The online world solves this problem. This is a classic foothold market for disrupting traditional schools; and the advent of this computer capability has fueled, in part, the recent spurt in home schooling.

Another big nonconsumption opportunity is students who need to make up credits. There is a large block of students in this group, as credit recovery problems plague students from the rural Midwest to many urban school districts.[5] For a variety of reasons, there is not always a remedial class available for students who fail a course. This creates big problems as students move toward their senior year in high school, and it creates a need for an alternative to nothing at all before it is too late. Online learning can fill in the gaps. And its modularity means that students do not have to waste instructional time on concepts they've mastered; they can simply take the modules with which they struggled in order to pass the class—or at the very least breeze through the parts they already understand or that come easily to them.

There is a host of other areas of nonconsumption where student-centric online technology can make a big impact. Roughly 30 percent of high school students drop out of school—and the number of dropouts is even higher in urban areas. Private tutoring and prekindergarten similarly offer big zones of nonconsumption. For example, 43 percent of children ages 3 to 5 do not enroll in any prekindergarten program— this includes day-care centers, Head Start programs, preschool, and so forth. Children from wealthier families attend these programs more than do those from poor families. As we increasingly recognize the importance of early childhood development's impact on future learning, a movement is growing to universalize prekindergarten. Student-centric technology has a revolutionary opportunity here. We address these last two areas in Chapters 5 and 6, as this chapter focuses more on disruptions currently taking place within public high schools.[6]

❖ MEETING THE DEMAND

Together, these venues of nonconsumption constitute a booming market in which school districts can welcome computers as the primary delivery platform for learning—in contrast to the way they are now deployed in mainstream classrooms. Some evidence: Apex Learning is a for-profit company. Apex began by developing a product that allows secondary schools to offer more AP courses to more students by placing the courses online. So Apex's strategy was to market courses that schools cannot offer. In 2003–2004, enrollments in Apex's AP classes were 8,400; by 2006–2007, that number was 30,200—a compounded annual growth rate of over 50 percent.[7] Apex allows school systems to aggregate the demand for AP courses over an entire school district where there is insufficient demand in individual schools to merit having a dedicated teacher—or where budget cuts have slashed these offerings. It has expanded well beyond AP courses by offering core classes for secondary schools as well. These often target students needing to make up credits or needing remediation in certain subjects, which has fueled Apex's explosive growth. Indeed, enrollments in AP courses make up only a small fraction of Apex's total enrollments today, as in the 2006–2007 school year Apex served 304,000 enrollments. By the 2008–2009 school year, Apex served roughly 200,000 students in more than 700,000 enrollments.[8]

Apex is far from the only online course provider. K12, Inc., is a publicly traded company that CEO Ron Packard and former Secretary of Education Bill Bennett founded in 1999. K12, Inc., has a variety of offerings, from its bread-and-butter full-time virtual schools that serve home-schooled students to online supplementary courses. It serves students from kindergarten through twelfth grade. From its 2006 fiscal year to

2009, the number of students it served in its virtual schools grew from 20,000 to 55,000. Connections Academy, Advanced Academics, KC Distance Learning, Insight Schools, and many others are significant for-profit players in this space as well.[9]

More than twenty-five states have supplementary virtual schools as well. The Florida Virtual School (FLVS) is the best known of these. Begun in 1997 as a pilot project with two school districts, FLVS has had wide appeal. Under the motto, "any time, any place, any path, any pace," FLVS today offers over 100 courses, which range from the traditional staples like algebra and English to the noncore ones like AP and business technology courses. Under this guiding light, FLVS has attracted students who otherwise would be nonconsumers of various classes for a variety of reasons, from not being able to be in school during certain hours to having difficulty completing their full course load. By the 2008–2009 school year, FLVS was serving more than 71,000 students in 154,125 course enrollments—throughout and outside of Florida.[10]

❖ FOLLOWING A DISRUPTIVE PATTERN

All disruptions share a pattern. Disruptions first compete against nonconsumption in a new "plane of competition." In that plane, the technology improves, and the underlying cost declines. The technology begins drawing applications from the original plane of competition into the new one—in this case, from the traditional monolithic classroom to online learning and then, shortly, to student-centric technology.

But this transition is neither abrupt nor immediate. When a new approach or technology substitutes for an old one because it has a technological or economic advantage over the old, the substitution pace almost always follows an S-curve,[11] as depicted on the left side of Figure 4.1. Here the vertical axis measures the percent of the market for which the new approach accounts. The S-curves are sometimes steep; other times they are gradual. But disruptions almost always follow this pattern: the initial substitution pace is slow; then it steepens dramat-

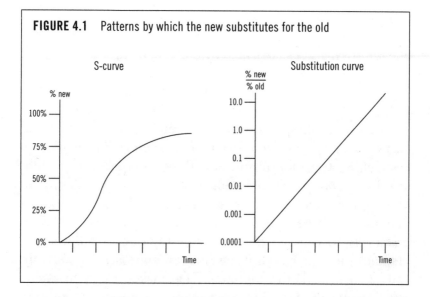

FIGURE 4.1   Patterns by which the new substitutes for the old

ically; and, finally, it asymptotically approaches 100 percent of the market.

A consistent problem emerges for the industry leaders when one of these substitutions occurs, however. When the nascent technology accounts only for a tiny fraction of the total market (when it is on the flat part at the bottom of the S-curve), the leaders project linearly into the future and conclude that there is no need to worry about the new approach because it will not be important for a long time. But then the world flips fast on them and cripples the established companies. For example, after a decade of incubation on the curve's flat portion, digital photography flipped on the film companies *very* rapidly. The result? Polaroid's core was wiped out. Agfa is gone. Fuji is seriously struggling. Kodak alone caught the wave—but even here it's been a rough ride.[12]

You might think that companies would learn from this experience, but the S-curve adoption pattern does beg a vexing question. If I'm on the initial flat portion of the curve, how can I know whether the world will flip on me next year, in 10 years, or at all?

It turns out there is a way to forecast the flip. First, as shown on the right side of Figure 4.1, one must plot on the vertical axis the *ratio* of market shares held by the new, divided by the old (if each has 50 percent, this ratio will be 1.0). Second, the vertical axis needs to be arrayed on a logarithmic scale—so that 0.0001, 0.001, 0.01, 0.1, 1.0, and 10.0 are all equidistant. When plotted in this way, the data always fall on a straight line. If the first four or five points do not lie in a line, it is a signal that there is no compelling driver for substitution. But the line is always straight if a disruption is occurring. Sometimes the line slopes upward steeply, and sometimes it is more gradual. The reason the line is straight is that the mathematics "linearizes" the S-curve. When the substitution pace is plotted in this way, one can tell what the slope of the line is even when the new approach accounts for only 2 to 3 percent of the total. That makes it easy to extend the line into the future to get a sense of when the innovation will account for 25 percent, 50 percent, and 90 percent of the total. We call this line a *substitution curve*. Whether it's the substitution of 5.25-inch for 8-inch disk drives, VoIP (Voice over Internet Protocol) for circuit-switched telephone calls, or the substitution of women's sportswear for dresses, the slope is so clear within the first few years of the substitution that people can make reasonable estimates for when the innovation will achieve increasing percentages of the market.

Although the data are hard to aggregate on a consistent basis, Figure 4.2 gives our best sense for the pace of substitution of online-delivered learning for live-teacher instruction. From 45,000 enrollments in fully online or blended-online[13] courses in the fall of 2000, that number had grown nearly 22 times to 1 million by the fall of 2007. Roughly 70 percent of these were for high school students. A significant 43 percent of rural schools already provide students with access to online courses that would not otherwise be available.[14] Even with this rapid growth, however, online courses[15] accounted for just 1 percent of all courses in 2007. Not much change is on the horizon if one projects linearly into the future. But when viewed from the logarithmic perspective, the data suggest that by 2019, about

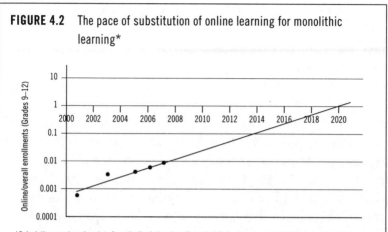

FIGURE 4.2   The pace of substitution of online learning for monolithic learning*

*Calculations are based on data from the North American Council of Online Learning and the U.S. Department of Education statistics. There are other numbers floating out there as well. In June 2007 the Washington, D.C.–based think tank Education Sector released a report titled, "Virtual High Schools and Innovation in Public Education." Written by its chief operating officer, Bill Tucker, it said that roughly 1.5 percent of all school enrollment is online today, but it has doubled in the past three years. The report says, "Virtual schooling is driving the same sorts of transforming changes in public education as Apple's iTunes has been producing in the way people collect and listen to music." Virtual schools are, "personalizing student learning and extending it beyond the traditional school day" (http://www.educationsector.org/usr_doc/Virtual_Schools.pdf).

The graph when converted to an S-curve will look like the following:

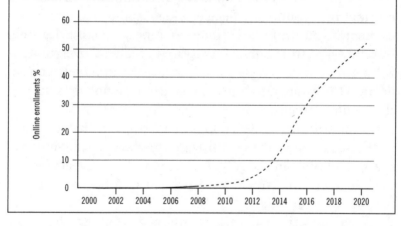

50 percent of high school courses will be delivered online. In other words, within a few years, after a long period of incubation, the world is likely to begin flipping rapidly to student-centric online technology.[16]

This substitution is happening because of the technological and economic advantages of online learning, compared to the monolithic school model. Online technology provides accessibility for those who previously would not have been able to take the course. It provides convenience for a student to fit the course into his or her schedule at the time and place that is most desirable. To varying degrees, it is simpler because it offers comparatively greater flexibility in the pace and learning path. And when it is software-based and online, it can scale with ease. Economically, it is often less expensive than the current model, even at today's limited scale. Estimates of the costs vary depending on circumstances, but on average, online courses cost between $200 and $600 per course. At the low end of this range, that is considerably less expensive than the present model; at the high end, it is comparable.[17]

Factors That Will Accelerate the Substitution

Four factors will drive the substitution. First, online learning will keep improving, as all successful disruptions do. It will become more enjoyable and take full advantage of the online medium by layering in enhanced video, audio, and interactive elements. Currently, according to reports, online learning works best with the more motivated students; over time, it will become more engaging so as to reach different types of learners. Software developers must also take full advantage of the medium to customize it by layering in different learning paths for different students. Figure 4.2 suggests that the "flip" in the substitution curve will begin in about 2012—just two years from now. In the subsequent six years, the technology's market share will grow from 5 percent to 50 percent. It will become a massive market.

A second driver of this transition will be the ability for students, teachers, and parents to select a learning pathway through each body of material that fits the learners' needs—the transition from computer-based to student-centric technology.

The third factor that will likely fuel the substitution is a looming teacher shortage. In the past, shortages have been in specific subjects or school types and mostly attributable to the revolving door of teacher turnover. And although many have forecast mass doom-and-gloom teacher shortages before, this is now more likely to happen. The baby-boomer generation of teachers will start retiring en masse soon, even as the student population, which is the highest it has ever been, will not decline in any proportional way. In 1999, 29 percent of teachers were over 50 years of age. In 2007, it was 42 percent, which suggests that a decade hence, there will be a wave of teacher shortages across the country. Unless computer-based learning has been honed in the foothold markets described above, it won't be ready for the mainstream when school districts will need the accessibility that it brings.[18]

The fourth factor is that costs will fall as the market scales up. Different industries have characteristic "scale curves" that allow executives to estimate quite accurately the degree of cost reduction per unit produced each time the scale of the market doubles. In assembled products like automobiles, the downward slope of this scale curve is 0.85—meaning that each time the quantity produced doubles (from 1 to 2; 2 to 4; 4 to 8; for example), cost per unit declines by 15 percent—to 85 percent of what it used to be. In the semiconductor industry, costs fall by 30 percent at each doubling; and in chemical plants, the scale curve slopes downward at a 40 percent pace of reduction for each doubling of scale.

Developers keep trying to improve their products so that more people will buy them. Improving computer-based learning technologies to become student-centric is likely to be quite expensive. And the costs of managing an organization as its market scales up also are significant. In addition, teachers will always remain in schools, as we note in Chapter 1—increasingly functioning as one-on-one tutors rather than teaching mono-lithically—and computer-based and student-centric learning will enable a teacher to oversee the work of more students. All of this means that the cost per student per course over the next 10 years is likely to decline by 15 percent for each doubling of volume, so that the cost will be one-third of today's costs, and the courses will be much better.[19]

Local government budget crises will add further fuel to this transition. In 2004, the Government Accounting Standards Board issued new rules that required public agencies to disclose, starting in 2008, the future costs of all postemployment benefits. The effect will be staggering. The unfunded liabilities for retiree health-care costs have been mounting unnoticed for years because many state and local governments have not made allowances for these liabilities in order to "balance" their budgets. JPMorgan estimates the present value of unfunded government employee health care and other non-pension benefits to be between $600 billion and $1.3 trillion, with the result that many state and local governments could go bankrupt—or at the very least plunge more deeply into debt to meet the costs. As a result, already tight public education budgets, of which state and local governments fund roughly 90 percent, will most certainly face cuts.[20]

The result of these four factors—technological improvements that make learning more engaging; research advances that enable the design of student-centric software appropriate to each individual learner; the looming teacher shortage; and inexorable cost pressures—is that 10 years from the publication of this book, online, student-centric learning will account for 50 percent of the "seat miles" in U.S. secondary schools. Given the current trajectory of substitution, about 80 percent of courses taken in 2024 will have been taught online in a student-centric way. Given how long some have been in the trenches of school reform, this will be quite a breathtaking "flip."

The Sequence of Substitution

Veterans of the battles for school reform with whom we've consulted for this project have been uniformly skeptical about these predictions, primarily because, as evidenced by their battle scars, the teachers unions will not allow it. While not minimizing the self-protective power that these institutions can wield in political processes,[21] if the substitution is managed disruptively, it will happen.

Because most organizations have limits on their resources, they allocate their priority resources to those customers whose business is most critical to their continued prosperity—or, in the language of disruption, they focus up-market. And they under- or disinvest in those less-profitable products or services whose sales actually pull profit margins down.

The evidence shows that school districts are doing something similar.[22] Recall from Chapter 2 that political or societal importance determines the metric on the vertical axis of the disruption graph in public education. School districts are responding to the scarcity of resources by investing in what they judge to be most important. The overriding concern among school leaders is to improve the test scores in the subjects on which schools will be judged. Schools are doubling up on reading and math at the expense of other subjects. The Center on Education Policy released a survey in March 2005 that showed that 71 percent of the nation's school districts are spending more time on math and reading, to the exclusion of other subjects.[23] The core subjects on which standardized achievement tests are administered are where priority resources are being focused.

To do this, schools are disinvesting in those "nice-to-have" courses that are less critical to the mandates of improving test scores and leaving no children behind. A darkening budget picture could make this focus on the core even more dramatic. The good news for managing the transition to student-centric learning is that as schools stop teaching certain courses, it creates a vacuum of nonconsumption—the ideal place for student-centric online technology to be deployed. Schools should greet these pressures as opportunities to implement a long-range plan to shift the instructional job to student-centric technology step by step and course by course. Disruptive innovation requires targeting not those courses that the public schools *want* to teach in-house. They must instead focus on courses that the public schools would be relieved *not* to have to teach, but do feel the need to offer. If officials target online courses at the core curriculum, however, it will elicit intense opposition by the teachers unions.

The growth path for online learning providers such as Apex is to figure out how to teach more courses more effectively. As schools face more budget pressures and the need to axe another course that lacks a critical mass of students, online learning providers want to say, "Hey, that previous course you outsourced worked so well. Let us do this one for you, too." The online providers would be motivated to add the very course the school would be motivated to drop. And these courses will keep improving as districts cut more offerings. Through a rational and incremental process, schools would outsource more and more of the instructional job to virtual providers. One day, schools will find themselves using most of their resources to do the noninstructional jobs that *cannot* be done online and find themselves teaching fewer and fewer courses through traditional monolithic instruction.

One of the most consistent findings in our studies of innovation is that although consumers are typically reluctant to pay higher prices for product "improvements" that they don't need and can't use, they generally are very willing to pay for improvements that *do* matter.[24] Recall, for example, that in the early years of the disruption of the music distribution industry, owners of early MP3 players could download and share music for free. But it was time-consuming and inconvenient. When Apple introduced its iPod and iTunes music store, millions of people gladly paid significant prices in order to get exactly what they wanted and none of what they didn't want as conveniently as possible. We suspect that during the initial period of substitution, many students' families would react similarly if they were asked to shoulder some of the cost of courses taught in a student-centric way.

❖ THE FUTURE CLASSROOM

If student-centric technology remains on this trajectory, what might the classroom of the future look like? Students filter into their room. Chemistry workbenches, complete with such things as test tubes, reagents, pH meters, and a bomb calorimeter, greet them. The students conduct experiments in which they measure the effect of changes in the pressure, volume, and temperature of gases. They record their experiments in their lab workbook, and the teacher grades them and returns the workbook to the students.

This might not sound too different from the everyday happenings many of us recall from chemistry class, but there is a big difference. This all takes place in the Virtual ChemLab. The classroom of the future is, in this case, present and accounted for.

Begun by a chemistry professor at Brigham Young University, as of 2006 the Virtual ChemLab served some 150,000 students seated at computer terminals across the country. The professor took 2,500 photographs and 220 videos, and, along with some video-game designers, created a simulated laboratory to allow students to do all the above and more. Although it is not as good, perhaps, as doing the experiments hands-on (some have pointed out that these students could enter college science courses without having used a real Bunsen burner), the virtual lab allows students to try experiments that would be too costly or too dangerous to do at their local high schools. What is more, it is infinitely better than many students' alternative—nothing at all. For resource-constrained schools in isolated rural areas or impoverished urban ones, this is a big improvement. And as technology improves over time, who knows how good the virtual re-creation of a lab might become? Maybe one day the students will be able to feel the heat from the Bunsen burner and smell the chemical reaction.[25]

In another classroom, students are learning Mandarin grammar. The students are wearing noise-canceling headphones and working with laptop computers. The teacher is kneeling beside a particular student. The student is directing the work of a brick mason on his computer screen by having him assemble a sentence in the same way that he would construct a wall—block by block. There are stacks of blocks with words on them in the background of the screen, each colored for its potential role in the sentence. The student has been directing the mason to pick blocks out of the appropriate stacks and put them in the correct order of a Mandarin sentence. When all the required blocks have been assembled in the proper sequence, the Mandarin word replaces the English on each block and the student joins the brick mason in reading the sentence (which is written phonetically in the Roman alphabet). When the student doesn't get the pronunciation right, the brick mason looks pained. The mason then repeats the correct pronunciation, and when the student gets it right, the brick mason gives a high five. Mandarin is a tonal language, so the blocks then tilt to help the student see and feel the tones.

Another student in the same classroom is learning the same material from the same software program by rote memorization—listening to a native Mandarin speaker and then repeating the sentences, in a mode of learning familiar to her parents' generation. Both students are learning to put together sentences that they'll use in a conversation together in front of the rest of the class—some of whom are using the same learning tools as these two, but many of whom are learning Mandarin in other ways that are tailored to the way they learn.

In contrast to the Virtual ChemLab, this Mandarin classroom is indeed a classroom of the future—we've not seen it yet. But it can emerge, provided the technology is introduced disruptively.

Where do teachers fit in this futuristic classroom? One, of course, is the teacher who developed the Virtual ChemLab. Another, in the room with the Mandarin students, was walking from student to student, helping each one, individually, to stay focused and to master the material in a manner consistent with each student's way of learning.

As the monolithic system of instruction shifts to a learning environment powered by student-centric technology, teachers' roles will gradually shift over time, too. The shift might not be easy, but it will be rewarding. Instead of spending most of their time delivering one-size-fits-all lessons year after year, teachers can spend much more of their time traveling from student to student to help individuals with individual problems. Teachers will act more as learning coaches and tutors to help students find the learning approach that makes the most sense for them. They will mentor and motivate them through the learning with the aid of real-time computer data on how the student is learning. This means, however, that they will need very different skills to add value in this future from the skills with which education schools are equipping them today. Since customization will be a major driver and benefit of this shift to student-centric online technology, increasingly teachers will have to be able to understand differences in students and be able to provide individual assistance that is complementary to the learning model each student is using.[26]

There is another potential benefit for teachers. Because student-centric technology allows for far more personalized attention from a teacher, we can do something counterintuitive in education—increase the number of students per live teacher. Facilitating this disruption of instruction has the potential to break the expensive trade-offs in which school districts have been trapped so that individual teachers can do a better job and give individual attention to *more* students. As a result, there potentially will be more funds to pay teachers better.[27]

❖ THE FUTURE OF ASSESSMENT

With the change to student-centric learning, assessment—the art and science of testing children to determine what they have learned—can and should change, as well. Student-centric learning should, over time, obviate the need for examinations as we have known them. Alternative means of comparison, when necessary, will emerge.

In the past, testing has been used to do two jobs for students, teachers, and administrators. The first has been to determine the extent to which students have mastered a body of material and are ready to progress. The second job is to compare students against one another. Student-centric technology can fulfill both of these purposes.

The conventional teacher-administered examination doesn't do the first job well. Regardless of whether students have mastered the material in a unit, they all move on. Teachers don't find out what students have actually learned until an exam is administered and graded, which tends to be some time after the unit or class is already complete. If students haven't mastered all the material but know it well enough to get a passing grade, the students still must move on. And even if they fail an exam, the students typically must move on, because moving on is inherent in the model of monolithic instruction. This teacher-administered examination tells teachers and administrators only what percentage of the students has demonstrated mastery of what percentage of the material. The amount of time in which to learn the material is fixed, but the amount of learning varies significantly.

In his book *Chasing the Rabbit*, Steven Spear, a senior lecturer at MIT, recounts an experience that has helped us frame the trap of monolithic instruction that we've gotten ourselves into in public education. While doing research in 1996 as a doctoral student studying Toyota's famed production system, Steve took temporary jobs working on an assembly line at Toyota and at one of the Detroit Big Three plants at the passenger-side frontseat installation point.

At the Detroit Big Three factory, the worker doing the training essentially told Steve, "The cars come down this line every 58 seconds, so that's how long you have to install this seat. Now I'm going to show you how to do it. First, you do this. Then do that, then click this in here just like this, then tighten this, then do that," and so on, until the seat was completely installed. "Do you get how to do it, Steve?"

Steve was quite certain he could do each of those things in the allotted time, given that he had earned a master's degrees in mechanical engineering from MIT. So when the next car came down the line, he confidently picked up the seat and did each of the preparatory steps. But when he tried to install it in the car, it wouldn't fit. For the entire 58 seconds he tried to complete the installation but couldn't. His trainer had to stop the assembly line to fix the problem. He again showed Steve how to do it. When the next car arrived, Steve tried again but didn't get it right. In an entire hour, he installed only four seats correctly. One reason why it historically was so important to test every product when it came off the end of a production line like the Detroit Big Three's was that there were typically hundreds of steps involved in making a product, and the company could not be sure that each step had been done correctly. In business, we call that end-of-the-line activity "inspection." In education, we call it "assessment" or "testing."

When Steve went to work at the same station in Toyota's plant, he had a completely different experience. First, he went to a training station, where he was told, "These are the seven steps required to install this seat successfully. You don't have the privilege of learning step 2 until you've demonstrated mastery of step 1. If you master step 1 in a minute, you can begin learning step 2 a minute from now. If step 1 takes you an hour, then you can learn step 2 in an hour. And if it takes you a day, then you can learn step 2 tomorrow. It makes no sense for us to teach you subsequent steps if you can't do the prior ones correctly." Testing and assessment was an integral part of the process of instruction. As a result, when he took his spot on Toyota's production line, Steve was able to do his part right the first time and every time. In fact, Toyota had built into its process a mechanism to verify immediately that each step had been done correctly so that no time or money would be wasted fixing a defective product. As a result, it did not have to test its products when they came to the end of the production process.

What a contrast between the two methods for training Steve Spear. At the Detroit Big Three plant, the time was fixed, but the result of training was variable and unpredictable—just as it is in the public schools' assessment systems. The "exam"—installing the seat—came at the end of Steve's training. At Toyota, the training time was variable. But assessment was interdependently woven into content delivery, and the result was fixed; every person who went through the training could predictably do what he had been taught to do (although Toyota's instructional methods might not be customized for the way Steve learns best, the point of this anecdote is to focus on the end implication for examinations and the opportunity to shift to a mastery-based system along the lines of what FLVS has done through online learning). Toyota follows that principle in all its training, for every activity in the company.[28]

We note in Chapter 1 that through the 1800s, there was little monolithic instruction in public schools because students of many ages were in the one-room schoolhouse together. Most instruction occurred at the individual level at individualized rates. Educators borrowed the concept of monolithically processing students in batches, with a fixed time spent in each stage of the process of assembling an educated person, from the concept of batch processing in industry so that they could cope with the burgeoning student population in the early twentieth century. Just like Steve Spear's experience at the Detroit Big Three plant, schools similarly acquired the character of "fixed time, variable learning." Just as manufacturers had to test each product when it came off the end of the production line because they couldn't predict which products had been made correctly, educators had to test their students because they couldn't predict which of those in each batch had learned what. Repair, rework, and rejects became costly elements of both systems. Just as a professional discipline of inspection emerged in industry, a professional discipline of assessment has emerged in education.

This shift from individualized instruction to monolithic content delivery targeting batches of students changed the teacher's job. We estimate that at least 80 percent of the typical teacher's time is now spent in monolithic activity—preparing to teach, actually teaching, and testing an entire class. Far less than 20 percent is available to help students individually. A profession whose work primarily was in tutoring students one on one was hijacked into one where some of the teacher's most important skills became keeping order and commanding attention.

When students learn through student-centric online technology, testing doesn't have to be postponed until the end of an instructional module and then administered in a batch mode. Rather, we can verify mastery continually to create tight, closed feedback loops. Misunderstandings do not have to persist for weeks until the exam has been administered and the instructor has had time to grade every student's test. Rather than a fixed time to learn with variable results student by student, the amount of time to learn can vary, but the resulting learning can be much more consistent. In other words, assessment and individualized assistance can be interactively and interdependently woven into the content-delivery stage, rather than tacked on as a test at the end of the process. And the software makers can also use the feedback loop to learn how to improve their product for different kinds of learners.

We mention above that the second job for which examinations are used is to compare students—and there are lots of sound reasons why we want to compare students. College admission decisions are built around test scores. The evaluation of which schools and districts are doing satisfactory jobs educating their students depends upon standardized exams. Even the assembly of honor rolls—whose purpose is to compare students—is largely based upon performance on exams.

As student-centric online technology becomes dominant, we can fulfill this need—to the extent it persists in today's framing—to compare in different ways. Because learning will no longer be as variable, we can compare students not by what percentage of the material they have mastered, but by comparing how far they have moved through a body of material.

If we indeed want to begin teaching subjects to students in ways that correspond to how their minds are wired to learn, it means that the science of assessment will need to evolve significantly. If we want to teach chemistry differently to people like Rob James, who struggles with conventionally taught math and science but was blessed with bodily-kinesthetic intelligence, then we'll need to find ways to compare his mastery of a body of material with the mastery demonstrated by someone whose intelligence is in the logical-mathematical realm.

Maurice Maeterlinck, the Belgian Nobel Laureate in literature, once observed, "At every crossway on the road that leads to the future each progressive spirit is opposed by a thousand men appointed to guard the past." Educators, like the rest of us, tend to resist major change. But this shift in the learning platform, if managed correctly—which means *disruptively*—is not a threat. It is an opportunity. Students will be able to work in the way that comes naturally for them. Teachers can be learning leaders with time to pay attention to each student. And school organizations can navigate the impending financial maelstrom without abdicating their mission.

The disruption of instruction by student-centric online technology that we chronicle in this chapter has been driven, to date, by its having taken root in competition against nonconsumption. Online learning already has transformed learning where the alternative has been nothing at all. We've noted that this is how all disruptions start. And we've shown that, given the shape of the substitution curves, this transition is likely to pick up substantial momentum in the coming years. The budgetary economics of states, cities, and towns will drive part of the substitution. The improving technology will drive much more of it.

This chapter paints a picture of the first phase of the disruption, which we have labeled computer-based, or online, learning. We've also mentioned the second phase, student-centric technology, in this chapter. At the end of the second phase of a disruption, the landscape often looks very different from what preceded it. Much of the opportunity for student-centric technology to take root and transform the learning landscape is outside the present K–12 public education system. This is an exciting opportunity, which we detail more in the next chapter.

NOTES

1. A report by Anthony G. Picciano and Jeff Seaman shows the precise instances of how and why schools would use online learning and confirms what the theory predicts. This provides a solid grounding for many of the assertions throughout the chapter on why school districts are motivated to use these courses as well as what the potential and pitfalls are for these solutions. Anthony G. Picciano and Jeff Seaman, *K–12 Online Learning: A Survey of U.S. School District Administrators*, Hunter College-CUNY, Babson Survey Research Group, The Sloan Consortium, 2007.

2. Mark Schneider, *The Condition of Education 2007*, U.S. Department of Education, National Center for Education Statistics, May 31, 2007, briefing.

   In addition, a 2007 U.S. Department of Education report indicates that a stunning 26 percent of high school students attend schools that offer no advanced courses—those math courses that follow algebra and geometry, honors English classes, and science courses more advanced than general biology—at all. See *Connecting Students to Advanced Courses Online: Innovations in Education*, prepared by WestEd for U.S. Department of Education Office of Innovation and Improvement, 2007, pp. 3–4.

3. The amount of nonconsumption because of shortages of highly qualified teachers is greater than one might imagine. According to an article in *Threshold* ("The Future of Online Learning: A Threshold Forum," Fall 2008, p. 20), there are more than 440 high schools in Georgia with only 88 highly qualified physics teachers in the entire state.

4. *The Condition of Education 2005*, U.S. Department of Education, National Center for Education Statistics, 2005, http://nces.ed.gov/fastfacts/display .asp?id=91. Brian D. Ray, "Research Facts on Homeschooling," National Home Education Research Institute, July 10, 2006, http://www.nheri.org/ content/view/199/.

5. Interview with Richard Siddoway, founder of Utah's Electronic High School, interview by Michael Horn, November 26, 2007.

6. *The Condition of Education 2007*, U.S. Department of Education, National Center for Education Statistics, 2007, http://nces.ed.gov/fastfacts/display .asp?id=78.

Also, there are many opportunities further outside the school system for student-centric technology to make a positive impact. Marc Prensky, a noted thinker and author on the impact technology can have in learning, calls the space outside the school system "after-school." After-school education is whatever students learn when they are not in class or doing their homework or preparing for tests. From science and robotics clubs to blogging, social networking, and playing video games, children spend lots of time learning outside of school. There are lots of areas of nonconsumption here to make a positive impact and revolutionize how we think about learning. Because the focus of this book is on our schools, we do not have the opportunity to delve deeper here, but interested readers can explore this further by visiting Prensky's Web site at http://www.marcprensky.com.

7. Rhea R. Borja, "Students Opting for AP Courses Online: Enrollment Takes Off as High School Students Burnish College Resumes and E-Learning Opportunities Boom," *Education Week*, vol. 26, no. 31, March 30, 2007, pp. 1, 16, 18.

Apex Learning also licenses its AP online courses to other online providers, like the Iowa Online Advanced Placement Academy and Michigan Virtual School. *Connecting Students to Advanced Courses Online: Innovations in Education*, p. 23.

8. An enrollment is defined as any instance of a student taking a semester-long (or half-credit) class, so one student can be responsible for several enrollments. The information on the total number of enrollments Apex has served are from Apex's internal data, which Innosight Institute research fellow Katherine Mackey acquired via interviews over e-mail with Apex employees in April 2010.

9. See K12, Inc., *Annual Report 2009: Strengthening the Promise of Education*, Herndon, Virginia, p. 2.

In another example, Massachusetts-based Virtual High School (VHS) started teaching virtual classes in 1996. In 2003, VHS offered 120 courses to 3,200 students in 175 schools. It now has 12,893 students enrolled in 336 course sections from over 662 schools spanning 32 different states and 61 international schools. VHS has an innovative membership model. Schools pay a yearly membership to join a consortium. Most members of the consortium provide a course to the other consortium members. Students can take courses on topics such as the literature of Charles Dickens, AP biology, or the Vietnam War. VHS found success in rural and so-called urban fringe schools, which lacked the critical mass to offer these courses. The VHS model plays off the economic interest of school districts by presenting a disruptive path for introducing distance learning by targeting nonconsumption. See "About Us," and "Member Profile" on the Virtual High School Web site, http://www.govhs.org/Pages/AboutUs-ParticipatingSchools (accessed on July 1, 2010).

10. Florida Virtual School, http://www.flvs.net/areas/aboutus/Pages/Quick
    FactsaboutFLVS.aspx (accessed on July 2, 2010).

    Also, see Katherine Mackey and Michael B. Horn, "Florida Virtual School:
    Building the first statewide, Internet-based public high school," Inno-
    sight Institute, http://www.innosightinstitute.org/media-room/publications/
    education-publications/florida-virtual-school/ (October 2009). The case
    study profiles FLVS's innovative performance-based funding model that has
    spurred the school's success, as well as a prudent step by the Florida legis-
    lature and Governor Jeb Bush to establish FLVS as an autonomous entity,
    equivalent to a school district, so that it could set up its own disruptive business
    model with a unique value proposition. As we discussed in Chapter 3, setting
    up an autonomous division is critical for an entity to disrupt itself.

    Other state virtual schools of note include Michigan Virtual University and
    the Idaho Digital Learning Academy.

    Districts are increasingly spurring the adoption of online learning as
    of the publication of this book. An interesting scenario the authors have
    observed is in a district, Houston, Minnesota, that started its own online
    operation to supplement its offerings. The district was losing more children
    each year as the population of children diminished. Under Superintendent
    Kim Ross's leadership, the district started two online schools—one for
    K–8 and the other for the high school level. The participation numbers
    have grown to dwarf the traditional school-attending enrollment in this
    district. *The Minneapolis Star Tribune* reported in 2006 Education Com-
    missioner Alice Seagren's explanation for the explosion in enrollment: "If
    you've got a kid who's interested in calculus or Chinese, you can't hire a teacher
    for one kid . . . But you can provide that student with an online class, and
    that kid will stay in that school district." See John Reinan, "Small Town Min-
    nesota School Is Big on the Web," *The Minneapolis Star Tribune*, November 10,
    2006. The story continues to unfold, as Ross left the district when his
    contract expired June 30, 2010, "amid concerns about his involvement
    with a private online-learning consulting firm." See "Superintendent's
    Online-Learning Business Raises Concerns," eSchoolNews, http://www
    .eschoolnews.com/2010/06/22/superintendents-online-learning-business
    -raises-concerns/ (June 22, 2010).

11. Everett Rogers, *Diffusion of Innovations* (New York: Free Press of Glen-
    coe, 1962). Richard Foster of McKinsey has also studied this phenomenon
    thoroughly. See *The Attacker's Advantage* (New York: Summit Books, 1986).

12. Another example is AT&T, which relied on a 1984 McKinsey study that
    advised AT&T that there would be fewer than 1 million wireless phone
    units by 2000. There were 740 million—reminiscent of IBM CEO Thomas
    Watson's forecast that the world would not need very many computers.

13. A blended-online course means that 30 to 80 percent of instruction is
    delivered on the Internet. We suspect—and the evidence suggests—that the

vast majority of online learning enrollments will in fact be in brick-and-mortar environments to some degree and will not be pure distance learning instances.

14. Thirty-seven percent of "town" schools provide online course access; 25 percent of "city" schools do; and 24 percent of "urban fringe" schools do. See National Center for Education Statistics, U.S. Department of Education, 2006.

15. There is a distinction between computer-based courses and online-delivered courses. Computer-based instruction is instruction that is delivered digitally, not by a person—live or remote. An online-delivered course is neutral on this point, although most online learning today utilizes a teacher in a very different role from a traditional instructor. In theory, delivering a course online should allow the provider to collect data to improve the course in real time, although in practice, today few online learning providers in the broader field do this.

16. Other numbers have emerged since we calculated this initial S-curve that have bolstered the general direction of the prediction. For this edition, we have chosen not to update the calculation because the data remain uncertain, even though they all point toward rapid growth. For example, a report by research firm Ambient Insight says that by 2014, 10.5 million PreK–12 students will attend classes online. According to *THE Journal*, Ambient Insight's chief research officer says that as of the publishing of the report in 2009, 450,000 K–12 students were already attending virtual school full time and another 1.75 million were taking some of their classes online. See http://www.innosightinstitute.org/education-blog/10 -5m-preK–12-students-to-take-online-courses-by-2014-research-firm -predicts/ (accessed July 3, 2010). Another report, Project Tomorrow's annual Speak-Up Survey, reported that 27 percent of all high school students took at least one online course in 2009, nearly double the 14 percent it reported for 2008, the year prior. Ultimately, this online learning growth, although explosive and in accordance with a disruptive innovation, does miss the point to some extent, which is that the ultimate goal should be a student-centric system that responds to the needs of each individual student.

17. By way of one example, when an apples-to-apples comparison is made between FLVS and brick-and-mortar school per-pupil costs (netting out costs that are unique to brick-and-mortar environments like transportation and building costs), FLVS is less expensive. See Katherine Mackey, pp. 12–13.

18. Richard Ingersoll, *Is There Really a Teacher Shortage?* Center for the Study of Teaching and Policy and The Consortium for Policy Research in Education, September 2003. Penelope M. Earley and Susan A. Ross, "Teacher Recruitment and Retention: Policy History and New Challenges," *Teacher*

Recruitment and Retention (Amherst, Massachusetts: National Evaluation Systems, 2006), p. 2. Andy Tompkins and Anne S. Beauchamp, "How Are States Responding to the Issue of Teacher Recruitment and Retention, and What More Needs to Be Done?" *Teacher Recruitment and Retention* (Amherst, Massachusetts: National Evaluation Systems, 2006), p. 31.

John Chambers, the chairman and CEO of Cisco Systems, has also talked at great length about the need to catch the market transition and prepare now for a true use of technology in education. See his article in *Forbes* online, http://www.forbes.com/2008/01/23/solutions-education-chambers -oped-cx_sli_0123chambers.html.

19. Of course, whether public systems have policies that allow them to realize or react in an efficacious way to these savings remains an open question.

20. Bob Porterfield, "Retiree Health Care Costs Overwhelming: Governments Could Be Overwhelmed by Retiree Health Care Burden over the Next 3 Decades," The Associated Press. ABC News Internet Ventures, September 24, 2006, http://abcnews.go.com/Health/WireStory?id=2485444&page =1. David Denholm, "New Accounting Rules to Identify Unfunded Pension, Benefit Liabilities," *Budget & Tax News*, The Heartland Institute, December 1, 2006, http://www.heartland.org/Article.cfm?artId=20235.

In addition, when we first authored this section, the United States had not yet experienced the massive economic difficulties that continue to hang over the system today. The resulting financial shortfalls have made this general point truer today than when we first wrote the section—and some have argued may have increased the adoption of online learning faster than what we projected.

21. At the 2000 Democratic National Convention in Los Angeles, NEA and AFT union officials held 457 of the 4,338 delegate slots. As former U.S. Education Secretary William Bennett once said, the National Education Association is "the heart and center of the Democratic Party." See The National Education Association, http://www.leaderu.com/orgs/probe/docs/ nea.html (accessed on April 3, 2008).

22. Labor-intensive industries are well known for trying to solve fiscal crises by scrambling for more money, even as the world has seen so many sectors over the last decade accomplish more with fewer resources. Economists are familiar with this behavior and often explain it by citing the early work of Princeton economist William J. Baumol.

Baumol famously invoked an analogy from a music performance, as he asked how one would improve the productivity of a string quartet playing Beethoven. Would you drop the second violin or ask the musicians to play the piece twice as fast? The Baumol analogy comes from the book authored by William J. Baumol and William G. Bowen, *Performing Arts: The Economic Dilemma* (Cambridge, Massachusetts: MIT Press, 1966).

Schooling as currently arranged is in the same trap. While costs for school bus fuel rise, health-care insurance premiums soar, and buildings wear out, the big money still goes to pay the teaching and administrative staff. As the public stiffens its resistance to paying more each year for what seems like the same service, what can educators do, particularly in the classroom where most of the expense lies? Add another row of paying customers (sometimes that's exactly what's done—a form of "labor productivity" increase that is anathema to school professionals)? What we instead see is a slow but steady trimming of the service package schools offer—cutting out extracurricular options, reducing course offerings, the ability to attract high-quality teachers perhaps first and foremost, and so on.

Is Baumol's pessimism the last word? Not if we shift the focus away from the traditional producer to what technology makes possible, says Education Evolving founder Ted Kolderie. Starting with Baumol's example of music concerts, he asks:

> What if we thought instead about the listeners and about their experience? Then surely we would contrast the cost and quality of a trip to the concert hall—the money costs and time costs of the drive and of the parking and of the tickets (one for each listener) to hear what might or might not be a world-class performance— with the cost and quality of putting on a CD, which can play and replay a world-class performance for multiple listeners without additional charge, in one's own living room, with nothing spent for driving or for parking and quite possibly with no people rattling programs or talking in the next seat. Consider what it would cost to have had top-class musicians perform Mozart's piano concerto No. 21 for as many people as now listen to it in a year, recorded? It seems impossible not to regard the shift from live to recorded music as a productivity improvement for the listener, simultaneously improving quality and reducing cost. The option remains, of course, for those who prefer that experience, to go to the concert hall for a live performance.

Fascinating questions arise when we turn this analysis to education. Here, too, the traditional analysis has focused on the "performer" and has assumed the technology of teacher instruction. And the essential Baumol questions arise. What would you have the teacher do: Skip every other chapter? Talk twice as fast? If instead we focused on the "listener" and thought about connecting the student directly with information through digital electronic technology, would that necessarily degrade the quality of the learning experience? Or might that disintermediation, the shift of work to the student, actually enhance it?

The source of Kolderie's quote here is the occasional papers of Education Evolving, as posted on its Web site—www.educationevolving.org.

23. "Students Getting Double Dose of the Three R's," Associated Press, August 4, 2006, http://cnn.com/2006/EDUCATION/08/04/double.dose education.ap/index.html, accessed on August 25, 2006.

According to a *Time* magazine article, "Martin West of Brown University found that, on average, from 1999 to 2004, reading instruction gained 40 min. a week, while social studies and science lost about 17 min. and 23 min., respectively. But the decline of science and social studies is often much steeper in schools struggling to end a record of failure. At Arizona Desert Elementary in San Luis, Arizona, students spend 3 hours of their 6½-hour day on literacy and 90 min. on arithmetic. Science is no longer taught as a stand-alone subject. . . . The payoff for this laser-like attention to reading and math: the school went from failing in 2004 to making AYP [Average Yearly Progress] and earning a high-flying 'performing plus' designation by the Arizona department of education last year." Claudia Willis and Sonja Steptoe, "How to Fix No Child Left Behind," *Time*, May 24, 2007, http://www.time.com/time/magazine/article/0,9171,1625192,00.html.

24. Picciano and Seaman, pp. 11, 16, and 17.

25. See Virtual ChemLab, http://chemlab.byu.edu/Tour.php (accessed on October 22, 2006). Sam Dillon, "No Test Tubes? Debate on Virtual Science Classes," *New York Times*, October 20, 2006.

26. In a different twist, Robert Wedl, a former Minnesota commissioner of education who is now working for the Education Evolving network, recalls a discussion with some 50 teachers in April 2007. These teachers had been laid off from rural schools with declining enrollments, despite having an average of 12 years of experience and most having advanced degrees. They banded together in a chartered online school called Blue Sky, governed by a board consisting mostly of teachers. The big surprise, Wedl reports, is how these teachers describe the bond they have with individual students, whom they have never met face to face. They have about the same ratios to handle as they had in traditional schools—roughly 150 students a day—but online, each one is truly an individual. The students call or e-mail at all hours because they are doing their schoolwork at all hours. Even children who were formerly behavior problems in school seem to have shaped up. It's hard to be a behavior problem in a class of one. (Conversation with Robert Wedl, notes by Curtis W. Johnson.)

27. "Personalization in the Schools: A Threshold Forum," *Threshold*, Winter 2007, p. 13.

28. Steven Spear, *Chasing the Rabbit: How Market Leaders Outdistance the Competition and How Great Companies Can Catch Up and Win* (New York: McGraw-Hill, 2008).

One of Professor Spear's core findings is that the principles or "rules in use" that guide the way Toyota's people do their work can be robustly applied to a very wide spectrum of situations—from the running of a hospital, to the process of aluminum smelting, to the making of integrated circuits. For those readers with an interest in Spear's work, we recommend first reading Steven Spear and H. Kent Bowen, "Decoding the DNA of the Toyota Production System," *Harvard Business Review*, September 1999.

Chapter 5

The System for Student-Centric Learning

At the library, Maria logs in with great excitement and barely even notices that Rob is at the computer across from hers. But he sees her.

"Don't you have class?" he asks.

"We were registering for classes for next term. And then I have lunch next," she says.

"What are you doing in here then?"

"Allston told me about this way to take Arabic online for credit!" Maria says, and then lowers her voice, uncomfortably aware that most of the people in the library can hear her and probably already think she is a dork. "It's going to customize a lesson plan for me."

"What? That must cost a fortune."

"It's free," Maria says. She is on the opening screen now. She chooses a log-in—ArabicMaria—and clicks through to the first screen.

"Pick a conversation companion," the screen suggests. Glancing over it, Maria realizes that part of the class requires regular Web camera conversations with a native Arabic speaker who is trying to learn English.

"This is so, so awesome," she says, forgetting to keep her voice down again. A librarian shoots her a meaningful look. "This is so awesome," she whispers, and Rob laughs.

"What?"

"I get to make a friend overseas who speaks Arabic."

"That's great! Hey, and look. I think I found someone who will tutor me in chemistry for free if I just speak English to him. Japanese guy." Rob turns his monitor around so Maria can see. "Mr. Alvera suggested it. Dude seems really nice."

"Mr. Alvera or the Japanese guy?" Maria asks.

"Both."

Walking behind them, Alvera grins. The state teachers' conference was useful after all. He'd spent a chunk of last night online himself. Reading through the international tutors material that had been provided, he finally felt like he'd found something tailor-made for Rob. There wasn't much he could do about having 120 students himself, but at least Mr. Nice Japanese English Student Dude had only one study buddy.

■ ■ ■

Disruption is often a two-stage process, and, as we note in Chapter 4, we expect this to be the case in education. In the first stage of disruption, an innovator makes a product much more affordable and simpler to *use* than what currently exists. But *making* the product is still complicated and expensive. When Microsoft disrupted IBM and Digital Equipment in the operating system business, for example, Microsoft's products (DOS, Windows) were a lot easier to afford and *use*. But they still were expensive and difficult to *make*. Similarly, companies like Silicon Graphics and Sun Microsystems made the early microprocessor-based workstations that disrupted the mini-computer business. While they were more affordable and simpler to use than the earlier computers, these machines were still expensive and hard to design and build. The reason is that, just like Microsoft's Windows, their products' architecture was proprietary and interdependent—meaning that the design of each part of the product depended on the design of every other part of the product (as we learned in Chapter 1). As a result, you had to be integrated to play in the game—you had to design everything in order to design anything.

The same appears to be true in the computer-based and online learning industry today. Although many products are simple to use, just like the best video games, rich and robust online learning products are expensive to build. They are also expensive to maintain across successive releases of the products.

In the second stage of disruption, however, additional technological change in the industry, which, as noted in Chapter 1, is called modular design, makes it simple and inexpensive to *build and upgrade* the products. The operating system business is going through this second-stage disruption now. Linux is a modular system composed of "kernels" that fit together in well-defined ways. This makes it simple for application developers to design and build their own customized operating system. Modularity also simplified computer design so that Michael Dell could slap together personal computers in his University of Texas dorm room.

This also will be the case in education, we believe, and it will be the key to making student-centric technology a reality. Even now, platforms are emerging that will make it simpler to build online learning products so that students will be able to make tools that help their fellow students learn. Parents will be able to assemble products that cater to the individual needs of their children; and teachers will be able to design programs that help their students learn as well as build their own brands and connect with students around the world regardless of geography or formal program. In terms of the substitution curves shown in Chapter 4, it is this second stage of disruption in public education that will cause the world to "flip" and make student-centric online technology a reality.

In this second stage of disruption, the existing value chain, which we call a "value network," is almost always disrupted as well. It is rare for a disruption to appear in just one part of a value network without the rest of the system changing, too. It is the disruption of the full value network that ultimately enables these modular solutions to emerge. Embedding a disruptive product in an entirely disruptive value network is key to achieving a less expensive solution than was possible in the first stage of disruption.

As with the first wave of disruption, some of the earliest applications of student-centric learning will arise outside the public schooling system. The adoption decisions in this stage will be dispersed, as shown in the vignette at the beginning of this chapter. On a just-in-time basis, they will be made principal by principal, teacher by teacher, parent by parent, student by student, and subject by subject. This is likely to occur in such a decentralized way that it will not require—and will even proceed in spite of—central bodies of authority such as school boards and teachers unions.

To understand how student-centric technology will first take root outside the K–12 system and then permeate it, we first need to detail what a value network is and why, when a disruption arises, a new value network almost always emerges to replace the existing one if the disruption is to be successful. We also describe the three fundamental types of business models. With these lenses at our disposal, we look at public education's value network to understand why the integrated software players can be successful in the first phase of disruption, but why we likely need significant changes elsewhere to unlock student-centric learning's full promise. Understanding the three basic business-model types will also give us some clues as to what student-centric technology might look like in the future.

❖ DISRUPTING THE VALUE NETWORK

A value network is the context within which a firm establishes its cost structure and operating processes and works with suppliers and channel partners to respond profitably to customers' common needs. The reason the whole value network must be replaced for a disruption to occur is that, in each stage, the actors' business models, economic incentives, and rhythms of innovation and technological paradigms are consistent and mutually reinforcing. Companies with disruptive economics simply are not plug-compatible with the old value network.[1]

What this means is that the entire system for creating education materials, making the decisions about which materials to adopt, and delivering the content to students must and will change.

Here's a simple example to illustrate why. As we discuss in Chapter 3, the transistor was disruptive to the vacuum tube because it couldn't handle much power. Hence, transistors couldn't be used to make large products—the sorts of floor-standing televisions and tabletop radios that the leading consumer electronics companies of the day, such as RCA and Zenith, made. These companies built their products with vacuum-tube technology and sold them through appliance retailers. Appliance stores made most of their money not from selling televisions and radios, but from repairing the burned-out vacuum tubes in the products they had sold. (Those of our readers with a few flecks of grey hair will remember that TVs and radios in that era were disabled with maddening frequency when a random vacuum tube burned out.)

When Sony developed the world's first miniature transistor radio in 1955 and the portable television four years later, it tried to distribute them through appliance stores, too. But the appliance stores wouldn't give the time of day to Sony. Why? Because Sony's solid-state products contained no vacuum tubes that would burn out. Luckily for Sony, however, discount retailers such as Kmart, Wal-Mart, and Target were emerging at that time, and they had not been able to sell vacuum-tube-based products because they couldn't service them in the aftermarket. It was a marriage made in heaven—products that needed no service sold through a channel that could offer no service. By the mid-1960s, solid-state electronics had progressed to the point that they could handle the power large televisions needed. In the ensuing transition it wasn't just Sony and Panasonic that disrupted RCA and Zenith; the miniaturized solid-state component suppliers disrupted the high-power component makers, and the discount sales channel disrupted the appliance stores. An entire value network disruptively displaced an entire value network.

Three Types of Business Models

To understand how the value network of developing, producing, and selling instructional materials is likely to be disrupted by the next system, we must first understand the business models involved in the current value network. Professors Øystein Fjeldstad and Charles Stabell have developed a framework of three generic types of business models. We call the three business types *solution shops, value-adding process (VAP) businesses*, and *facilitated networks*.[2] Disruption can occur within each of these types of business model. When the disruption entails solution shops giving way to VAP businesses and VAP businesses giving way to facilitated networks, however, the change in the industry is even more profound.

Solution shops employ experienced, intuitively trained experts whose job is to diagnose problems and recommend solutions. High-end consulting, law, and advertising firms; R&D organizations; and specialist physicians' diagnostic activities in hospitals all are examples of this type of business model: They diagnose problems and recommend solutions. These firms' abilities to deliver value to customers are largely resident in the people who work there; standardized processes are uncommon in solution shops. We typically treat special education as a solution shop. Each student's challenges are diagnosed and treated uniquely.

Manufacturing, retailing, and food-service companies are examples of the second class of business models, which we call *VAP* businesses. These companies bring inputs of materials into one end of their premises, transform them by adding value, and deliver higher-value products to their customers at the other end. In contrast to solution shops, much of the ability to deliver value in a VAP business is embedded in strong, standardized processes. Its capabilities are not nearly as people-dependent as are those of solution shops. The production and distribution of textbooks is a VAP business. Most schools currently operate like a VAP business, too. Students are herded into a classroom at the beginning of the school year, value is added to them, and they're promoted to the next grade at year's end.

In the third type of business model, *facilitated networks*, customers exchange with each other. Telecommunications is a facilitated network: we send information to you, and you send it to us. So is insurance: we pay our premiums into the pool, and our claims are paid out of the pool. Banking is also a facilitated–network business. Participation in the network typically isn't the primary profit engine for participants. Rather, the network is a supporting infrastructure that helps the buyers and sellers make money elsewhere. The company that makes money in a facilitated network is the one that *facilitates* the network.

Public Education's Value Network

Public education's present value network is largely a VAP business. This has implications for what types of learning can and cannot be introduced into the present system. We summarize the companies and committees of public education's value network—all of the activities entailed in decisions about what to teach and how to teach it—in Figure 5.1. First, subject-matter experts create textbooks and other instructional tools, which codify the concepts to be taught and the methods used for teaching them. Curriculum experts at the state and local levels then make decisions about which textbooks to adopt. Teachers then deliver the content to the students—typically en masse, though sometimes individually—and the extent to which students learned what they were taught is assessed. Teacher training sits in the middle of this and reinforces how all these steps work.

In Figure 5.1, the single arrows that link different activities signify that those activities' economics propel the participants toward large-scale products. Multiple arrows signify that the technology and economics at that interface are amenable to small-scale products. In the following sections, we focus on how the technology and economics at key interfaces of these stages work, and how those forces limit the type of disruptive products that can appear in the current K–12 system. We also discuss how these interdependent forces have historically reinforced public education's monolithic system.

FIGURE 5.1 The existing value network for developing, adopting, and using instructional materials

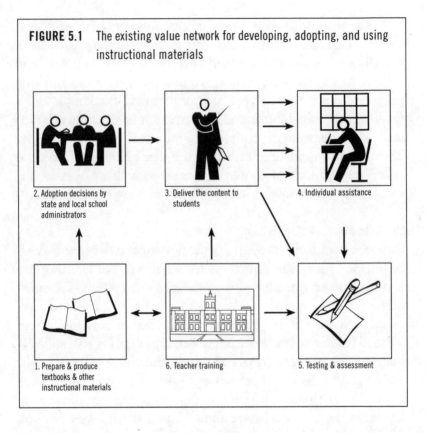

Step 1: Producing and Distributing Textbooks and Instructional Materials
The first step in the value network is textbook creation. Generally one or a few expert teachers write a text. Other experienced teachers and subject-matter experts edit and review the texts. The textbook's architecture typically reflects the architecture of knowledge in its domain or field. The book defines the sequence in which key concepts will be introduced and how they are related to one another. Textbooks often come with teaching aids, suggested examinations, and other materials to enrich the learning experience.

Because these experts are from the "intellectual cliques" we talk about in Chapter 1, instructional materials in the school curriculum are developed by and taught to a "dominant intelligence"—the type of brain whose wiring is most consistent with the methods used to solve problems in the field, as the domain experts have framed them. Textbooks and instructional materials are one of the primary vehicles in which these methods of understanding and problem solving are codified. Hence, physics, economics, and mathematics teachers tend to have high degrees of logical-mathematical intelligence, and those who write texts in those domains draw upon this intelligence type to frame and explain the problems in that field.

The textbook industry is a scale-intensive VAP business—properties that reinforce these intellectual cliques to the exclusion of people who are stronger in other kinds of intelligence. The costs of writing, editing, and setting up to print and bind a book are roughly the same, whether 1,000 or 1 million copies are sold.[3] The pharmaceutical and commercial aircraft manufacturing industries also are scale-intensive businesses marked by high fixed costs. Bigger companies can spread those fixed costs over higher unit volumes. Therefore, big companies make products at significantly lower costs than do smaller competitors. Industries with steep scale economics tend to be highly concentrated. In large commercial aircraft, all but two (Boeing and Airbus) of the approximately 20 companies that once populated this industry have dropped out of the race through bankruptcy or consolidation into larger firms. The textbook industry exhibits the same pattern, as evidenced by the mergers and consolidations in which smaller firms are folded into those with greater scale. These are blockbuster-seeking businesses. A large, monolithic market for a single bestselling title is just as attractive to a textbook publisher as the blockbusters Zantac and Lipitor are to a drug company.

There is little dispute among textbook providers that because individual students learn differently, they need differentiated learning options. But the textbook companies can't get there from here. Were they to focus on developing different books for each type of intelligence, their volume per title—and their profitability—would decline markedly. Because this would be so disruptive to their business models, most of the intellectual and financial energy of this formidable industry focuses on creating and commercializing still more blockbuster books for large, undifferentiated masses of students. They might attempt to pack in features to appeal to different types of learners, but textbooks by their very nature are fixed and static. Adding materials to a textbook increases its size, weight, and complexity. Many a student drags home a backpack full of fat texts containing hundreds of pages he or she will never read.

Step 2: Marketing and Distribution

The second step in the existing value network is the sale and distribution of the teaching material. This step, even more than the development of the instructional material, cements the system in monolithic, large-scale products. The reason is that curriculum experts at the school district level—and, with increasing frequency, at the state level—almost always make the textbook adoption decision. If a textbook author and its publisher can get their book selected by Texas's State Board of Education, for example, and then if the boards of three or four other large-population states or districts adopt the book, its financial success is guaranteed. And once a few large boards have made an "adoption decision," many other states and school districts tend to follow their lead rather than go through their own evaluation processes.

Why are so many engineers notoriously bad at spelling? Why do so many students who love literature struggle to master mathematics? Why are so many labeled as "dumb athletes" in the classroom when their bodily-kinesthetic intelligence scores at the genius level in game after game? One critical reason lies in the textbook-adoption process. The committees at the district and state level that make textbook adoption decisions typically are composed of the most highly regarded experts available in the subject matter. They are charter members of the intellectual cliques in their fields. And, consciously or not, the members of these adoption panels tend to choose those texts and instructional materials that are best at teaching the material to the dominant intelligence of each field.

Administrators have centralized textbook adoption decisions to address cost and quality control concerns. The cost advantages are obvious—with the scale of an entire district or state behind them, they can negotiate much better prices. When judging quality, it is a complicated challenge to decide what is the best textbook, because it's not just the ways of learning that are at issue. Standardized tests loom at regular intervals. Funding and reputation hinge so decisively upon students' performance on these exams that texts that don't explicitly prepare students for those standardized exams simply can't be adopted. Administrators understand that no single text can be effective for each student because different students learn differently. But needing to choose a single text for all students to use, the best they can do is a one-size-fits-as-many-as-possible solution. The very process of reaching an adoption decision mandates standardization in the way subjects will be taught.

If authors and a publisher develop a textbook or other teaching material that caters to one student segment that has a specific, nondominant intelligence type in that subject matter, they will find it almost impossible to sell that book or material within the mainstream school system. It cannot get through the adoption process because it does not fit the criterion of addressing the dominant intelligence in the field, as well as the economic and test-score appeal of one-size-fits-as-many-as-possible. As we show, the way for student-centric products to find the customers who need them will be for a new value network to emerge—one that has a facilitated network at its core, rather than a VAP business.

Subsequent Steps

The remaining four steps in the value network, as depicted in Figure 5.1, are instructing the students in a monolithic mode, offering individualized assistance where possible, and then monolithically testing to measure the number of students who can demonstrate understanding of some portion of the material delivered to them. We also depict as the sixth step in this diagram the training of new teachers. This occurs in colleges around the world, even as steps 1–5 are taking place in the public school system. Much of teacher training is to prepare teachers to function in this monolithic system—for example, how to hold the rapt attention of a classroom of students when teaching about covalent bonds in chemistry.

Note how everything in the system (except step 4, the small amount of time teachers have available to offer individual help) is designed to treat all students the same.

How Integrated Software Solutions Fit into This Value Network

Most people who develop online learning products of the sort we discuss in Chapter 4 will attempt to commercialize them within the system depicted in Figure 5.1—for very rational reasons. Complex software, like textbooks, is a VAP business. It is also scale-intensive because of the high fixed costs incurred in the development phase (the scale economics are particularly steep because software generates virtually no costs in replication and distribution). Integrated software, more easily than textbooks, can incorporate pathways for different types of learners as methods for teaching in these different ways become understood. This increases the size and complexity of the software, but the student does not have to deal with this increased complexity directly. Programmers can build multiple paths into a program to adjust for a student's progression; students need not see whole swaths of the software that are not relevant to their personal pathway.

That's the good news. Now the bad. This technology will be expensive, and there are massive entry barriers. School districts' funding and reputations hinge upon how students do on standardized exams. Although online learning tools can build in real-time assessments, these are unlikely to replace the standardized exams that are mainstays of the existing system anytime soon. Software will therefore have to correspond directly to these tests, or districts simply cannot adopt it. There are other mandates and regulations required by district, state, and federal policies that further define—both implicitly and explicitly—what computer-based technology must do. These policies will confine this software within the traditionally defined subject disciplines. For example, do you recall from Chapter 1 the teacher who hoped to teach algebra in the context of chemistry? Innovations like this would be *very* difficult to do.

The evidence on this topic is overwhelming in our research on disruptive innovation. When disruptive innovators target nonconsumption for their foothold applications, they have a good chance of succeeding. But if those applications are then ensconced within a value network—a chain from suppliers to customers whose definitions of quality and profitability were honed in the established way of doing things—the disruption won't fly unless it conforms to the rest of the players' needs and expectations. That typically limits the scope of the innovation. And it is expensive. It is for these reasons that disruptive growth is truly unleashed only when the new technology is taken to the market not only through a disruptive business model, but also by utilizing a disruptive value network—from suppliers through distributors—whose economics are consonant with the disruption. We now turn to suggest how this disruptive system will likely look in the second phase of this disruption.

❖ DISRUPTION TOWARD STUDENT-CENTRIC LEARNING

We state above that in the first phase of disruption of the instructional system, the software will likely be complicated and expensive to build. The reasons for this can be traced to the use of the existing value network when marketing the software, as noted previously, as well as to the relative immaturity of Web 2.0 software. Within a few more years, however, two factors that were absent in stage 1 that are critical to the emergence of stage 2 will have fallen into place. The first will be platforms that facilitate the creation of user-generated content. The second will be the emergence of a facilitated network, whose analogues in other industries would include eBay, YouTube, and dLife (for patients with diabetes and their families). The tools of the software platform will make it so simple to develop online learning products that students will be able to build products that help them teach other students. Parents will be able to assemble tools to tutor their children. And teachers will be able to create tools to help the different types of learners in their classrooms. These instructional tools will look more like tutorial products than courseware. But rather than being "pushed" into classrooms through a centralized selection process, they will be pulled into use through self-diagnosis—by teachers, parents, and students. Facilitated networks, not VAP businesses, will be the business models of distribution. This will allow parents, teachers, and students to offer these teaching tools to other parents, teachers, and students.

We illustrate these stages of disruption in Figure 5.2 as successive planes of competition, where each plane comprises a value network. The rearmost plane of competition represents the present public school systems, as well as most private and chartered schools. They are characterized by monolithic instruction, as noted previously. Textbook development and production, school district adoption decisions, the systems of instruction, and assessment are all monolithic because customization is prohibitively expensive.

The middle plane, representing the first stage of instructional disruption that we call computer-based, or online, learning, takes root competing against nonconsumption. It is already underway and is being fueled primarily by the economics of the teacher-led model—by the inability of schools to offer the courses that students want or need to take, just as happened in our vignette when Maria wanted to take Arabic. The courses in this stage look a lot like the courses in the back plane in that they tend to be designed by and taught to people

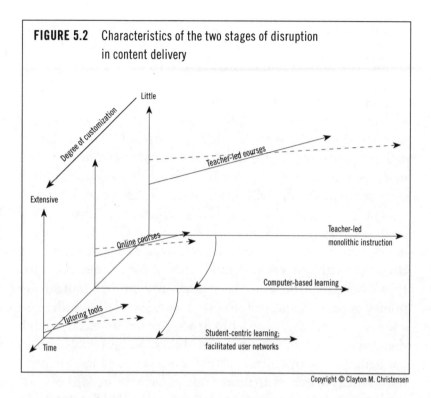

FIGURE 5.2   Characteristics of the two stages of disruption in content delivery

Copyright © Clayton M. Christensen

with the dominant type of intelligence in the field. They constitute complete courses and tend to be made and marketed by companies with VAP business models.[4]

The front plane in Figure 5.2 depicts the second stage of disruption. As we discuss next, the products in this wave will be user-developed online tools for *tutoring*. They will be distributed to students, teachers, and parents through a facilitated network, not a VAP business. The products will be modular, which will make customization easy. In a manner analogous to the way that software developers can build their custom operating systems by inserting kernels of Linux exactly where they are needed, users will select these tutorial modules and then insert them, like "kernels," to augment and customize the courses to the learning needs of each different type of learner.

Ultimately, people will assemble them together into entire courses whose approach is truly student-centric—custom-configured to each different type of learner.

The Technological Platform

Platforms that enable nonprogrammers to build remarkably sophisticated software for specific purposes (called "applications") are becoming increasingly common in software markets. One such platform is Intuit Inc.'s *QuickBase*, an online software platform that allows anyone to develop her or his own system to manage a small business's resources. Imagine, for example, that you were running the annual Girl Scout cookie sale for your state. You need to keep track of what orders have been submitted by each of thousands of Girl Scouts for each type of cookie. You must keep track of who has sent in the money collected, and who hasn't. You must add the orders up and send the aggregate order to headquarters. You need to track them to ensure that the hundreds of thousands of cookie boxes are delivered, with exactly the right mix, to local leaders, who in turn deliver exactly the right mix to each of the Girl Scouts' homes. You must ensure that the girls actually deliver to their customers the cookies they had ordered and that money is collected from customers who had not yet paid. You also must ensure that thank-you notes are sent to all the leaders for their volunteer efforts and that special rewards are given to those girls who achieved certain sales benchmarks. And, incidentally, you know nothing about software, and you have a family of your own to raise. This is a *very* complicated problem, but you cannot justify what it would cost to get an off-the-shelf enterprise resource planning software package from a vendor like SAP. But with QuickBase, you simply hop online and create the program for your unique needs.

Platforms of tools that are similar in character to QuickBase will enable nonprofessionals to create software that helps different types of learners master topics that they would otherwise have struggled to learn. These will be simple products at the outset, experimentally devised by those who live face to face with students' learning problems. These might come from a father of a mathematics genius; he has figured out why his daughter is such a horrific speller and doesn't seem to care, and he has devised a method to teach spelling to his differently wired daughter. They might come from a high school sophomore who barely understands Algebra 2 and yet has found a way to teach the concepts to her friend, who is struggling even more in the class. Or they might come from a history teacher, who, in do-or-die desperation, finally figured out a way to inspire her students to become inquisitive about the Spanish Inquisition.

Notice that these sound more like tools for tutors—and that's the point. We'd love for every student to be able to afford personal tutors who have the skill to tailor the way they teach each subject to their students in a manner that matches the way the students learn. But this is too expensive; hence, we've settled for monolithic instruction. These stage 2 tools disrupt the tutoring business; they can make it so affordable and simple that each student can have a virtual tutor through these tools. Over time, the modules that students, parents, and teachers employ to help students solve individual learning problems in individual courses will be combined into complete custom-configured courses—the consummate purpose of modularity.

Far-fetched? We don't think so. It's not just QuickBase that enables build-your-own software. A generation ago, it was inconceivable that anyone could create animated movies that could compete with Disney's artists. But digital animation technology enabled Pixar to create *better* movies—to the point that Disney had to buy Pixar in order to stay in the game. Now the technology is making it so simple that *lots* of people can create their own animations. Check them out on YouTube. Second Life is a very popular online, three-dimensional world that is "imagined and created entirely by its residents."[5]

Distribution through Facilitated Network Business Models

The initial motivation for creating these tutoring tools could very well be "local"—for family, friends, or a teacher's own students to use. If history is any guide, however, the best of these tools will spread in popularity very quickly, and exchanges will emerge through which this user-generated content can be offered to others for free or for a fee. By illustration, the software-as-a-service company Salesforce.com features an "AppExchange" on its Web site. There, people who have developed programs from QuickBase or platforms like it can post the applications they have created, and other users can join and find applications that fit their needs.

Though still in their infancy, facilitated networks such as these—user-generated, collaborative learning libraries through which participants worldwide can instruct and learn from one another—are emerging.[6] These networks will harness the innovative energies of a much larger group of insightful people than is possible in today's VAP business models that dominate the creation and sale of traditional textbooks and their use in monolithic instruction. As these networks become known and platform tools for building these products become easier and easier to use, a user who figured out how to teach spelling to people strong in logical-mathematical intelligence could go to an exchange, develop a tool, post it, and see what happens. As content is used over time, users will rate it, as they rate books on Amazon.com and movies on Netflix, so that others can easily find the tools that match the way they best learn.

One insight that educators can glean from the health-care industry is that people are quite good at self-diagnosis when they are given adequate tools. They often can feel their symptoms much more comprehensively and subtly than can be articulated to a doctor. That's why pharmaceutical companies have begun to spend so aggressively on direct-to-patient advertising for certain maladies. Historically, patients simply put up with disorders and discomforts because they did not know that there was a remedy for the problem. The advertisements that communicate that a solution exists typically also teach the patient about the problem. In the past, drugs were "push-marketed" through the professionals—the doctors—and patients generally received therapy if and when the physician prescribed it. Increasingly, patients are "pulling" the solution from their doctors after they've made a preliminary diagnosis themselves.

The analogous case in education is that historically, because they haven't known of the existence of remedies for learning problems, students and their families typically put up with poor grades and the low self-esteem spawned by feeling stupid. These facilitated networks will be designed to help students and their families diagnose why they're finding it so difficult to master a subject and then find their own solution. Just as in health care, students and their families will not wait for their teaching professionals to prescribe a "therapy." They will pull the solution out of the facilitated network themselves.

The Benefits of User-Generated Content

We mention above that these software platforms will enable students to teach other students by developing tools and putting them into the facilitated network. Isn't it better to have the professionals teach, and the learners learn? No, not necessarily. We often learn better when we teach than when we listen to a teacher.

Consider this illustration of this principle. A friend of ours, whom we call Dan, studied accounting at a junior college in the western United States. Through intense effort he graduated with mediocre grades and somehow got himself admitted, on probation, to a nearby four-year university, where he planned to finish the final two years of upper-division courses required to earn a bachelor's degree in accounting. Married and 23 years old, Dan was a mature student who worked hard at his studies. But after his first semester at the university, Dan had logged a GPA of 1.5. His academic advisor called Dan into his office and asked, "What does your father do for a living?"

"He's a rancher," Dan replied.

"I think you should go home and work with your father," the advisor counseled. "You're just not cut out for university work. I've seen a lot of students just like you, and you'll be a lot happier if you do something you're good at."

Dan replied that he wasn't stupid and that he wanted to pursue a career in business. "You just watch me," he countered to the advisor. "I'm going to do well, and I'm going to graduate!"

Dan redoubled his efforts. By working 80 hours each week at his accounting homework, he graduated and remarkably got himself admitted to the university's Masters in Accountancy program—again on probation. By dint of extraordinary effort and willpower, Dan earned his master's degree.

A few weeks after Dan graduated, an accountancy instructor at the junior college Dan had attended became ill unexpectedly. While they were exploring whether there was anyone else in that small community qualified to step in to teach his courses, one of the faculty said that someone had told him that Dan had earned his master's degree. "Maybe he'd come home and teach for us—at least for a year, until we can find someone else," he posited.

With no other options, the faculty agreed. Dan accepted the offer.

Dan recounted to us that as he began to teach accounting, "All of a sudden, I understood it! I had grunted through all those years as a student by sheer guts and willpower, memorizing all the rules. But I never understood why we had to do all of those things. As soon as I had to prepare for class and teach it, I understood it!"

We now have a language to explain what happened to Dan. His brain was wired to learn in a way that didn't match the standard approach by which accounting was taught. While many of Dan's fellow students digested the rules and the reasons quite naturally, Dan struggled because his brain just didn't work that way. But when he had to teach the same material, the only way he could do it was to format the rules of accounting in a way that was consistent with his intelligence type. When Dan had to teach the material, he was finally able to learn it well.

Most of us have had the experience that Dan had: we learn material much better when we teach it than when we're sitting passively in a classroom listening to someone explain it to us. That's why technologically enabling students to create content for this second stage of disruption will be so healthy for student-centric learning.

❖ DISRUPTING REGULATED MARKETS: LESSONS FROM OTHER INDUSTRIES

Untold numbers of school reformers and philanthropists have bloodied themselves by bashing the barriers that bar change in the existing system. Changing the textbook adoption process, confronting the demand for standardization, and countering the power of teachers unions are just three of a litany of factors that have rendered change a seemingly hopeless cause for many. And yet disruptive change has swept through many other heavily regulated and unionized industries. How did it happen? Never did success come through a head-on attack against the regulations and network effects that constituted the power of the status quo. Rather, the disruption prospered in a completely independent value network outside the reach of regulators. Once the new value network had proven itself to be viable and better and the bulk of the customers had migrated to the unregulated system, its regulators responded to the fait accompli. Rarely has revised regulation preceded disruptive revolutions.

For example, Southwest Airlines didn't disrupt the airline industry by seeking approval in the early 1970s from the federal Civil Aeronautics Board for discount prices on long, interstate routes. It began flying short routes within the state of Texas, where the federal regulators lacked jurisdiction. The rates and route structures of interstate trucking collapsed under their own weight in the late 1970s after corporations began operating their own truck fleets, which fell outside the jurisdiction of the Interstate Commerce Commission. The regulation of bank interest rates was toppled when Merrill Lynch—not a bank and therefore not regulated by the Federal Reserve—introduced its interest-bearing cash management account. We could cite dozens of comparable examples. In each case, markets that were dominated by entrenched competitors surrounded by powerful network effects and protected by regulation have ultimately given way to the fait accompli of a new network, and to efficient, safe markets that emerged by circumventing regulation. Head-on attacks almost never work.

In public education, the influence that teachers unions possess and that the entrenched parties can wield over textbook and instructional software adoption decisions looms so large that many would-be school reformers have abandoned hope of significant change. We suspect, however, that when disruptive innovators begin forming facilitated networks through which professionals and amateurs—students, parents, and teachers— circumvent the existing value chain and instead market their products directly to each other as described above, the balance of power in education will shift. Administrators, unions, and school boards will capitulate to the fait accompli of larger and larger numbers of students acquiring and using superior, customized learning tools on their own.

This also points to a road forward for those venture capitalists, foundations, and philanthropies that hope to invest with impact in education. Many of these have shied away from education software because development and large-scale adoption are expensive. If our assessment of the future is correct, it suggests that there are two types of investments that can have great impact. The first is in the development of a technological platform that nonprofessionals can use to create student-centric learning tools. The second is in building a facilitated network. We suspect that many thousands of teachers, as individuals, will begin using student-centric tools that they find in these networks and will put content that they develop onto the network for other teachers to use.[7] In powerful ways, the participation of teachers in these facilitated networks will diminish the opposition of their unions to this transition to student-centric learning.

Introducing student-centric learning through facilitated networks, instead of through the VAP system of curriculum adoption, satisfies the litmus tests of competing against non-consumption. Teachers, parents, and students, who previously could not develop or market these learning tools, will now be able to do these things. Rather than expecting that in one fell swoop computers will be in and textbooks out, the user-generated tools will be used independently as tutorial tools. For several years, most teachers and students will still have conventional textbooks. But little by little, textbooks will give way to computer-based online courses—increasingly augmented by user-generated student-centric learning tools. The second, or student-centric, stage of this disruption will move to the mainstream when users and teachers start piecing together enough tool modules to create entire courses designed for each type of learner.

At some point, administrators, school committees, and teachers unions will recognize that even without explicit administrative decisions ever having been made, student-centric learning has become mainstream. The substitution curve analysis in Chapter 4 suggests that this will happen in approximately 2014, when online courses have a 25 percent market share in high schools—six years from the original date of publication of this book. Student-centric learning is not far away.

NOTES

1. Clayton M. Christensen, *The Innovator's Dilemma* (Boston: Harvard Business School Press, 1997), pp. 29–59.
2. We thank our friend, Professor Øystein Fjeldstad of the Norwegian School of Management, for teaching us this typology of business models. It is a useful concept in many fields beyond education—one of which is health care. Professor Fjeldstad gives different names to these types of models: value shops, value chains, and value networks. Starting with his first published studies of disruption in 1995, Clayton Christensen has applied the

term *value network* to a very different phenomenon—a vertical commercial system of suppliers and customers whose economic models are interlaced and congruous. To avoid confusion among those who have studied Christensen's earlier research, we reluctantly decided to relabel Professor Fjeldstad's concepts for the purposes of this book. We highly recommend his work to interested readers. See, for example, Øystein Fjeldstad and Espen Andersen, "Casting Off the Chains: The Value Shop and the Value Network," *European Business Forum*, June 2003.

3. There are, of course, variations across different books, but if we assume quality as a constant, this is roughly true.

4. It is quite common for there to be two stages of disruption in an industry, and there are remarkable parallels with the patterns we expect to see in education. For example, in computers, the wave that destroyed minicomputer makers was composed of workstation companies like Silicon Graphics, Sun Microsystems, and Apollo (which was acquired by Hewlett-Packard). Workstation computers had proprietary architectures and were therefore not easily customized. And they were quite expensive—typically costing $75,000–$100,000 in today's dollars. Dell typified the second wave of disruption. Dell's product architecture was consummately modular; this made customization easy. Its computers sold for less than $1,000 apiece.

5. Quotation taken from SecondLife.com home page, March 7, 2008.

6. Since the writing of this book, the number of companies trying to introduce a platform similar to what we describe in this chapter has grown significantly. Some start-up players have emerged with the aim of introducing a next-generation learning management system (LMS) that serves as a facilitated network similar to what we describe in this chapter. Agilix's BrainHoney is among the leaders in this area. With all of the standards mapped out, a user can click on a standard and see several different pathways through different content modules—either in proprietary online courses or through open-source ones that have been matched to the standard—to learn and master that standard. Renzulli Learning, for example, is another facilitated network that possesses some similarities.

Others have sought to create student-centered facilitated networks through the tutoring path, as we suggest in this chapter. Guaranteach is one example of this. Started by Innosight Ventures, which was cofounded by Clayton Christensen, Guaranteach allows teachers to create online video lessons that teach math concepts in a variety of ways. It is built such that, over time, the data engine behind Guaranteach "learns" what an individual student's learning preferences are, and delivers 90-second videos best tailored to those preferences. Students also have lots of autonomy in finding math concepts explained in different ways until they understand them. See http://www.guaranteach.com/welcome/about.

Another facilitated network, Knewton, began by targeting test preparation—a market full of nonconsumption outside of school—with a product that was significantly more affordable than the test preparation offerings of the traditional players. As of this writing, it is gearing up to move into the K–12 market. Knewton is built to tag content from anywhere at the metalevel and then track how students respond and learn from it so as to create a real-time individualized learning engine.

Still another platform is Immersive Education, which allows users to create virtual reality environments similar to Second Life, but specifically for learning. Relatively speaking, there appear to be fewer authoring tools such as this one. Another is Mangahigh, which allows teachers to create math games. Still another is Bloomfire.

Another take on the facilitated networks with some promise is that of companies creating platforms by which teachers can create their own businesses online to reach students directly. Students can pick and choose among the different teachers to find the one who works best for them. Megastudy in Korea has become a booming business with this type of business model. Many in the United States have sought to copy the model, but without much success to date. One interesting player that is similar is start-up Presence Telecare, which offers speech language pathology instructors and services to school districts remotely. In targeting this market, the founders have found an area of both nonconsumption in school districts—many schools cannot afford a full-time speech pathologist or are not located near one—as well as an area where some students are overserved by a school district's offerings, and therefore districts and students are delighted with the Presence Telecare model that gives them what they actually need for less money.

7. This will happen even if they do not receive royalties for their work. As evidence, there are dozens of Web sites today on which teachers make their teaching plans available to other teachers—not in search of profit, but because their primary motivation is to help more children learn more effectively. One such facilitated network for teachers to do this is Curriki, which is the result of work done for the Global Education and Learning Community, an online project that Sun Microsystems started. Others include BetterLesson and The School Collective. Also see Winnie Hu, "Selling Lessons Online Raises Cash and Questions," *New York Times*, November 14, 2009.

Chapter 6

The Impact of the Earliest Years on Students' Success

Sitting in her office, flush from the vindication of having given Maria the Arabic class she'd wanted, Stephanie Allston gets up, closes the door, kicks her heels off, and puts her nylon-clad feet up for just a moment.

Ah, Maria Solomon. If only all students were wired to go like her.

After a moment, Stephanie flips forward and puts her feet back down, simultaneously reaching forward to yank open a file cabinet. Maria's problem had worked out, but not everyone's did. Stephanie pulls out a folder of records for a freshman named Sam Spitz. What a contrast! She'd already thrown every option she had at Sam, a student who had had trouble reading, but to little avail. His third-grade test scores had been low, his fifth-grade test scores had been low, his seventh-grade test scores had been low—and it wasn't because he wasn't trying. He worked hard, and his record showed that he had been getting great extra help throughout his schooling. It was as though his learning processes had been shaped so early that very little could be done to change them.

What had happened to Sam when he was younger? What was the missing piece to a puzzle that had begun so long ago? Stephanie reaches again for Sam's file, puts her feet up, and turns to the very beginning.

...

For much of the book so far, we've focused on changes that schools need to undertake in order to help more students come closer to maximizing their potential and realizing the other goals we propose on the first page of the Introduction. As we suggest in the last chapter, however, much of the opportunity to revolutionize education lies outside of the K–12 school system. And a rather stunning body of research is emerging that suggests that starting these reforms at kindergarten, let alone in elementary, middle, or high school, is far too late. By some estimates, 98 percent of education spending occurs after the basic intellectual capacities of children have been mostly determined.

One could argue that a chapter on early childhood education belongs in a textbook on parenting or child development. But the topics are no longer separable for two reasons. First, we note in Chapter 2 that schools now have been assigned the job of leaving no child behind—therefore eliminating poverty. If this is the job, and if indeed what happens before kindergarten heavily influences a child's prospects for prosperity, then this topic is salient to improving the schools' performance. Second, a groundswell is mounting among politicians and policymakers in favor of universal prekindergarten as a mechanism for boosting the chances of scholastic success for children who otherwise would be unprepared for school. As we discuss later, we have concluded that such programs are an ineffective mechanism for addressing the challenge of better preparing children for school. In an era of limited school budgets, diverting money to programs that cannot work is the second reason for this chapter's salience to schools.

If we can do well what must be done before kindergarten starts, we will make schools' jobs considerably easier. We see three core elements of this preschool job:

1. Creation of intellectual capacity in early childhood.
2. Cultivation of strong, positive self-esteem—a child's core belief about himself or herself. Building self-esteem

is a lifelong process, but its foundation is established in childhood.

3. Stimulation of intellectual curiosity, which will serve as a lifelong motivator for continued learning.

The subject of what changes must occur before school starts, during ages 0 to 4, demands at least a book-length treatise. In this brief chapter, we simply hope to inform our readers about one of the many important sets of findings emerging from this research and to help those who devise policy and allocate resources in public education to spend money where it has maximum impact and not waste it on programs that will fail.[1]

This particular strand of research is teaching us that a significant portion of a person's intellectual capacity is determined in his or her first 36 months. Two of the principal researchers of how intellectual capacity is determined, Todd Risley and Betty Hart, observed and recorded the physical and verbal interactions between a significant sampling of parents and their children in their homes for the first two and a half years of the children's lives. They calculated that, on average, parents speak 1,500 words per hour to their infant children. But that's the average. "Talkative" college-educated parents spoke, on average, 2,100 words to their infants per hour; whereas children in what the researchers termed "welfare families" heard their parents speak only 600 words to them per hour. Risley and Hart estimated that by age 36 months, children of talkative college-educated parents had heard their parents speak 48 million words to them. In contrast, children in welfare families had heard 13 million words. Interestingly, the most powerful of these words, in terms of subsequent cognitive achievements, seemed to be those that were spoken in the first year of life—when there was no visible evidence that the child could understand what the parents were saying. The children whose parents did not begin speaking seriously to their children until their children could speak, at roughly age 12 months, suffered a persistent deficit in intellectual capacity, compared to those whose parents were talkative from the beginning.

What impact did these different conversational experiences have? Hart and Risley tracked the cognitive achievements of the children in their study as they grew older. They administered the Stanford-Binet IQ test to these children at age 3 and found a powerful, direct correlation coefficient of .6 between the number of words the child had heard and the size of the child's vocabulary. When they eliminated "business talk" from the word count that the children had heard and looked only at what they termed "extra talk" (discussed below), the coefficient of correlation between the words spoken to the child and the child's measured IQ was .78—about the highest correlation that could plausibly be measured.[2]

The researchers continued to follow the children as they progressed through school. The correlation between the amount of extra talk before the children were age 3 and their scores on the Peabody Picture Vocabulary Test that was administered at age 9 (in third grade) was .77. There is a strong and well-documented correlation between the breadth of vocabulary and performance on examinations for reading comprehension.

❖ LANGUAGE DANCING

So what is this "extra talk" that is so strongly related to a child's intellectual capacity? Hart and Risley observed two sorts of conversations occurring between parents and their infants in their study. Parents they described as "taciturn" often limited their conversations with their children to "business"—statements related to what needed to be done. "Finish your food," "Hold out your hands," "Let's get in the car," and, "Time for bed," are examples of business conversations. Business conversations with infants are not rich or complex; they are simple, direct, here-and-now conversations. As suggested above, the impact of "business" interactions on cognitive development is relatively limited.

The words that truly matter are spoken in a posture that Hart and Risley term "language dancing," where the parents are engaged face to face with the infant and speak in a fully adult, sophisticated, chatty language—as if the infant were listening, comprehending, and fully responding to the comments. Language dancing can occur in a shopping cart, while folding laundry, while being fed, while having a diaper changed, or while being cuddled. It is deliberate, uncompromised, personal adult conversation.

Language dancing is not talking more business. It is talking about "what ifs," "do you remember," "shouldn't you," "wouldn't it be better if," and so on. These often take the form of questions that invite infants to think deeply about what is happening around them. Language dancing entails chattiness, thinking aloud, and commenting on what the child is doing and on what the parent is doing and planning. Interchange of this sort has been shown to cultivate curiosity in children.

If the number of words spoken to children so heavily determines their vocabulary and cognitive capacity, could a busy parent simply turn on the television and put the infant in front of it? Or put it in an infant seat on the next chair while engaging in a business meeting? No, it's not so easy. That sort of "background noise" has insignificant impact on the child's intellect.

Other scholars have shown that the most powerful factor influencing reading skills is auditory processing skill—the very skill that is honed as infants listen to parents speak to them in sophisticated, adult language.[3]

Neuroscience and Language Dancing

There is a strong connection between what neuroscientists are learning about how the physical brain functions and the observations that extra talk, or language dancing, leads to keen auditory skills, which in turn leads to improved learning capacity. Our brains are composed of between 10 and 100 billion neurons, or brain cells, which spend their days and nights sending and receiving messages to and from each other. Each neuron has an axon, which is a single tubular filament that is responsible for sending signals, and dendrites, which are extensions structured like a tree with a "baseball mitt" of sorts on the end of each one, that are responsible for receiving signals. The site at which one neuron's axon forms a functional connection with a neighboring neuron's dendrite is called a *synapse*. This is the site where virtually all important brain activity occurs.

When one cell communicates with another one, it sends an electrical signal down its axon to one of the tiny branches or terminals at the end of the axon that is positioned close to a neighboring cell's dendrites.[4] At this synapse, or gap, between the message-sending axon and the message-receiving dendrites, the electrical signal triggers the release of chemicals called *neurotransmitters*. The neighboring cell receives the message if and when these neurotransmitters are detected by and bound to receptors on its dendrite.

A substantial body of evidence exists that shows that when the synaptic pathway between any two cells or systems of cells has been repeatedly activated, those neurons will become "associated," so that activity in one makes it more likely that the other will become active. Scientists believe that repeated coactivation of connected cells creates physical changes in the synapse so that neurons can fire signals across the synapse much more efficiently than was possible before the connection had been forged. Conversely, when two cells aren't in the habit of firing signals to each other, the gap between them, called a *synaptic cleft*, isn't very efficient. Signals can get lost.

When a parent engages in extra talk—speaking 48 million words to an infant in its first 36 months of life—many, many more of the synaptic pathways in the child's brain are exercised and refined. This makes subsequent patterns of thought easier, faster, and more automatic. The major cognitive task for infants is to develop and use the synaptic pathways that will facilitate their thought processes. A child who has heard 48 million words in its first three years won't have just 3.7 times as many well-lubricated synaptic connections in its brain as a child who has heard only 13 million words. Each brain cell can be connected to hundreds of other cells by as many as 10,000 synapses. This means that children who have been lavished with extra talk have an almost incalculable cognitive advantage compared to those who have not been. Their brains have been "wired" to think in much more sophisticated ways than those of children whose synaptic pathways have not been extensively developed and lubricated through use.[5]

Strong self-esteem is a foundation that can give children the confidence they need to successfully grapple with difficult educational challenges and life issues as they are encountered. When children whose cognitive capacities have been expanded as described above confront and succeed at the initial academic challenges they encounter in school, their sense of self-efficacy—their excitement and confidence in their ability to succeed at difficult intellectual tasks—can blossom. When they enter school without this preparation, their initial academic experiences consist of struggle and failure, which destroy self-esteem and make further academic work seem intimidating and unexciting. We discuss this important point further in Chapter 7.

❖ A CASE OF MULTIGENERATIONAL ENTRAPMENT?

We might reach a frightening conclusion from this combination of findings from neuroscience and the way that cognitive capacity is developed in infancy: the children of lower-income, poorly educated, inner-city parents are trapped in a multigenerational cycle of educational underachievement and poverty. If their parents are not prone to engage in sophisticated, fully adult extra talk, their children will start school seriously disadvantaged and fall further behind from there. The children's self-confidence and enthusiasm for academic effort, in turn, will dissipate, so that by the time they become parents, they inflict the same disadvantages on their children. This is, unfortunately, a generally sound explanation for why improving inner-city schools has proven to be an almost insurmountable problem.

"The first three years are unique in the lives of humans because infants are so utterly dependent on adults for all their nurture and language," according to Hart in a *New York Times* article. "By age 4, the best that can be expected from education or intervention programs is to keep less advantaged children from falling even further behind."[6] Indeed, 80 percent of the variation in public school performance results from family effects such as those summarized above, not school effects.[7]

But there is hope. One of the most important findings of the Risley-Hart study was that the level of income, ethnicity, and level of parents' education had no explanatory power in determining the level of cognitive capacity that the children achieved. *It is all explained by the amount of language dancing, or extra talk, over and above business talk, that the parents engaged in. It accounted literally for all the variance in outcomes.*

"In other words," summarized Risley, "some working, poor people talked a lot to their kids and their kids did really well. Some affluent business people talked very little to their kids and their kids did very poorly. . . . And there is no variance left for race either. All the variation in outcomes was taken up by the amount of talking, in the family to the babies before age 3."[8]

❖ WHAT TO DO

If the definition of causality described above is generally correct, it becomes quite clear that some public policy and legislative initiatives are well intentioned but wrong-minded. They are grounded in correlation and not causality. For example, Massachusetts Governor Deval Patrick has staked out universal preschool as a centerpiece of his initiatives to improve public education. And he is not alone. Similar proposals are being weighed in several other states. The rationale seems clear: with such glaring disparities in the level of preparation when children begin kindergarten, perhaps if we begin teaching the disadvantaged ones sooner, we can eliminate some of the disparities in preparation for school. The Head Start program initiated by President Lyndon Johnson was similarly intentioned. The problem with programs like this is that unless they employ for each child an individual surrogate parent who has the instinct and aptitude to engage in hundreds and hundreds of hours of face-to-face language dancing, it won't do the trick. Indeed, much of the adult language used with children in preschool programs is, of necessity, "business." Programs such as these will cost billions of dollars, and we predict that they will have minimal effect.

The impact that fully adult conversation in the earliest years can have on a child's ultimate cognitive capacity is not well understood, even by highly educated parents who are motivated to do what is best for their children. Nor is it understood by the professionals who counsel those parents. For example, the American Academy of Pediatrics produces a monthly newsletter for pediatricians to send to parents with new babies during the first two years. This publication doesn't even mention the importance of talking to babies until the twelfth month because that's generally when the baby begins talking to the parents.

Rather than funding programs that hire people to substitute for parents who aren't succeeding at preschool talk, quite possibly we might have greater impact if we taught children how to be parents before they become parents. In the not-too-distant past, courses like home economics, auto repair, and wood- and metalworking were offered in most high schools to prepare young people for at least some of the mechanics of adulthood. Quite possibly, high school might be the place to teach courses that conveyed the methods of early cognitive development to tomorrow's parents. The benefits might be broadly felt. Young, single, inner-city mothers who otherwise would be trapped with their children in the multigenerational cycle of educational underachievement and poverty certainly would benefit from knowing how to shape their early interactions with their children to help them succeed in school. It would also likely help the professional couples of the future as well. These new parents often are so anxious to get back to their careers after childbirth that they hand their babies prematurely to caregivers whose responsibilities for multiple children give them bandwidth for little more than business talk. Perhaps a course like this in high school would help them, too, to make better-informed choices.

Two statements attributed to Albert Einstein are relevant to this chapter's topic. The first is, "The significant problems we have cannot be solved with the same level of thinking we were using when we created them."[9] The second statement Einstein is said to have made is his definition of insanity: doing the same thing over and over again and expecting different results.[10] We have for decades ignored the deteriorating preparation for parenthood that plagues so many families. If we don't change the level of our thinking to encompass the systemic problems within which our schools are embedded, and if we persist in believing that the problems of our schools can be solved by simply improving schools, we will never succeed.

NOTES

1. We refer interested readers to several informative sources on this topic. Drs. Betty Hart and Todd R. Risley began studying the way cognitive capacity is created in 1965, through studies conducted in Kansas City and at the Universities of Kansas and Iowa. Their book, *Meaningful Differences in the Everyday Experiences of Young American Children* (Baltimore: Paul H. Brooks Publishing Company, 1995), summarizes many of the findings from their research and that of their colleagues. The endorsement of this book from the *Journal of Early Intervention* said, "This book may very well change our thinking about how we arrange early experiences for our children, if not revolutionize our approach to childhood." Other research on this topic can be found at www.lenababy.com.

2. A correlation coefficient of 1.0 would be measured if there were a perfect, one-to-one correspondence between a change in one variable and a change in another. A correlation coefficient of .78 is about as high as one can find in explaining the variation in different students' scores on a test like the Stanford-Binet IQ test because the correlation of test-retest scores for the same student on that test is .81.

3. See, for example, Kurt J. Beron and George Farkas (2004) , "Oral Language and Reading Success: A Structural Equation Modeling Approach," *Structural*

Equation Modeling: A Multidisciplinary Journal, vol. 11, no. 1, pp. 110–131.

4. This explanation has been excerpted from the February 2008 issue of *Mind, Mood and Memory,* a newsletter from Massachusetts General Hospital, a leading center of excellence in the field of cognitive fitness. (For more information, click on http://www.mindmoodandmemory.com.)

5. Each of these fields about the brain and learning is so young that these thoughts have not been well researched. It is possible, however, that the existence of multiple types of intelligence has its roots in this process by which neural pathways are emblazoned in the brain. In other words, it seems possible that the children of parents who engage in the sorts of extra talk that Hart and Risley observed will have strong verbal-linguistic intelligence. At points in the past, various experimenters have noted that exercise, listening to music (the Mozart effect), cuddling, light, color, exposure to the out-of-doors or to media (fingerpaints, water play, sand), tastes through food, and a variety of voices, places, languages, and people can benefit children. Other researchers have questioned the conclusions of many of these studies. If in fact the patterns by which neurotransmitters connect across synapses in the brain are influenced by these experiences, cultivating certain types of intelligence and not others, quite possibly the measurements taken in these studies have been flawed—the wrong type of intelligence was being measured. We feel that sound research that addresses these questions could be of inestimable value.

6. Sandra Blakeslee, "The Power of Baby Talk," *New York Times,* April 20, 1997, http://query.nytimes.com/gst/fullpage.html?res=990CE3DB1F3FF9 33A15757C0A961958260.

7. Daniel M. O'Brien, "Family and School Effects on the Cognitive Growth of Minority and Disadvantaged Elementary Students," prepared for presentation to the American Education Finance Association, March 18–20, 1999. This paper was summarized in George Farkas and L. Shane Hall, "Can Title I Attain Its Goals?" Brookings Papers on Education Policy, v. 2000.

8. This and much of the other wording used in these paragraphs has been excerpted from an unedited interview of Dr. Todd Risley by David Boulton. See www.childrenofthecode.org/interviews/risley.htm (accessed on April 3, 2008). For further reading on the research cited in this chapter as well as other salient research and a discussion of the possibilities for low-income children escaping the trap of a multigenerational cycle of educational under-achievement and poverty, we highly recommend Paul Tough's *Whatever It Takes: Geoffrey Canada's Quest to Change Harlem and America* (New York: Houghton Mifflin, 2008), in which he details the story of the Harlem Children's Zone and its theory of action in combating this problem.

9. See www.quotedb.com/quotes/11 (accessed on April 3, 2008).

10. www.quotationspage.com/quote/26032.html (accessed on April 3, 2008).

Chapter 7

Why So Many Students Seem Unmotivated

A short time later, as Stephanie sits at her desk writing a quick memo that needs to go out to her staff later today, the solemn atmosphere is broken by the usually reserved Alvera bursting through her door, talking fast, waving his hands. "You won't believe what I just learned," he gushes. Allston leans back in her chair as she hopes that this news flash won't mean she will be wrestling some hairy public relations problem all afternoon.

As though he were reading her mind, Alvera quickly says, "No, it's not a problem. It's just, well, it's such a surprise, and I couldn't wait to tell you."

"About?" she asks, holding up both hands in a "bring it on" gesture?

"Well, it's that kid that always tries so hard but just doesn't ever seem to keep up, you know, Sam Spitz."

Allston shoves her keyboard back into its desk slot and reaches up to take off her glasses. She feels a little startled herself. "That's a coincidence," she says. "I was just looking at his file and wondering if the system hadn't let him down from the very beginning. But what's this all about?"

Alvera, still standing, grabs a chair and pulls it up to the side of All-ston's, loosens his tie, and spills it out: "I was covering the study hall period this afternoon, and I saw a couple of kids go over to Spitz's desk and hand him small packages. I thought, what's that about? Of course I wondered if it had something to do with drugs; you hear all these rumors about what kids are doing."

"So what did you do?" Allston was getting impatient for him to get to the point.

"I went over and asked what was going on. It turns out that Spitz is a media geek of some kind. Other kids give him their memory cards with video and photos and he downloads just the right music to go with them and does something, I think these kids called it 'mash-ups.'"

Allston had heard the term, was never sure what it meant, and sure didn't want to risk asking one of the students. Alvera knew only a little more: "Sounds like he's hooked up with one of the small media arts firms in the warehouse district and hangs out there in all his free time. These kids say if you get him talking about music and video and creating new stuff to upload on people's Web sites, he's all animated and very smart."

That is so not the Sam Spitz I have a file on, Allston thinks to herself. Apparently Sam has his own path to success, and school isn't yet a part of it, she says out loud to herself, as Alvera rushes off to his next class.

■ ■ ■

In most school reform efforts, the focus is on the schools. The question we typically ask is, "Why aren't schools performing as they should?" Perhaps a key reason why we're so dissatisfied with the state of public K–12 education is that we've been asking the wrong question. If we asked instead, "Why aren't students learning?" perhaps we might see things that others have yet to perceive. After all, it's the children's performance that should concern us. The performance of a school is little more than the sum of the performance of its students.

In the Introduction, we explain that one of the bittersweet rewards of prosperity is that poverty serves as an extrinsic motivator for some students, as it causes them to endure monolithic, batch teaching of subjects like math and science. When prosperity has removed this source of motivation, the solution must be to make learning *intrinsically* motivating. Student-centric learning will play a key role in addressing this challenge. The purpose of this chapter is to draw upon other models from our research on innovation to dive more deeply into students' motivation to learn. If children are motivated to learn, and if we enable each one to learn effectively, we will have an education system with a great performance record. As the late educator Jack Frymier often said, "If the kids want to learn, we couldn't stop 'em. If they don't, we can't make 'em."

The challenge of student motivation is a pervasive and increasingly problematic barrier to improving students' learning. Whether it is manifest as inattentive ennui on the faces of affluent suburban students, attendance and dropout problems in inner-city schools, or simply "forgotten" homework assignments, making students excited to learn is a challenge that most have not cracked. Teachers and parents "offer" education, but many students are not buying what is being offered.[1] A few outlier parents, teachers, and schools actually seem to have solved the motivation problem, but in most of these instances their solutions haven't yet seemed to scale—as if there is a secret sauce in student motivation that defies codification.

❖ WHAT WE'VE LEARNED IN OTHER CONTEXTS ABOUT MOTIVATING CUSTOMERS TO BUY

The problem of motivating customers to buy what companies are trying to sell them is not a problem that is unique to education. Over 75 percent of all new products and services that established companies launch into their markets fail. Year after year, those that champion and fund the development of these products are convinced that if the products are "good," demand for them will materialize. If demand is insufficient, a typical solution is to make the product even better in the belief that the reason why customers were not motivated to buy the original version is that it wasn't yet good enough. Rarely do subsequent improvements right a sinking ship, however. Why is it so hard to crack the puzzle of customer motivation?

A model from our research on innovation goes a long way toward explaining why the inability to anticipate customer motivation correctly is such a common cause of failure in innovation in general. And specifically, this model can help us see the danger in our tendency to blame students' poor performance on a simple lack of motivation, without questioning whether waning motivation might be the result of deeper causal factors. As we have elsewhere in this book, we first describe and illustrate the model in the context of corporate innovation and then examine the challenge of student motivation through the lens of this model.

❖ THE IMPORTANCE OF GETTING SEGMENTATION RIGHT

The way in which companies choose to define market segments influences which products they develop, determines the features they incorporate in those products, defines who the customer is and isn't, and shapes how they take the products to market. Segmentation schemes define who is and is not framed as a competitor and how large specific market opportunities are believed to be. In other words, the market segmentation scheme that companies adopt is a decision of vast consequence. Yet many managers give little thought to whether their segments-in-use—which is essentially their theory of the structure of their markets—are leading their marketing efforts in the right direction.

Most marketers behave as if the world is structured by product category or by customer category. Auto companies, for example, typically segment their markets by product category: there are subcompact, compact, midsized, and full-sized sedans; minivans; SUVs; luxury cars; sports cars; light trucks; and many more. They can tell you how big each segment is, how fast it is growing, and who has what market share. Other companies (and these are not mutually exclusive) frame their market's structure in terms of customer characteristics by using demographic attributes like age, gender, marital status, and income level. Business-to-business (B2B) enterprises typically use corporate demographics like small, medium, and large enterprises or industry "verticals" to define the structure of their markets. The reason these choices are salient to innovation is that they define the targets, in terms of customers and competitors, for the innovation. Slicing markets along these dimensions makes sense because when you're inside the company looking out on the market, this indeed is how it appears to be structured. What is more, when data are collected about the size of markets, they come structured by product and customer category, because that is the easiest way to collect and analyze data.

Segmentation schemes such as these are static, in that customers' behaviors change far more often than their demographics do. The segment between the ages of 18 and 34 is often used in consumer marketing, for example. But it lasts 17 years—during which time attitudes, behaviors, and needs change dramatically. Demographic data cannot explain why a man takes a date to a movie on one night, but orders in pizza to watch a DVD from Netflix the next.

The reason why it often seems difficult to explain whether a customer within a given demographic category will buy a new product from within a given product category is that from the customers' perspective, the market is not structured by product and customer category. Rather, customers just find themselves needing to get things done. Jobs arise in their lives that demand resolution, and they hire products or services to help them do these jobs. Marketers who seek to develop products and services that their customers will buy predictably need to see the world through the eyes of those customers. This means that they need to understand the basic jobs that their customers are confronting and the results they need to achieve for which their products might be hired as a solution. In other words, the *job*, and *not the customer or the product*, should be the fundamental element of a marketer's understanding.

Most of the "home runs" of marketing history occurred when people sensed the fundamental job that customers were trying to do and then found a way to help more people do it more effectively, conveniently, and affordably. The strikeouts and singles of marketing history, in contrast, generally have been the result of developing products with better features and functions than other products in the same category, or of attempting to decipher what the average customer in a demographic wants.

A job is the fundamental problem a customer needs to resolve in a given situation. To illustrate what a job is and how much clearer the path to successful innovation can be when marketers understand the job, we offer illustrations from the fast-food and photography industries, where companies traditionally have segmented their markets by product and customer categories, but would benefit greatly if they segmented by job.

Hiring Milkshakes

Some time ago, a fast-food restaurant resolved to improve the sales of its milkshakes.[2] Its marketers first defined the market segment by product—milkshakes—and then refined it further by profiling the customer most likely to buy milkshakes. Next, they invited people who fit this profile to evaluate whether making the shakes thicker, cheaper, or chunkier would satisfy them better. The panelists gave clear feedback, but the consequent improvements to the product had no impact on sales.

A new researcher then spent a long day in a restaurant to understand the jobs that customers were trying to get done when they "hired" a milkshake. He chronicled what customers were wearing, when they bought their milkshake, what other products the customers purchased, whether they were alone or with a group, and whether they consumed it on the premises or drove off with it. He was surprised to find that nearly half of all milkshakes were purchased in the early morning. These customers almost always were alone; they did not buy anything else; and they promptly got in their cars and drove off with their milkshakes.

To understand what job these early-morning customers were hiring the milkshake to do, the researcher returned the next morning, confronted these customers as they left the restaurant, milkshake in hand, and essentially asked (in language that they would understand), "Excuse me, but could you please tell me what job you were trying to do when you came here to hire that milkshake?" As they struggled to answer, he helped them by asking, "Think about a recent time when you were in the same situation, needing to get the same job done, but you didn't come here to hire a milkshake. What did you hire?" Most of them, it turned out, bought it to do a similar job: They faced a long, boring commute, and they needed something to keep that extra hand busy and to make the commute more interesting. They weren't yet hungry, but they knew that they'd be hungry by 10 a.m.; they wanted to consume something now that would stave off hunger until noon. And they faced constraints: They were in a hurry, they were wearing work clothes, and they had (at most) one free hand.

In response to the researcher's query about what other products they hired to do this job, the customers realized that sometimes they bought bagels to do the job. But they were dry and tasteless. Spreading cream cheese on the bagels while driving caused serious problems. Sometimes these commuters bought a banana. But it didn't last long enough to solve the boring-commute problem, and they were starving by 10 a.m. Doughnuts were too sticky and made the steering wheel gooey. Candy bars made them feel guilty, and coffee didn't fill them up. The milkshake, it turned out, did the job better than any of these competitors. It took people 20 minutes to suck the viscous milkshake through the thin straw, which gave them something to do with that extra hand while they drove. They had no idea what the milkshake's ingredients were, but that didn't matter. All they knew was that at 10 a.m. on days when they had hired a milkshake, they didn't feel hungry. It didn't matter that it wasn't a healthy food because becoming healthy wasn't the job they were hiring the milkshake to do. And all of these characteristics fit cleanly in their cup holder.

The researcher observed that, at other times of the day, parents often bought milkshakes, in addition to a complete meal, for their children. What job were the parents trying to do? They were exhausted from repeatedly having to say no to their kids. They hired milkshakes as an innocuous way to placate their children and feel like loving parents. The researchers observed that the milkshakes didn't do this job well, though. They saw parents waiting impatiently after they had finished their own meal while their children struggled to suck the thick milkshake up through the thin straw.

Customers were hiring milkshakes for two very different jobs. But when marketers had asked a busy father who needs a time-consuming milkshake in the morning (and something very different later in the day) what attributes of the milkshake they should improve upon, and when his response was averaged with those of others in the same demographic segment, it led to a one-size-fits-none product that didn't do well either of the jobs it was being hired to do.

Once marketers understood the jobs that the customers were trying to do, however, it became clear how to improve the milkshake to do the job even better, and which improvements were irrelevant. How could they better tackle the boring morning commute job? Make the shake even thicker, so that it would last longer. Swirl in tiny chunks of fruit so that the drivers would occasionally suck chunks into their mouths, which would add a dimension of unpredictability and anticipation to their monotonous morning routine. Just as important, they could move the dispensing machine in front of the counter and sell customers a prepaid swipe card so that they could dash in, gas up, and go, without getting stuck in the drive-through lane.

Addressing the other job to be done would require a very different product, of course.

Hiring Photos

It is easy for marketers to become confused by thinking that just because people *should* want to do something, they actually *will* do it. Accurately predicting what customers actually will buy and use typically requires that we watch what they do because we often are misled when we succumb to this logic that *should* do it equals *will* do it.

Recall, for illustration, what life was like before digital photography. We took our roll of film to a store to be developed. Most of us chose to get double prints, because the second one was almost free, and in case one of the prints turned out to be especially good, we wanted to be able to send that extra one to Grandma. When you picked the prints up, what did you do with them? You flipped through them, and then put them back in the envelope, which you then put in a box or a drawer. The overwhelming majority of all photos that have ever been taken were looked at only once. Only the most conscientious people took the trouble to mount the most memorable photos in an album to look at again. The rest of us knew that we should keep albums, but we just didn't—or we planned to start tomorrow. If you watched what people did, it was very different from what they knew they should do or said they wanted to do.

When digital cameras emerged to disrupt film photography, companies offered several value propositions to camera users based on what the technology was capable of offering and what their market research said customers wanted. One was, "You can click 'attach,' and e-mail photos to friends and family whenever something interesting or important happens!" Another was, "If you'll just take the time to learn how to upload these photos, you can edit the red eye out of all those pictures that you used to look at only once!" A third proposition was, "You can keep all those images in this online scrap book that makes it easy to sort, search, and print from your gallery of thousands of photos!"

If you watch what most digital camera users actually do, a large majority of them have not learned to use photo editing software and have not created online photo albums. Why? These just weren't things that were priorities in their lives before the new technology arrived. The feature that most digital camera users actually use is the facility for e-mailing images to family and friends or for posting photos on social networking sites. Why? Because these uses represent the same job that we were trying to do when we ordered double prints and then mailed one of the copies to Grandma. An innovation that makes it easier and cheaper for people to do what they're trying to do is what is called a *killer app*(lication). An innovation that makes it easier and cheaper for people to do what they're *not* trying to do, in contrast, faces an uphill death march through knee-deep mud before it fails.

People who don't want to do something that they know they should do or are told they should do have marvelously inventive abilities to not do it or ignore the advice. They resolve to start tomorrow or conclude that it's okay if they just don't do it. We rationalize the rules to comply with our desired behavior. Marketers in every industry must confront this reality: Consumers demonstrate daily the propensity to prioritize what they want to accomplish, not what they are told they should accomplish. College students should be motivated to expand their learning by delving into the online expansions of their textbooks. Drivers should obey speed limits for their own good. But they don't. It's human behavior, not the behavior of diabetics, smokers, and the obese with which we're dealing. Most of us are frightfully guilty of believing that we don't need to follow certain rules that it is demonstrably important for everyone else to follow.

One of the reasons why the jobs-to-be-done concept is proving to be powerful in directing successful innovation within so many companies is that it gets directly at the *cause* of action. The fact that someone is in a particular demographic segment is often *correlated* with a propensity to buy certain products and not others. But what *causes* the purchase is that the customer has a job that needs to be done.[3]

❖ WHAT JOBS ARE STUDENTS TRYING TO DO?

We believe that a core reason why so many students languish unmotivated in school or don't come to class at all is that education isn't a job that they are trying to do. Education is something they might choose to *hire* to do the job—but it isn't the job. While we continue our research to understand this crucial issue, we hypothesize that there are two core jobs that most students try to do every day: They want to feel successful and make progress, and they want to have fun with friends.[4] Just as the milkshake competes with bananas, doughnuts, bagels, candy bars, and coffee for the morning commute job, schools compete with gang membership as something that students can hire to experience success and to have fun with friends; other choices are dropping out of school; buying a car, and cruising around town; joining athletic teams—whether they are school teams, AAU-sponsored, or of the pickup or sandlot variety— and playing video games. Others languish in boredom and do not experience success because they can learn much faster than the rate at which their teachers are pacing class.

How do schools fare against these competitors as something that students can hire to be successful and have fun with friends? Miserably, in many cases. The primary mechanisms in most schools for doing these jobs are explicitly separated from education. Activities such as athletic teams and musical and dramatic arts performance groups, which are mechanisms for feeling successful and making progress, are "extracur-ricular" activities rather than "curricular" ones, which speaks volumes. The key events embedded within our curricula that could help students feel successful—examinations—occur every few weeks. Feedback on whether students actually succeeded is often delayed by another one to two weeks while the teacher does the grading. And when the grades are handed out, the privilege of feeling successful is reserved only for the best students. By design, the rest experience failure.

We often conclude that the top students succeed because they are motivated, and the rest languish in the middle or the bottom of the pack because they aren't. The jobs-to-be-done perspective leads us to a different conclusion. All students are likely to be equally motivated to feel successful. For some, school is a viable candidate to hire for this job. This group likely includes those whose parents provide a clear link between academic achievement and career success; those whose intellectual capacities were honed through repeated, sophisticated verbal interaction with adults before the age of three; and those whose way of learning or passion matches that of their particular teachers. The students who do not hire school to feel successful are not unmotivated to feel successful. They just don't or can't feel successful at school—often it makes them feel like failures. School does not motivate intrinsically. For these students, schools just can't compete against other vehicles that they can hire for feeling success. Motivation operates through a different causal mechanism from the one most of us have assumed traditionally.[5]

❖ INTEGRATING TO DO THE JOB

One of our most important observations in the jobs-to-be-done dimension of our innovation research has been that most companies are not integrated correctly, given the job for which customers are hiring their product. When a company understands the job its customers need to do and then integrates its activities to enable customers to do the job as well as possible, it typically develops strengths that competitors struggle to copy.

There are three levels in the architecture of a job. At the highest level is the job itself—the fundamental result that the customer needs to achieve. Every job has a functional, a social, and an emotional dimension—and the importance of these elements of the mix varies from job to job. For example, "I need to feel like I belong to an elite, exclusive group" is a job for which products with luxury brands such as Gucci and Versace are hired. In this case, the *functional* dimension of the job isn't nearly as important as its social and emotional dimensions. In contrast, the jobs for which a delivery truck might be hired are dominated by functional requirements.

The second level in the architecture is composed of all of the experiences in purchasing and using the product or service that its vendor must provide so that they add up to "nailing" the job perfectly.

Once innovators understand what these experiences must be, they can then implement the third level in the architecture of a job: They can *integrate* properly by knitting together the technologies, ergonomic features, packaging, training, support and service capacities, distribution and retailing systems, and branding and advertising strategies that are required to provide each of the experiences necessary for customers to do the job perfectly.

If you don't understand what the customer is trying to accomplish, you don't know what experiences in purchase and use you need to provide. And if you don't understand what these necessary experiences are, you are likely to integrate the elements of your enterprise in ways that are irrelevant to what your customers are trying to accomplish. By illustration, consider what the understanding of the "morning commute" job that the customers were hiring milkshakes to do for them enabled the fast-food restaurant to do: (1) it improved the product in ways that otherwise would have been counter-intuitive (making it more viscous; stirring in tiny chunks of fruit); (2) it could move the dispensing machine in front of the counter so that customers could serve themselves; and (3) it could equip the machine with a prepaid "swipe card" system so that customers could dash in, "gas up," and go, without ever having to wait in a line. Each element of this system had existed before, but integrating them in this way was an insight that could have emerged only through understanding the job that customers were hiring the milkshake to do. Providing the experiences in purchasing and use to do the job of placating children (the other job that customers hired the milkshake to do) would entail a very different sort of integration.

In our research, companies in industries that seem to be notorious for high prices and poor customer service almost always aren't integrated to help customers get a specific job done. We suspect that executives of the companies that comprise these industries think that they are integrated, in that each element that is required for customers to buy and use their product or service exists. But the elements are not knitted together in a way that provides the experiences required for the customer to do the job perfectly.

Consider colleges and universities, by illustration. Their major lines of organizational structure are typically drawn by academic field: departments of mathematics, physics, French, economics, classics, and so on. The reason for structuring universities in academic departments is to facilitate the faculty's ability to interact with others who share common interests and expertise and to help them publish in specialized academic journals so that they can achieve tenure. As a result of these structures, college education for most students entails repeated bouncing back and forth in a cumbersome way between departments and administration to get their education. And colleges incur extraordinary overhead expenses to deal with the fact that few of them are organized in ways that optimize the flow of students through the requisite experiences.[6]

In contrast, when we see companies that have reputations for delighting their customers with their quality and cost, the root cause of this ability generally is that they view their market's structure—intentionally or unintentionally—in terms of jobs to be done. This enables them to integrate, or tightly couple, the relevant functions in their companies to provide the experiences in purchase and use that add up to nailing different jobs perfectly.

As an example, IKEA is organized to do very well a particular job: "We need to furnish this apartment today!" Consequently, it is integrated *very* differently from other low-priced furniture retailers. IKEA engages its own designers directly and exclusively to create knockdown lightweight furniture kits that customers can retrieve from the warehouse, take home, and assemble themselves, without having to wait for delivery professionals. They design furniture that is explicitly meant to be temporary, not to become heirlooms. IKEA offers child care because unfettered concentration on furniture purchases is an important experience; and it positions an affordable cafeteria at the midpoint of the winding journey through the store so that customers can refuel for the second half. Although IKEA has been slowly rolling out across America for 30 years, even though its "formula" is open for all to inspect, and despite the fact that its owner is the third wealthiest man in the world, *nobody* has copied IKEA. *Nobody*. The reason? We believe that because other furniture retailers regard their market as structured by product category and price point, they don't even see the need to integrate differently; and they therefore rarely are hired to do this job.

If IKEA executives someday were to decide that they wanted to diversify into other jobs, they would need to set up separate business units in order to achieve the integrated structure required to provide the experiences appropriate to those jobs. For instance, there is another job in the furniture realm that might be characterized as, "For 20 years we've been living with the furniture we bought in graduate school. It's time that we furnished our house with nice furniture that we'll spend the rest of our lives with—heirlooms that we can give to our children." Helping customers do this job would entail a very different type of integration that would have to be achieved within a different business unit.

Schools Are Integrated Incorrectly

Just as the companies that offer poor service at high prices do, K–12 educators have, by and large, framed the structure of their world by product categories and by demographic—the subjects taught in the curriculum and the different aged students sorted by grade level, for example. Because of this framing, instead of viewing their task as enabling their students to do the job that they're trying to do, educators operate as if the delivery of education (their product) is their objective. The activities in schools generally are not integrated in ways that would help students be successful every day—even though doing so is crucial to having schools nail their own jobs, which are increasingly to educate every student adequately and have each one graduate from high school.[7]

Do you recall how, in response to customer feedback in our milkshake story, the company kept improving the features of the product, and yet had no impact on sales? It wasn't until the restaurant understood what the "morning commute" job was that it became clear that it had been improving the milkshake along dimensions of performance that were irrelevant to the job for which it was being hired. Understanding the job helped it see that it wasn't just selling a product. It needed to provide the experiences required to *do* the job perfectly.

When unmotivated student "customers" aren't buying what the schools are offering—as evidenced by where they are spending their time and attention—school administrators and teachers often have worked extraordinarily hard to improve the features of their products, in the hopes that more interesting or compelling lessons, textbooks, and media might resolve the problem of student motivation. They are solving the wrong problem.

What might correct integration that helps students feel successful every day look like? Some schools, like the Big Picture schools, follow a "project-based" learning strategy, in which students are organized into teams and then undertake meaningful projects that require them to master the reading, writing, math, science, and social science skills that the school wants them to learn. This integrates the delivery of curriculum with experiences that enable students to feel successful and have fun with their friends every day.[8]

One reason why we take an assertive position in this book on the wisdom of using computer-based learning as the mechanism for achieving student-centric learning is that by the very nature of software, achievement can be integrated with the delivery of content in ways that help students feel successful while they learn, every day. Often this comes in the form of reviews or examinations that are built into the software, which require students to demonstrate mastery before they can move to the next body of material. Feedback can be delivered frequently and in bite-sized pieces, as necessary, to help each student feel successful. In traditional monolithic batch instruction, in contrast, examinations are offered every few weeks. Then, because this system is designed to categorize students as excellent, average, and below average, it causes most students not to feel successful as they learn.[9]

There is mounting evidence that students' learning is maximized when content is delivered "just above" their current capabilities—not too much of a stretch, and not too easy. Customization to the "just above" level for each student is much easier to achieve in software than in the current monolithic delivery model of most schools.[10]

Couch Potatoes and Jobs to Be Done

An important implication of the jobs-to-be-done model of market structure is that a job can exist independently of a market for products or services that might be hired to do that job. When we see a customer not hiring anything to do a particular job, it does not necessarily mean that he or she does not have that job to do. Rather, it may simply mean that there is nothing available for hire.

Here is an example. One of the most publicized successes in the economic development of impoverished nations is

Grameen Telecomm in Bangladesh, launched by Nobel laureate Muhammad Yunus. After building out a wireless infrastructure, the company loaned money to a carefully chosen woman in each village so that she could buy a wireless telephone. Others in the village could then pay a fee to this "telecomm entrepreneur" in order to use her telephone.

One of the most common uses was by farmers who were ready to take their crops or animals to market. Prior to the Grameen phone, the farmers had to choose which town to go to without knowing in advance what was being paid in that town for their particular animals or crops. And when they arrived in that town, the buyer had all the pricing leverage because the buyer could decline to buy, whereas the farmer needed to sell. The Grameen phone enabled farmers to call to each town in their region before starting their journey to learn where the best prices were being paid and to lock in a price before they made the trip. The job—to know in advance of travel where the best prices were—had existed for centuries. But the *market* of services that could be hired to do this job did not exist until Yunus and his colleagues conceived of and implemented this service.

We hypothesize that the need to feel successful is a job that every child has. When children listlessly spend hours each day watching television, we do not believe that it is evidence that those particular children don't have the "feel successful" job to do. Rather, we suspect that there just isn't anything in their lives, given their circumstances or the context, that can enable them to do the job. School might cause them to feel like failures; athletic team membership might similarly cause them to feel like failures; and so on. The fact that there is no "market" in those particular homes for academic, athletic, or work activities whose wages include feelings of success and accomplishment does not mean that the job doesn't exist in the lives of those children.[11]

Scaling a Solution to This Problem
We note at the outset that certain teachers in certain schools, by dint of their charismatic teaching style or unique abilities

to teach in an engaging way, seem to have "cracked" the motivation problem—but that their solutions or methods seem not to scale well. Do the findings summarized in this chapter scale any more readily?

We believe that there are two things that can and must scale. First, the *principle* must scale—and it can. We must start by correcting the notion that nearly all teachers and administrators hold, which is that education *itself* is the job. It is not. Rather, it is one of many competing activities, most of which are not educational, that students can hire to do the jobs of feeling successful and having fun with friends. The principle of correct integration can also be taught—the notion that what must be learned can be knitted together with experiences that help students whiff the sweet smell of success every day. We have cited above different examples that have done this knitting. There are many, many other examples of which we are not yet aware.

Second, we have observed repeatedly in our studies of innovation that in the beginning stages of an industry, the basic technical problems typically can be addressed only by experts who draw upon their deepest experience and intuition to solve the problems inherent in designing products or services. In the earliest days of the synthetic fibers industry, for example, there were just a few chemists in the world who could create the molecules that comprise the fibers known as nylon, polyester, acetate, and Kevlar—and DuPont employed most of them. There was a similarly small and elite cadre of engineers with the intuition to design mainframe computers—and IBM employed most of them. The same could be said for the early stages of most industries. One result of this expertise-intensiveness was that the initial products were expensive and inaccessible to many people. A second result was that nobody could play these games like DuPont and IBM—because intuition doesn't scale well.

In most of these industries such as synthetic fibers and computers, the technical problems that once required the intuition of the world's best have now become so well understood that the science underlying their design and manufacture has become rules-based, which has enabled people with much less training and expertise to design and deliver products whose quality is better and whose price is much lower than the experts could achieve in the early years. Their products became affordable, accessible, and consistently high in quality not because the expertise of DuPont's scientists and IBM's engineers was replicated over and over. It was achieved by *commoditizing* their expertise, so that many people could achieve it.

A great advantage in creating software that has been designed with success embedded within it is that it scales readily and economically. The intuition of those elite teachers who have the instinct to conquer motivation does not. Online learning changes a teacher's job, and, as it improves, it will enable far more people to do what only the expert intuitive teachers could do before.

As hundreds of thousands of teachers and parents develop methods for knitting success and education together in the years ahead and as many thousands of them make their solutions available to others in the facilitated networks that we describe in Chapter 5, we believe that this integrated solution of success and education will be found to have scaled magnificently against the challenge of student motivation.

NOTES

1. We use the term *buy* in this paragraph in the general sense of giving up something in order to get another thing. Students themselves don't pay for their education, but they certainly give up time and energy, and incur opportunity costs that to them are significant, in order to get what schools offer. It is in this sense that we consider students to be customers of our schools. They may or may not "buy" what the schools are offering. And although society is the ultimate customer of public schools, if students do not buy what is being offered, schools will likely not accomplish what society is demanding of them either; those expectations—or jobs—are discussed in Chapter 2.
2. The descriptions of the product and company in this example have been disguised.

3. We describe and discuss the importance of this distinction between causation and correlation in the following chapter.

4. That "seeing their friends" is a principal motivation for kids to come to school has become accepted wisdom among educators. But we thank one of Clayton Christensen's former students, Gunnar Counselman, for the profound reminder to us that the job-to-be-done model would be useful in framing the challenge of motivation.

    In addition, Bob Moesta—one of the original collaborators who created the Job to be Done framework and an honorary fellow of Innosight Institute, a nonprofit think tank devoted to applying the theories of disruptive innovation to solve problems in the social sector—is conducting ongoing research to understand further the jobs that children—and others connected to the education system—have. Moesta's early work confirms that the jobs referenced in this chapter are indeed among those that children are trying to do.

    Furthermore, when we use the phrase "want to feel successful," we do not mean the kind of surface-level idea of success that constitutes praising a child no matter how she performed on a given activity under the mistaken idea that building "self-esteem" in this vein is a good idea. Instead we mean true success, where the student in fact accomplishes and achieves something real and makes progress. A discussion of the perils of the former can be found in George Will's discussion of Po Bronson and Ashley Merryman's book, *NutureShock: New Thinking about Children*. See George F. Will, "How to Ruin a Child: Too Much Esteem, Too Little Sleep," *The Washington Post*, March 4, 2010, http://www.washingtonpost.com/wp-dyn/content/article/2010/03/03/AR2010030303075.html.

5. We believe that the thesis of this chapter is one of the most important assertions in this book. Yet like most of our other assertions, this one has not been inductively derived from large-n studies of students. Rather, it is drawn primarily from looking at the education industry through the lens of one of our theories on how successful innovation works. We invite other scholars and foundations to explore and test these ideas, and pledge our support to their efforts.

6. Important exceptions, as we write this chapter, are Western Governors University, an online university, and Brigham Young University-Idaho. The leaders of these schools, whose mission is to help students learn rather than to facilitate faculty research, are designing models that optimize the learning flow for students. For certain research universities, the traditional departmental structure is more appropriate. Findings that breakthrough insights typically occur at the intersection of disciplines, however, suggest that the departmental structure doesn't optimize the productivity of research, either.

For a rich discussion of the history behind the university's structure and its evolution—as well as more information about Western Governors and BYU—Idaho, see Anya Kamenetz's *DIY U: Edupunks, Edupreneurs, and the Coming Transformation of Higher Education* (White River Junction, Vermont: Chelsea Green Publishing, 2010).

7. As mentioned above, we discuss the jobs that society has historically hired schools to do in Chapter 2. An interesting case study emerges from this perspective. College Summit is a national nonprofit organization that helps high schools raise their college enrollment rates by building a college-going culture. College Summit does this by attacking the jobs that high school students have so that schools can in turn accomplish their jobs. Its founder, J. B. Schramm, has observed that most high schools try to lower their dropout rate by encouraging students to "not drop out." The problem with this approach, however, is that "not dropping out of high school" is not a job that students have to get done. In high school, their jobs are much more around gaining *access* to a better future—through either attending college or getting a job. When the schools with which College Summit works change their approach to help the students solve their jobs—by being relevant to helping them attend college or gain access to a better job—dramatically higher numbers of students stay in school and graduate. As a result, schools accomplish their job, too, which is to raise their graduation rate.

This illustrates a point that plays out in many industries. When offering a product or service that will rely on the adoption and use of multiple stakeholders, for the product to take off, it must fulfill the jobs of all the stakeholders or else it will not work for any of the stakeholders.

Another interesting case history to consider along these lines is that of the beginning of Wireless Generation. Many companies have offered products or services that they could see would improve student learning—if only teachers would just use them correctly! Many an education technology company has struggled with this—and few have lived to tell about the struggles. Wireless Generation had such a product with its mobile educational assessment solutions, but unlike most education technology companies, its product became a success. What was the difference? Just as in the story about digital photos, most education technology companies are not offering a product that helps teachers do more efficiently what they are already trying to do and prioritizing, but instead have the result of layering "just one more thing" on top of a teacher's already busy work day. By contrast, Wireless Generation's handheld device, discussed in Chapter 1, helps its target teachers do more easily something that they were already doing—and it allows them to improve and simplify their lives rather than further complicate them.

8. In Chapter 9 we discuss examples of some schools—the Met school and High Tech High in particular—that are designed in accordance with these principles. Dennis Littky, the cofounder of the Met school, also makes the

point that another key element for students is to feel important and intrinsically valued. As a result, for them to hire schools, the work often needs to be meaningful and valuable to the larger community beyond the school. Extracurricular activities do this well in many cases, but regular schoolwork often does not.

9. We suspect that some of our readers will skeptically want to remind us that Asia is filled with classrooms filled with attentive students sitting row-by-row in large classrooms, being lectured to in a monolithic manner, and yet seeming to be highly motivated. We would remind these readers that poverty is still a powerful extrinsic motivator in many of these countries and explains much of this.

10. This idea relates closely to the notion of the Zone of Proximal Development, which was developed by Lev Vygotsky, a Soviet psychologist. See the Wikipedia entry, "Zone of proximal development," for a high-level summary of the concept at http://en.wikipedia.org/wiki/Zone_of_proximal_development#cite_note-4, accessed April 7, 2010, 1:43 p.m. An often cited definition of this term is, "the distance between the actual developmental level as determined by independent problem solving and the level of potential development as determined through problem solving under adult guidance, or in collaboration with more capable peers," as written in his own work (see L. S. Vygotsky: *Mind in Society: Development of Higher Psychological Processes* (Cambridge, Massachusetts: Harvard University Press, 1978), p. 86.

   In addition, another way to talk about this concept can be found in an excerpt from Harvard Professor Paul Peterson's engaging new book, *Saving Schools: From Horace Mann to Virtual Learning*, in which Peterson quotes cognitive scientist Daniel T. Willingham from his book *Why Don't Students Like School? A Cognitive Scientist Answers Hard Questions about How the Mind Works and What It Means for the Classroom* (San Francisco: Jossey-Bass, 2009). Peterson says: "Cognitive scientist Daniel Willingham provides an explanation for the power of customized learning. Working on problems that are of the right level of difficulty is rewarding, but working on problems that are too easy or too difficult is unpleasant." Paul E. Peterson, *Saving Schools: From Horace Mann to Virtual Learning* (Cambridge, Massachusetts: Harvard University Place, 2010) p. 253.

11. As Terry Behrendt, the founder of the Learning Centers program in Wichita Public Schools that offers an opportunity for dropouts to earn high school diplomas and at-risk students to recover credits through the use of online learning, said in an Innosight Institute case study: "I have yet to meet a kid that did not want to succeed in their own way. Most of the time they just do not know how to succeed or what the next steps are." Katherine Mackey, "Wichita Public Schools' Learning Centers: Creating a New Educational Model to Serve Dropouts and At-Risk Students," Innosight Institute, March 2010, p. 5.

Chapter 8

Improving Education Research

Stephanie sighs. She's still pondering how it is that Sam Spitz gets what he's looking for outside of school, while she's been able to help Maria inside, though admittedly by using resources from outside. Maybe it wouldn't be such an uphill battle to turn this school around after all. Maria is a smart and adaptable kid, but Allston knows enough to see that she's not the only one in the school who will be excited about these steps forward.

Allston remembers back to her own family and schooling. Her whole family had done well—her brother Dave is an engineer, and her sister Eleanor, a doctor. She'd thought long and hard about the law, but after volunteering with teenagers during college, she knew her heart lay with education. After a few years of teaching history at another high school, she'd been sent to the middle school as a new principal. Then, last spring, the superintendent had called her into his office for a meeting.

"What do you know about Randall Circle High?" he'd asked her.

"It's the one on the verge of failing, right?" Stephanie had asked.

"That's right."

"What a tough gig," Stephanie said sympathetically.

"Well, it looks like Tom Briggs wants to retire. So what if it were your tough gig? A tough person for a tough gig?"

"More than half the kids at Randall are failing to show proficiency in math and reading!" Stephanie said.

"Uh-huh," said the superintendent. "Want to change that? Consider it a vote of confidence."

Allston had spent the summer doing research for her new job. She'd even found a boot camp for educational administrators working on "turnaround" skills. She couldn't think of anything that needed more of a turnaround than Randall Circle. She signed up, showed up, and found herself receiving pile upon pile of books. Weighed down with the research she'd been given, she'd gotten even more frustrated when she realized that the boot camp had given her the research, but no way through it. The contradictions were absurd: one study praised breaking large schools into smaller schools, and then another, from the influential Gates Foundation, indicated that the small schools it had created had been a mixed bag—some were great, whereas others had been academically disappointing. Some books touched on her own favorite issue—better use of computers—but then other research said that technology did not change performance significantly. She'd always believed in being a strong principal, and she had taught well herself in schools with strong administrators. But another new movement got its energy from the idea that teachers should operate collegially without a principal. Thinking back over what she had read, Allston knew that she had tried many of these things at her middle school; she'd seen some of her former bosses try out new approaches to technology, class size— even school hours. But many of them, even ones she admired, had implemented these strategies, only to face failure.

Allston sinks back in her seat and makes a face at the pile of "best practices" studies in front of her. What do they all mean, anyway? Thank goodness she's found at least one idea that might work—one practical, usable solution for a real student. And Maria is down the hall, logging onto the Arabic 2000 Web site.

■ ■ ■

Stephanie Allston's frustrations are real. There is lots of education research. Some is filled with mountains of statistical evidence, whereas other research examines case studies of randomized control trials. But the statistically valid research too often leads nowhere. Much of it is contradictory. Other times, when a principal or teacher or policymaker applies some of it, it just doesn't work. Given this, what can we reasonably expect someone like Allston to do? So many talented, committed people work so hard to improve public schools and yet get disappointing results because the research they follow is preliminary and incomplete.[1]

Why is this? And are the conclusions you've read in this book any different? Other fields have bodies of research that allow people to predict with great certainty the results of actions. Many people in education—from teachers to researchers—say that it is impossible to build models of this sort in education because education is unique. It is not a science, they say. It is an art. Certainty is impossible.

We disagree. Education is certainly unique, and many elements of it will remain an art. Having skillful teachers who use their judgment to understand and relate to students is terribly important, for example. But the prevailing paradigm in which education researchers have been trapped does not even give them a chance at producing research that can lead predictably to better schools. This is because the existing paradigm causes researchers to stop their work when it is half done. This gives us statements of correlation but not causality. Most—although certainly not all— education research consequently creates more contention than consensus. Much of the research on business is in the same boat, incidentally. It, too, stops at correlation and fails to seek causality. Much of it is not, therefore, helpful to managers in the field.

Interestingly, the contention that the phenomena are unfathomably complex, with unpredictable outcomes, is not unique to education. For example, prior to 1700, people said similar things about understanding the natural world. Some things seemed so inexplicable that the only plausible explanation was the wrath of gods. But the development of the scientific method changed all that, and now we understand and can predict with reasonable certainty many things in the world around us. For example, understanding gravity allowed humans to predict that if someone walks off a cliff, he or she will fall—and therefore we do not need to collect experimental data on that particular question. We can predict the level of stress at which a given material will fracture, the conditions under which certain elements will bond chemically with others, and so on.

Researchers can build the same rigorous understandings in education. Doing so, however, will require a shift away from the prevailing paradigm. No longer will research on best practices or what works best on average across education suffice. Just as researchers in medicine are working to understand disorders by their causes as opposed to their symptoms in order to move toward precision medicine, education research must move toward understanding what works from the perspective of individual students in different circumstances as opposed to what works best on average for groups of students or groups of schools.

So why include a chapter explaining good research, and why include it *now*? This book is a marked departure from the common pattern in education research described in the vignette at the beginning of this chapter. The theories we have been using about how to develop and implement successfully high-impact innovations were developed as general models of innovation that apply to for-profit, not-for-profit, and government organizations, whether regulated or not. For those who use them, they have made successful innovation much more predictable. This is research that has been built inductively and tested deductively across categories and through anomalies. For the previous seven chapters, we have delved into the promise disruption holds for education. The argument hinges on the notion that many students are not motivated to learn because schools teach in monolithic ways as opposed to ones customized by circumstance. Chapter 9 is based on other circumstantial arguments from theories also built outside of education research. Rather than compare the average performance of one set of schools, students, or methods against others, our approach is to examine the state of education through the lenses of these theories of innovation in order to understand more deeply why schools have struggled to improve and to predict what courses of action will and will not lead to the performance needed. We hope, as a result, that the prescriptions for change in policy and practice that we offer are not simply new or fresh. We believe that they hold the promise of the predictable improvement in schools that so many have been working so hard for so long to achieve. The purpose of this chapter is, therefore, to describe the process by which education research can become capable of predicting which initiatives will improve our schools, which will not, and why.[2]

❖ HOW DESCRIPTIVE BODIES OF UNDERSTANDING ARE BUILT

Researchers build bodies of understanding in two major stages—the descriptive stage and the prescriptive stage. The descriptive stage is a *preliminary* stage, as researchers generally must pass through it to develop more advanced, or prescriptive, bodies of understanding. Researchers engaged in descriptive research generally follow three steps—observation, categorization, and association—as they do their work.

Step 1: Observation

The first step in building a body of understanding, as depicted in the pyramid in Figure 8.1, is simply to describe the phenomena as accurately as possible. Schools, their buildings, the communities in which they operate, teaching methods, and the range of students, teachers, and principals are all phenomena whose careful chronicling is an important foundation. If subsequent researchers cannot agree upon the descriptions of phenomena, then improving the body of understanding is difficult.

To make sense of all the details, researchers in this stage develop *constructs*. Constructs are abstractions that help us understand the essence of the phenomena being studied. The

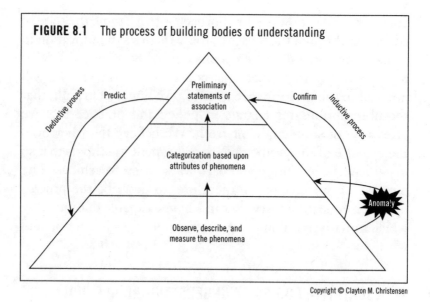

FIGURE 8.1   The process of building bodies of understanding

Deductive process

Predict

Preliminary statements of association

Confirm

Inductive process

Categorization based upon attributes of phenomena

Anomaly

Observe, describe, and measure the phenomena

Copyright © Clayton M. Christensen

notion we introduce in the first chapter, that there are different types of intelligence, for example, is a construct that synthesizes a range of specific observations that different students learn, or compute information, differently. Ethnicity similarly is an important construct, or abstraction, that captures an otherwise bewildering array of detailed descriptions.

Step 2: Classification

Having observed and described the phenomena, researchers then categorize the phenomena based on their characteristics. For example, researchers might look at schools and decide that those with less than a certain number of students are "small schools" and those with more than a certain number are "large schools." Other common categorizations in education research include chartered versus district, private versus public, and urban versus suburban versus rural.[3] Researchers frequently categorize by class size; by the type of training teachers have received; by the leadership styles of administrators; and on and on. Howard Gardner's multiple intelligences that we introduced in Chapter 1 are an illustrative system of categories. Many people are still arguing over and researching what the proper categories should be in this still nascent field of understanding how people think and learn.

Researchers categorize in an attempt to highlight possibly meaningful relationships between the characteristics of these categories and the outcomes of interest. They would categorize by size of school, for example, if they felt that the breadth of curriculum or the degree of personal attention given to students might differ and that those differences matter.

Step 3: Defining Relationships

With the phenomena observed and categorized, researchers then explore the association between the category-defining attributes and the outcomes of interest. Researchers might gauge the correlation between the test scores and dropout rates of large versus small schools. Studies of this preliminary kind are able to state that, on average, one group does better than another. But correlative measures cannot predict whether specific students, classes, teachers, or districts will or should conform to the average tendency.

Two studies posted by the U.S. Department of Education illustrate this. The first, released in July 2006, categorized schools by those that are private versus those that are public and compared fourth and eighth graders' reading and math National Association of Educational Progress (NAEP) scores as the outcomes of interest. After adjusting for factors of gender, race, ethnicity, disability, and language and for school characteristics such as size and location, public school scores ranked higher on math for fourth graders and not significantly better or worse on reading. Grade 8 results showed private schools better on reading but showed little difference on math.[4]

At about the same time, the department released another study that compared fourth-grade NAEP assessments of 150 chartered schools with those of 6,764 traditional public schools. Chartered schools affiliated with a traditional school district had comparable average scores, but chartered school scores in more independent settings were lower.[5]

Although correlative studies such as these are preliminary steps on the road to robust bodies of understanding, most education research is trapped in this stage and does not progress beyond it. This causes paralysis because correlative studies, or descriptive bodies of understanding, cannot tell specific people whether following that average formula will lead to the hoped-for outcome in a specific situation. Surely there are specific private schools that outperform specific public schools within the Department of Education study; yet we don't know which or why. All that the research paradigm in general—and this study in particular—can assert is that on average this was not the case. The ability to know what actions will lead to desired results for a specific school in a specific situation awaits the development of prescriptive bodies of understanding in this field, which we can get to only by improving the descriptive research.

❖ IMPROVING DESCRIPTIVE BODIES OF UNDERSTANDING

Preliminary, descriptive bodies of understanding almost always have *inductive* origins—that is, their correlations are derived from a set of data. All such research is a starting point and needs to be improved. Building understanding in education stalls, however, when people declare victory when they have run only this inductive half-lap up the pyramid. By stopping with their correlations, the game they play is, "My correlations are better than yours." It drives headlines, but it doesn't improve schools. The studies of private schools versus public schools and chartered schools versus traditional public schools did just this. While opponents of chartering policy asserted that these results should sink the whole chartering movement, advocates of chartering pointed to other studies that arrived at the opposite conclusion.[6]

The way that scholars in other fields improve their preliminary research is to seek exceptions, called *anomalies*, to the average tendencies identified in their descriptive work. They do this by cycling *deductively* down the other side of the pyramid shown in Figure 8.1 and stating, "If the correlations we observed are typical, then when we examine more phenomena, we ought to see the same relationships." If in fact the researchers do see the same relationships when they test their correlations on other data, it supports those relationships, *but it does not improve the body of understanding.*[7] It is only when we find something that the preliminary correlation *cannot* explain that the research can improve. Anomalies are actually good news because they allow researchers to say, "There's something else going on here," and *that* is what leads to better understanding.[8]

As Figure 8.1 suggests, discovering an anomaly typically means that the categorization scheme isn't quite right. Researchers use the anomaly to revisit the foundation layers in the pyramid so they can define and measure the phenomena less ambiguously, or sort those phenomena into alternative categories. Only then can researchers explain the anomaly *and* the prior associations of attributes and outcomes. Productive anomalies in the study comparing district and chartered schools cited above are lurking in certain independent chartered schools whose students outperformed students in other schools. Finding private and chartered schools that have indeed outperformed traditional public schools would lead researchers to realize that the preliminary categorization scheme can't be right. After all, calling a school "chartered," for example, tells us only how it was formed; it is simply a legal term. It reveals nothing about the school's learning strategy for students, its special offerings, or even anything about its size. As an information services officer for the Wisconsin School Boards Association said in 2006, "[The study] is like saying leased automobiles get better gas mileage than owned ones. The lease arrangement has nothing to do with the performance of the vehicle."

The Transition from Descriptive to Prescriptive Bodies of Understanding

Thomas Kuhn wrote 50 years ago that confusion and contradiction are the norm during this descriptive stage. As studies comparing the efficacy of chartered versus traditional public schools or small versus large schools illustrate, Kuhn's wisdom is still with us. This phase is often characterized by a plethora of categorization schemes because the phenomena generally have many different attributes. Often in this phase no model is irrefutably superior: each seems able to explain anomalies in other models, but suffers from anomalies in its own. This is the zone in which so many education studies remain stuck.

This confusion starts to clear when careful researchers using detailed empirical and ethnographic observation move beyond statements of correlation. As depicted in Figure 8.2, they leap upward to the top of the pyramid of prescriptive bodies of understanding, the capstone of which is a statement of what *causes* the outcome of interest. Prescriptive bodies of understanding have much greater predictive power than descriptive ones do, for reasons that become clearer below.[9]

Prescriptive understanding, like its descriptive predecessor, still needs to be improved. Researchers accomplish this by following the same steps used in the descriptive stage. They put on their statement of causality like a set of lenses and cycle deductively to the bottom of the pyramid to test the causal statement. They say, "When we observe these actions being taken, these should be the outcomes we observe." When they encounter an anomaly, they then delve back into the lower levels of the pyramid and account for the anomaly by revisiting the categorization stage.

But there is another significant difference here. Rather than categorizing by different attributes of the phenomena, researchers building prescriptive bodies of understanding categorize *the different circumstances* in which administrators, students, or teachers might find themselves. They do this by asking when they encounter an anomaly, "What was it about the situation in which those people found themselves that caused the causal mechanism to yield a different result?" As they cycle up and down the pyramid, anomaly-seeking researchers will ultimately define each of the different circumstances in which

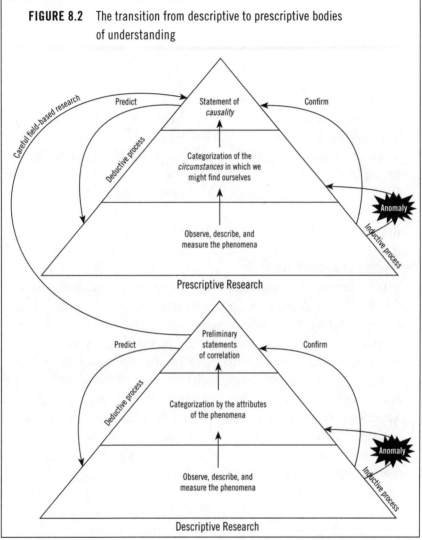

FIGURE 8.2   The transition from descriptive to prescriptive bodies of understanding

Careful field-based research

Predict   Statement of *causality*   Confirm

Deductive process

Categorization of the *circumstances* in which we might find ourselves

Anomaly

Observe, describe, and measure the phenomena

Inductive process

Prescriptive Research

Predict   Preliminary statements of correlation   Confirm

Deductive process

Categorization by the attributes of the phenomena

Anomaly

Observe, describe, and measure the phenomena

Inductive process

Descriptive Research

Copyright © Clayton M. Christensen

administrators, teachers, or students might find themselves when pursuing the outcomes of interest.[10]

This disciplined research method opens the door to contingent statements of causality—to show how and why the causal mechanism results in a different outcome in the different situations. Prescriptive research built upon well-researched categories of circumstances can allow administrators and teachers to predict what actions will lead to the desired result given the circumstance in which they find themselves—and thus know what they *ought* to do.[11] The work produced in this process results in a more nuanced and helpful statement than before. Whereas descriptive research might conclude, "On average, teaching reading using Phonics produces better results," prescriptive research would say something like, "If the student is strong in this intelligence, then teaching reading with Phonics produces better results; but if the student is strong in this other intelligence, then teaching reading with a Whole Language approach produces superior outcomes."

The History of Manned Flight

The history of manned flight provides a way to visualize how this transition from descriptive to prescriptive understanding occurs. During the Middle Ages, would-be aviators observed animals that could fly well and compared them with animals that could not. The vast majority of the successful fliers had wings with feathers on them; and almost all of those that could not fly had neither of these attributes. This was a descriptive statement. Outliers such as ostriches had feathered wings but couldn't fly; bats had wings without feathers and flew well. But the wings-feather-flight correlation was so high that aviators of the time copied the seemingly salient characteristics of the successful fliers in the belief that if they had wings and feathers like the "best practices" fliers, they could fly, too. So, ignoring the anomalies, they fabricated wings, glued feathers on them, jumped off cathedral spires, and flapped hard. It never worked.

There were disagreements about the categorization scheme—about which of the birds' attributes or actions truly enabled flight. For example, Roger Bacon wrote an influential paper asserting that the differentiating characteristic was that birds had hollow bones. Because humans had solid bones, Bacon reasoned, we could never fly. Bacon then proposed designs of machines that could flap their wings with sufficient power to overcome the disadvantage of solid bones. It still never worked.[12] Armed only with the descriptive statements of correlation, aviators kept killing themselves.

Then, through a careful study of fluid mechanics, Daniel Bernoulli identified a shape that we call an *airfoil*—a shape that, when it cuts through air, creates a mechanism we call *lift*, in which the air "pushes" the structure up. Identifying the causal mechanism (now called Bernoulli's principle) made flight possible. But it was not yet predictable. The statement predicted that aviators would fly successfully when they built machines with airfoils to harness lift. But there were still some crashes. These were anomalies that Bernoulli's principle could not explain. But crashes allowed researchers to revisit the categorization scheme. This time, however, instead of slicing up the world by the attributes of the good and bad fliers, researchers categorized the world by *circumstance*. They asked, "What was it about the circumstance confronting the aviator that caused the crash?" This then enabled engineers to improve equipment and techniques, as well as articulate circumstance-contingent statements of causality: "This is how you should normally fly the plane. But when you get in this situation, you need to fly it differently in order not to crash."

Discovery of the causal mechanism made flight possible. And categorization of the salient circumstances in which pilots might find themselves established the context from which *predictability* emerged.

If circumstance-defined categorization is so critical to the building of prescriptive research, how do people decide what boundaries best define the categories, and what potential definitions of boundaries are not salient to accurate prediction and understanding? In our aviation illustration, the boundaries between circumstances that matter are those that require the pilot to fly the plane differently. If a different circumstance does not require different methods of piloting, then it is not a meaningful category. The same holds true for administrators and teachers. If they find themselves in a circumstance where they must change actions or organization to achieve the desired outcome, then they have crossed a salient boundary into another category.

❖ MOVING FORWARD IN EDUCATION RESEARCH

So it is in any field or undertaking. Every action that policymakers, administrators, and teachers take is based upon one or more theories that if they do certain things, they will get the results they need. As pilots of their organizations, if policymakers and administrators possess a sound understanding of causality, then achieving the needed results is possible. And if researchers provide statements of what different actions are required in each different circumstance to get the results that are needed, efforts to improve can become more predictable.

We sense a new readiness to improve education research. Although there are still hundreds of descriptive studies being done where researchers correlate results with various school characteristics that are not necessarily causal, change may be afoot. Many federal K–12 grant programs now demand research that is based on randomized controlled trials. These trials—or "double blind" studies—are a significant step forward. Trials of this sort have made significant advances in such fields as medicine and welfare policy, but by no means does doing trials complete the research cycle—in education or medical research, for that matter. The result of most randomized controlled trials is that only a portion of those who receive the intervention in question respond favorably to it. If that percentage is high enough and the downsides are low enough, it gains traction. The fact that some portion of the people receiving the intervention do not respond is treated as probabilistic noise from which statistically significant signals of efficacy must be isolated. As a result, little is learned from the trial beyond the probabilistic profile of side effects and the proportion of people for whom the prescription is effective.

In other words, most clinical trials, by design, keep therapy safely on the descriptive side of the research pyramids. To move this forward one more step, the research community, foundations, and policymakers must frame these randomized controlled trials as an interwoven part of the research process rather than simply "tests" that occur at the end of the process. When some people respond to a program while others with the same symptom do not, it is evidence that there's more going on than meets the eye—there is an anomaly. Either multiple underlying conditions share the same symptom—as is the case with reading difficulties, for example—or there may be genetically or environmentally based differences in the people with the same underlying condition—or both. Regardless, the anomaly should be an invitation to explore what is different about those who respond versus those who do not in order to advance us further along the continuum toward prescriptive theories.[13]

Meredith I. Honig wrote about the deficiencies in education research in her new book, *New Directions in Education Policy Implementation: Confronting Complexity.* She says that some education research is targeted to helping educators and administrators take predictably successful actions that are appropriate for their situation. But most is not. If one looks at the state of education research optimistically, she says, we see that some policies get implemented and are "successful some of the places some of the time. . . . The essential implementation question then becomes not simply 'what's implementable and what works,' but what is implementable and what works for whom, where, when, and why?"[14]

❖ WHAT MAKES STATEMENTS FROM RESEARCH VALID?

How do we know when to *trust* a statement backed by research? There are three measures. We call the first metric the statement's *reliability.* For this measure, increasing the sample size as much as possible matters so that one can minimize the probability that the measured correlation isn't zero to be sure the observed relationships aren't a statistical fluke. The second measure is *internal validity*. An internally valid study is one in which the conclusions logically derive from the premises and where there are no other plausible explanations for the measured correlations.

The third metric of trust is *external validity*. External validity is *not* established with large data sets and measures of statistical significance. Rather, it is built when researchers have defined the complete set of situations or circumstances in which people might find themselves with respect to the outcomes of interest. It is only when the categories of situations have been defined in a collectively exhaustive and mutually exclusive way that we can say with confidence, "I'm in *this* situation, and I need to do it *this* way to be successful. But when I find myself in *that* circumstance, the same approach won't work. I've got to do it *that* way." External validity comes from getting the categories right—something the prevailing education research paradigm tends to ignore.

When the unit of analysis is a group of schools, the researcher can be specific only about the entire population of schools. Some administrators will find that following the formula that works best on average for the group works best in their situation as well, but sometimes the action that is optimal on average will not yield the best outcome in a specific situation. Jared Diamond had his own way of saying this in *Guns, Germs, and Steel*: "Before you read a whole book examining environmental effects on a very large scale—effects on human societies around the world for the last 13,000 years—you might reasonably want assurance, from smaller tests, that such effects really are significant."[15] Similarly, you might want to see whether one approach, like that of KIPP (Knowledge Is Power Program) schools, works at all for a particular kind of student. And then you might want to see how it works in a few other circumstances for a few more children before trusting another mountain of data.

As we'll see in Chapter 9, understanding what category one is in is key to determining how one should act to obtain the desired results. Many policymakers, administrators, and reformers often take actions that are inappropriate for their particular circumstance. The resulting failures could have been predicted if those who did the research—or, in many cases, those who wrote about the research in the press—from which these reforms were conceived had defined the categories or situations in which the recommended actions would be effective.

NOTES

1. There is a host of articles that criticize education research from vantage points different from ours. For example, several scholars point out that these research studies are often too narrowly focused on pedagogical or curricular factors with no reference to the underlying culture and its effects. See M. Fullan, *Change Forces: The Sequel* (London: Routledge, 1999). Seymour Sarason, *The Predictable Failure of Educational Reform* (Hoboken, New Jersey: Jossey-Bass, 1990).

2. There are many views of what theory is and how it is best built and taught. The model we offer here is a synthesis of what several other scholars have written about how valid and reliable theory can be built. Though there are other useful models of theory-building, the particular model we employ here has proven to be helpful to us and many students and colleagues as we have collectively conducted theory-building research, evaluated the work of others, trained our students, and designed and taught our courses. The scholars whose models of theory-building are synthesized here include Thomas Kuhn, *The Structure of Scientific Revolutions*, 1st ed. (Chicago: University of Chicago Press, 1962) and Karl Popper, *The Logic of Scientific Discovery* (London: Routledge, 1959) in the natural sciences; and D. T. Campbell and J. C. Stanley, *Experimental and Quasi-Experimental Designs for Research* (Chicago: Rand McNally, 1963); A. Kaplan, *The Conduct of Inquiry: Methodology for Behavioral Science* (San Francisco: Chandler, 1964); B. Glaser and A. Strauss, *The Discovery of Grounded Theory* (Chicago: Aldine, 1967); Arthur L. Stinchcombe, *Constructing Social Theories* (New York: Harcourt, 1968); F. J. Roethlisberger, *The Elusive Phenomena: An Autobiographical Account of My Work in the Field of Organizational Behavior at the Harvard Business School* (Cambridge, Massachusetts: Harvard University

Press, 1977); Herbert A. Simon, *Administrative Behavior: A Study of Decision-Making Processes in Administrative Organizations* (New York: Free Press, 1976); R. Yin, *Case Study Research: Design and Methods* (Beverly Hills, California: Sage, 1984); Robert S. Kaplan, "The Role for Empirical Research in Management Accounting," *Accounting, Organizations and Society*, vol. 11, nos. 4–5, 1986, pp. 429–452; Karl E. Weick, "Theory Construction as Disciplined Imagination," *Academy of Management Review*, vol. 14, no. 4, October 1989, pp. 516–531; K. M. Eisenhardt, "Building Theories from Case Study Research," *Academy of Management Review*, vol. 14, no. 4, October 1989, pp. 532–550; and Marshall Scott Poole, Andrew H. Van de Ven, and Kevin Dooley, *Organizational Change and Innovation Processes: Theory and Methods for Research* (New York: Oxford University Press, 2000), in the study of management and social science. To this synthesis we have added our own observations, derived from studying various doctoral students' research efforts at Harvard, MIT, Stanford, and the University of Michigan. Our purpose in these few pages is simply to suggest that education researchers historically have drawn upon a very limited source and that much can be gained from viewing inductive and deductive processes as interdependent, holistic activities in building bodies of understanding.

3. There actually has been only primitive work done on generating a sophisticated taxonomy of schools to this point; Mark Van Ryzin at the University of Minnesota has recently undertaken a study to create such a taxonomy. The purpose of his study is to find an empirically derived taxonomy so that there can be a much richer classification scheme for schools by drilling past the typological descriptors such as "traditional" or "progressive" and capturing the key structural and operational differences that may be related to student outcomes. Having identified the preliminary variables, this research is now headed to the field phase. It's online at http://taxonomy .pbwiki.com.

4. Henry Braun, Frank Jenkins, Wendy Grigg, and William Tirre, *Comparing Private Schools and Public Schools Using Hierarchical Linear Modeling*, U.S. Department of Education, National Center for Education Statistics, July 2006, http://nces.ed.gov/nationsreportcard//pdf/studies/2006461.pdf.

5. See Braun et al., *Comparing Private Schools and Public Schools*.

These sorts of studies are typical for the field. Another one came out in June 2007 when New York City Mayor Bloomberg's administration reported that the 47 small schools converted from larger ones since 2002 had a graduation rate of 73 percent, compared with a district high school average of 60 percent. Mayor Bloomberg and Superintendent Joel Klein hailed the percentages as proof that small school do better. Some, however, made the point that these schools tended to enroll fewer special education students or those with limited English ability. Julie Bosman, "Small Schools

Are Ahead in Graduation," *New York Times*, June 30, 2007, http://www
.nytimes.com/2007/06/30/nyregion/30grads.html?_r=1&oref=slogin.

6. To be more precise, according to a Charter School Leadership Council
report, of seventeen studies "that looked at a snapshot in time, nine studies
show charter students generally underperforming district schools, while
the other eight show comparable, mixed, or generally positive results for
charters." Greg Vanourek, *State of the Charter School Movement 2005: Trends,
Issues, and Indicators*, Charter School Leadership Council, May 2005, p. 14.

Another study by EdSource came up with this revelation about chartered
schools: "It all depends." It categorized chartered schools by level (ele-
mentary, middle, and high) to see if that mattered and generated a mix of con-
clusions that were still "on average" statements. Nanette Asimov, "Charter
Schools Outperform Regular Schools in Middle Grades: But Further
Study Needed to Find Out Why, Researcher Says," *San Francisco Chronicle*,
June 13, 2007, http://www.sfgate.com/cgi-bin/article.cgi?f=c/a/2007/06/13/
BAGQGQECQE1.DTL.

7. Popper, op. cit., asserts that a researcher in this phase, when the theory accurately predicted what he observed, can only state that his test or experiment
of the theory "corroborated" or "failed to disconfirm" the theory.

8. See, for example, Kuhn, op. cit., and Poole, Van de Ven, and Dooley,
op. cit.

9. As we have presented this model of theory building in various faculty seminars,
we have frequently become embroiled in esoteric discussions about whether
absolute truth exists, let alone whether we can ever discover what it is. We
have concluded from these discussions that we cannot judge the value of a
theory by whether it is "true." The best we can hope for is a body of understanding that asymptotically approaches truth. Hence, the value of a theory is
assessed by its predictive power. This is why we assert that prescriptive theory
is more advanced, and more useful, than descriptive theory is.

10. Whether this set can ever be defined in permanent, unambiguous ways is
addressed later in this chapter.

11. Bazerman has noted that one reason why the research of social science
researchers generally has had little influence on management is that most
of these researchers choose not to be prescriptive. In fact, a culture of sorts
has emerged among many social science researchers that descriptive theory
is as far as they should go. Bazerman shows that not only is it possible to
develop prescriptive theory in the social sciences, but it is desirable. M. H.
Bazerman, "Conducting Influential Research: The Need for Prescriptive
Implications," *Academy of Management Review*, vol. 30, no. 1, January 2005,
pp. 25–31. Ferraro, Pfeffer, and Sutton seem to agree that prescriptive
social science theories *can* profoundly influence behavior—sometimes in
self-fulfilling ways. See F. Ferraro, J. Pfeffer, and R. I. Sutton, "Economics

Language and Assumptions: How Theory Can Become Self-Fulfilling," *Academy of Management Review*, vol. 30, no. 1, 2005, pp. 8–24.

12. Brian Clegg, *A Brief History of Infinity: The Quest to Think the Unthinkable* (London: Robinson, 2003).

13. A U.S. Department of Education report details how conducting research of this sort has made significant gains in medicine and welfare policy, and how it can in education as well. One study, for example, reveals that one-on-one tutoring by qualified tutors for at-risk readers in grades 1–3 helped the average student read more proficiently than approximately 75 percent of the untutored students in the control group. Conducting research in this manner is an improvement in the education world, but it is still incomplete. While tutors broadly capture the causal mechanism of learning—tutors have a better ability to teach in a student-centric way and match a student's learning needs—this still only tells us on average what will happen when we implement a certain policy. It is still on the descriptive side of the research process depicted in Figure 8.2. Teachers and administrators need to know reliably what will happen if they implement a policy in their specific situation, not what will happen on average. We need to understand what circumstance students were in when they had a disappointing result after the tutoring. Were the tutors not as good? Did the tutors not adjust their teaching styles to match the students? Or was it something about those individual students? Understanding these outliers and revisiting the categorization scheme will improve the statement's predictability. *Identifying and Implementing Education Practices Supported by Rigorous Evidence: A User-Friendly Guide*, U.S. Department of Education, December 2003.

Another study in the military showed that the average tutored student's achievement is better than 98 percent of classroom students, according to Michael Parmentier, the former head of Readiness and Training Policy Programs at the office of the Secretary of Defense, Advanced Distributed Learning briefing, Spring 2000.

Also see Clayton M. Christensen, Jerome H. Grossman, and Jason Hwang, *The Innovator's Prescription: A Disruptive Solution for Health Care* (New York: McGraw-Hill, 2009), ch. 8, in which the authors discuss how the clinical trials process must change for pharmaceuticals. Part of this paragraph is paraphrased and adapted from a section in that chapter. In addition, the authors include a diagram in the appendix to the chapter that provides a suggestion for how the clinical trial process should look by focusing on the "Worse Responders" to a given treatment—and advancing past randomized controlled trials to enriched trials. We've replicated the diagram here because of its parallels to improving education research as a suggestion for those involved in the field who conduct or use education research.

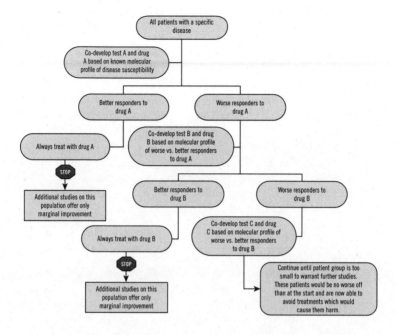

All patients with a specific disease

Co-develop test A and drug A based on known molecular profile of disease susceptibility

Better responders to drug A

Worse responders to drug A

Always treat with drug A

Co-develop test B and drug B based on molecular profile of worse vs. better responders to drug A

STOP

Additional studies on this population offer only marginal improvement

Better responders to drug B

Worse responders to drug B

Always treat with drug B

Co-develop test C and drug C based on molecular profile of worse vs. better responders to drug B

STOP

Additional studies on this population offer only marginal improvement

Continue until patient group is too small to warrant further studies. These patients would be no worse off than at the start and are now able to avoid treatments which would cause them harm.

14. Meredith I. Honig, ed. *New Directions in Education Policy Implementation: Confronting Complexity* (New York: State University of New York Press, August 2006), p. 2.
15. Jared Diamond, *Guns, Germs, and Steel: The Fates of Human Societies* (New York: W. W. Norton, 2005), pp. 54–55.

Chapter 9

Organizing to Innovate

Stephanie's hectic yet typical day of alternating between exhilaration and disappointment continues into the final class period when her secretary comes in with a note. Stephanie, on the phone with the principal of Matthew Keys about a transfer, glances at it: Second-string soccer forward Doug Kim's misbehavior has put his athletic eligibility up in the air again. She sighs. Doug's problems aren't just academic: they start at home. Sadly, Maria Solomon does not a school make.

She ends the conversation with the other principal as quickly as she can and calls Gladys, "Can you ask Doug to come to my office after soccer practice? I should be able to meet him right after the PTA meeting."

Allston looks at the clock and groans. It's going to be a long evening. "I am neither a parent nor a teacher. Discuss," Allston mutters to herself, as she imagines the issues that will be raised in the meeting—worried that neither the parents nor the teachers trust her yet.

At 5:30, when she walks into the spacious but grimy band room where the meeting is held, Patty Burkins is already there, talking to a few parents and gesticulating broadly. Allston has been part of the Randall Circle community for only a brief time, but already she sees Mrs.

Burkins's power—most of the parents and many of the teachers think Burkins knows more about how the school is run than Allston does. They might even be right: Burkins's accumulated knowledge about the school spans her own four children, two of whom have already graduated—plus the foster children her family regularly hosts and enrolls in the school. If it's happened to someone at Randall, Burkins knows about it. Allston smiles at her. She can't help but admire Burkins—the woman's fierce attitude about education rivals her own. In fact, Burkins reminds Allston of her own mother.

She hasn't met most of the other parents yet. Running a quick hand over her frizzing hair, she inserts herself into a circle of parents. "I'm Stephanie Allston, the new principal," she says brightly, and the parents introduce themselves.

"Barbara Solomon," says a black woman with Maria's face. Stephanie refrains from telling her what a pleasure her child is in front of all these other parents—she knows too well the backbiting that could lead to later. She grips the woman's hand firmly and turns to the man beside her.

"Ralph James," the man says. "My wife couldn't make it tonight, but welcome to the school, Dr. Allston."

As more parents stream in, Allston expertly wends her way into different groups, flashing her signature smile and offering her firm handshake. Her superiors often comment on her poise and bearing, but she knows that after her opening speech, her excellent schmoozing skills may not matter. She's here to deliver some unpleasant truths. The crowd's rumble begins to die down, and Patty Burkins beckons her to the front of the room.

"I think we're ready," she says into the microphone. "Another great year! Let's hear it for Randall Circle!"

The parents laugh, but clap enthusiastically. Burkins is a cheerleader, but they love her for it. They live in fear of her last child graduating: who will have this much enthusiasm then?

"I'm so happy to have our new principal here today. Thank you all for coming. I know Dr. Allston is excited to see you all!" And with that, she hands the microphone to Allston. Stephanie, standing there, remembers her days of high school debate. She has spoken at educational conferences and national universities, but this might be the most terrifying audience she's ever seen.

"Thanks, Patty." She pauses to brush the hair out of her eyes again. "I'm so pleased to be here and to be pursuing excellence for Randall Circle with all of you on my side. I look forward to talking with you about what the PTA can do this year.

"I want to talk about the biggest challenge facing Randall Circle right now: standards. I came to Randall Circle because it needs to take a new direction. That said, I want to add that I took this job because I believe the school can find a new path.

"Our school is tremendously diverse—we have kids from well-off families, but we also have many on the free and reduced lunch program. Over 50 percent of our students are not reading at grade level. We also have champion tennis players, Physics Olympiad winners, and a few kids who were arrested last week when the police found the beginnings of their makeshift meth lab. There's a lot going on here. So how do we meet the needs of all these kids, in one school, at once?"

Almost immediately, Ralph James shoots a hand into the air.

"How do we track kids by learning styles?" he asks. "My kid is smart, but he doesn't always do well with the traditional style of teaching."

"But teachers can't tailor everything to each student," Carlos Alvera immediately protests. "I have 120 students—and they all learn differently. The students just have to do the best they can, and no offense, Mr. James, but that attitude starts at home."

Barbara Solomon cuts in. "What can parents do to help the situation? We're all in different income brackets. We have different jobs. I went to this school 25 years ago, and my daughter does well here—but she does well because she's got certain tools at her disposal. What about the kids whose interests aren't being met here? Even my daughter— she often wants things that Randall doesn't have, and I bet she'd be a lot happier if there were a better writing program after school. Or what about expanding the art classes? If the kids were coming to school for things they were excited about—"

"Where's the money for that going to come from?" another parent asks.

"I didn't mean to launch a free-for-all here," Allston says, realizing her mistake too late. As the parents burst into argument, she fights the desire to put her head in her hands. That won't help Randall Circle. But what would?

An hour later, when the meeting ends, Stephanie heads back to her office. She has half an hour to figure out what to say to Doug, who had been caught vandalizing the fourth-floor lockers. He's such a nice kid, normally, that she knows that something else might be going on. And his attendance lately has put him right on the border of eligibility anyway. In just a day, Rob and Doug have switched fortunes—and all over a can of black paint. She doesn't regret allowing him that one final practice today.

Allston thinks back to the boot camp she'd gone to during the summer. When she was there, she'd met some fellow principals who were alumni of the Knowledge is Power Program (KIPP). The educators, who had come from Houston and New York, offered interesting ideas that spoke to the bigger advantages of chartered schools. At KIPP, they explicitly told kids that they were expected to follow strategies to help them learn—they taught kids how to pay attention, especially kids like Doug, who is falling through the cracks because his financially struggling parents haven't been able to spend the time with him that his peers' parents have spent with them. Knowing what she knows about Doug Kim's parents, Allston wishes she could keep him in school all day, watch him eat breakfast, holler at him herself to pay attention. She's seen Doug in class a couple of times—he's perfected the art of appearing to take notes, but unlike most of his teachers, she knows he's not. He's doodling. Fantastic, elaborate doodles. That first glimpse of his notebook had horrified her—how long had he been getting away with this? But she had also instantly known he was talented. Maybe Doug belongs in a school with more unconventional programming—more art, more creative kinds of writing, more music. Too bad Randall Circle doesn't have the infrastructure or funding for that stuff. If he had the right kind of attention—and he's such a good-spirited, distractible kid. In fact, when he arrives at her office door, blithely unconcerned, he's singing to himself.

"I heaaaaaaard it through the grapevine," he hums. "Hi, Dr. Allston."

"Come on in," she says.

He sits before she asks him to and looks at her smiling. With some effort, she manages not to smile back. His spiky hair is threaded with blue—a new addition since his last visit—and freshly wet from a post-practice shower.

"Doug, the paint is really a new step. Do you realize that vandalizing school property is an automatic five-day suspension?"

His face falls. "It was just for a team prank."

"Doug, no one else on the team did anything."

He's silent.

"What's your mother's number?" She picks up the receiver near her desk.

"Mom's at work, Dr. Allston. Evening shift. Don't need to bother her. I'll clean it up or pay for it or whatever." Doug's words speed into each other.

"Douglas Kim. This isn't about money, not really. And how much do you think that costs? Between the janitors and the new paint and the number of lockers you defaced, it's going to be easily $800."

Doug's mouth falls open a little. He mutters an expletive, which Allston chooses to ignore. He's in enough trouble.

"Either you can call your parents, or I call the cops."

There are days when she hates her job. In another school, at another time, she might be telling Doug Kim that he'd won an art award. Instead, she hands him the phone. Slowly, reluctantly, he dials. Rob James doesn't know it, but Doug's days of threatening his place as first-string forward are coming to an end.

■ ■ ■

Stephanie Allston is in a frustrating and familiar position: She sees a problem and knows there are some proven solutions for it. But within the constraints of her school, she can't implement those solutions. As we saw earlier, Allston had gotten some things done within the structure that was Randall Circle. She had made it more customizable by introducing online courses so that students could take classes they otherwise could not have. But student-centric computer-based learning can't touch many of the problems plaguing Randall Circle and its students. Some students' home environments were screaming for a very different sort of school—maybe a chartered school like KIPP—one that is structured to impart learning and life skills, not just content. But constrained by rigid rules, straitjacket budgets, and disparate opinions, she cannot bring a pervasive solution to problems like Doug's. The most she can hope for is to help one child at a time.

Why do solutions that transform one organization prove impossible to implement in another? Rarely is the root cause that employees in one institution are eager to improve and solve problems, whereas those in the other passively embrace mediocrity. Most often it relates to the willingness or ability of the managers in the different organizations to create organizational structures that enable new solutions to be formulated and implemented successfully. A crucial skill of managers is to change the organization's structure in ways that fit the problems to be solved.

THE SOUL OF AN ORGANIZATION

An incident in Tracy Kidder's Pulitzer Prize–winning book, *The Soul of a New Machine*, illustrates well how an organization's structure affects its ability to innovate. In the late 1970s, a Boston-area start-up company called Data General engaged in a competition to beat the industry leader, Digital Equipment Corporation (DEC), in designing a next-generation minicomputer. Tom West, one of Data General's employees, headed the project to beat DEC.

DEC had already launched its new minicomputer, so Data General had to play catch-up. By working long hours in a marathon effort, West's team finished designing its new product in record time, only to have the question of how good DEC's product was continue to gnaw at them. A friend's company happened to have purchased one of these new DEC products, so the friend gave West permission to sneak into his facility to take the DEC machine apart—to assess not just what the machine could do, but how it did it.

With the tension of Cold War-esque espionage filling the air, West unscrewed and lifted the cover off the DEC machine to scrutinize its internal architecture. As West looked through the machine, he could see that DEC had not in fact won the competition—Data General had engineered a much more performance-efficient, cost-effective design. "Looking into the [minicomputer], West had imagined he saw a diagram of DEC's corporate organization," Kidder remarked.[1] The way DEC's different engineering departments were organized determined the components it could and could not produce. The structure of DEC's organization had essentially dictated, and therefore handicapped, the design of its computer.

DEC had gone through a transition every organization experiences. A small team interactively designed its early products, as all members contributed to the specifications of each component and subsystem. When DEC began selling its first products successfully in the market, however, it had to parcel out responsibility to design its next-generation products. DEC formed subteams, or departments, to improve each subsystem's design—from that of the data storage system, to the logic circuitry, to the operating system, and so on. Engineers established rules or interface standards to define how each department's work would fit together with the subsystems that other departments were designing. In other words, the product's architecture drove the way the organization chart came to be configured—what the groups were, what their responsibilities would be, and how they would interact.

As the employees in these departments worked generation after generation to improve their respective pieces of DEC's computers, their subsystem expertise deepened because this was a task that they successfully addressed over and over again. But their abilities to reconfigure completely how the pieces of the computer could interact in a novel architecture atrophied because defining what the components and subsystems of the computer should be and how they would fit together was a task that the organization tackled only at its inception. Over time, as a result, the relationship between the design of the organization and its products turned on its head. The structure of the organization now determined the architecture of its products.

This change in the direction of causality occurs in every successful organization. When the task simply is to improve individual components, the organizational structure facilitates these improvements. But when the company's product needs to be fundamentally reconfigured to escape the trap described above, the organization's structure itself must be reconfigured to facilitate new patterns of groups working together.

❖ A MODEL OF ORGANIZATIONAL DESIGN

Those engaged in innovation confront four categories of problems. For each type, they need a different organization structure to address it successfully, as depicted in Figure 9.1. This diagram maps the nature of change vertically—from component-level problems at the bottom, to architectural and business model problems at the top.

The simplest category of improvement is called a *functional*, or departmental, problem. This type of problem occurs within components of a product or individual steps in a process.[2] Because the work is self-contained within each component, the work can be self-contained within each department. Interacting with other departments is not necessary to solve this sort of problem because the way each department's component must interface with the other departments' components does not change.

To visualize this problem type, imagine how you would design an improved personal computer at Dell. Its architecture is standardized.[3] This means that what the components are, and the specifications by which each interacts with each of the other components, are codified in great detail in industry standards. They are so detailed that the teams working on the improvements do not even need to work in the same *company*! Intel improves the microprocessor; Microsoft upgrades its operating system; Seagate adds gigabytes to its disk drives; Samsung adds megabytes to its DRAM chips; and so on. The thoroughly codified interface specifications obviate active coordination between these independently functioning organizations.

The type of team that works best with this sort of problem is a *functional team*, which we depict in the bottom-right corner of Figure 9.1. Managers tend to create functional groups around business disciplines like finance, marketing, manufacturing, engineering, and so on. Often they then subdivide these broad disciplines by specialized expertise, such as electrical, mechanical, and software in an engineering organization or cost accounting, budgeting, accounts payable, payroll, credit,

FIGURE 9.1 Relationships between the type of task and the type of organization

Dots in the diagrams represent members of the team; solid lines represent lines of authority and responsibility. Dotted lines represent lines of communication.

Level of change	Product Project	Process Project	Team Type
Context	*Business model* in which product is used	*Business model* in which process is used	Autonomous
	Product *architecture:* What are the components, and which ones interface with others?	Process *architecture:* What are the steps in the process, and what is their sequence?	Heavyweight
	Change the specifications for *how components must fit* together	How must the steps in the process *interface* in time and space?	Lightweight
Component	Improve performance of each *component*	Improve *individual steps* in the process	Functional

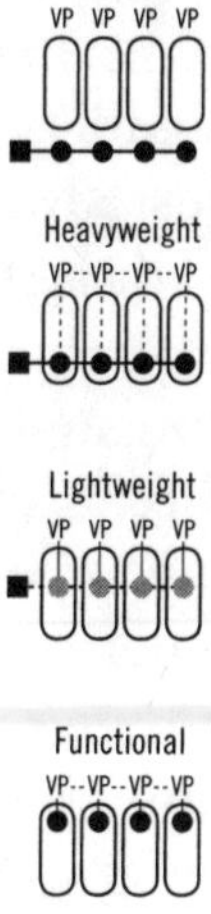

and collections in an accounting organization. Detailed specifications define what each functional group is supposed to do
and how each group's work must fit together with the other
groups' work. When people can specify this in advance and
there are no interdependencies, the groups can work independently and efficiently—with little coordinative overhead cost.

Sometimes a group decides to make improvements that will
affect how another group needs to do its job. When there is
predictable interdependence between groups, managers need
to organize a *lightweight team* to handle the project. We call
managers in lightweight teams coordinative or lightweight
managers—not because they have limited intellectual capacity,
but because of the nature of their responsibilities. Lightweight
managers shuttle back and forth among the units doing the
project to ensure that their work fits together temporally and
functionally. We depict their coordinative role in Figure 9.1
as a dotted line connecting the manager with team members.
The functional departments, however, retain primary responsibility for the work, as the solid vertical line in the diagram
shows. The mindset of team members is that the purpose of
their membership on the team is to represent the abilities and
interests of their departments. Most "matrixed" organizations
are coordinative and lightweight in character.

Improving components within a given product architecture typically results in incremental improvements. When
a significant or breakthrough improvement is required,
almost always the basic architecture of the product needs to
be rethought. When the architecture of a product or process
needs to change—which entails combining, eliminating, or
adding new components or requiring that components assume
different roles in the product's performance—the components
and people responsible for them need to interact with one
another in new ways that cannot be anticipated or specified
in advance. Resolving these unpredictable interdependencies
often means people must trade off one department's interests
in favor of another's to achieve an optimal level of system per-

formance. To address these challenges, organizations must create *heavyweight teams*. This structure enables its members to transcend the boundaries of their functional organizations and interact in different ways. To be effective, members of heavyweight teams often must co-locate, and a manager with significant clout must lead the team. Members bring their functional *expertise* with them as they join the heavyweight team, but their mindset must never be to "represent" the interests of their department during the team's deliberations. Rather, they think of themselves as having collective responsibility to figure out a better way to knit things together to meet the overall project's goals.

Heavyweight teams are tools to facilitate the new ways of working together that are required to generate new product architectures. In contrast, lightweight and functional teams are tools to exploit existing patterns of responsibility that match the existing architecture.

The fourth type of team is an *autonomous business unit*. Autonomous units are critical when, instead of innovating to create new products and processes, managers are tackling a disruptive business model innovation. A project is disruptive if the mechanism for making money in the new effort is incompatible with the profit formula by which established business units prosper. An autonomous team is a tool to create a new economic model that can profitably serve the new market; a classic example of this was Dayton-Hudson's decision to create an autonomous team called Target to enable the corporation to survive the disruption of department stores by discount retail. We gave other examples of this in Chapter 3. Figure 9.1 depicts this team as being totally independent of the mainstream departmental structure of the company—in commercial as well as technical dimensions.

Toyota's Teams

Historically, Toyota has provided a great example of the power of using the right team for the right purpose. Toyota designs its cars in functional teams. It can do this because its engineers have painstakingly detailed the required performance standards for each component in each car model. They also have specified how to manufacture each component to be assured of meeting those performance standards as well as of how each must interface, or fit, with each of the other components. These detailed specifications minimize the problems of coordinating among all the engineers and manufacturing workers. Everyone knows what he or she needs to do and how it fits with what the others are doing. This has enabled Toyota to design improved models of its cars quickly and cost-effectively with little coordinative overhead—an extraordinary capability for products of such complexity.

When Toyota developed its Prius hybrid car, however, it could not use functional teams because the hybrid entailed a completely different architecture. New components had to be developed that interfaced with other new components in novel ways. The internal combustion engine had to coordinate propulsion responsibility with an electric motor. The brakes didn't just slow the car; they needed to generate electricity. This, in turn, completely changed the role the battery plays in the system. With the components performing nontraditional functions, the engineers needed to find alternative ways of integrating them into a coherent whole.

To solve these problems, Toyota pulled key people from each department and put them together in a completely different location to serve as a heavyweight team. Although they brought their functional expertise to the team, their role was *not* to represent the interests or needs of their respective departments. It was to use their expertise to help generate a newly coherent product—an elegant machine. In contrast, most of Toyota's competitors designed their hybrid cars in lightweight teams. Their cars simply have not performed as well as the Prius—a fact that is reflected in Toyota's dominant share of the hybrid car market.

Toyota kept its heavyweight team intact for the second generation Prius just to refine the architecture and ensure that it knew how the pieces of the system worked with one another. But once its engineers sufficiently understood this, they codified how to make each component and how each component must interface with all other affected components so that they were able to design the third-generation Prius in a functional team, where the coordinative overhead could be minimized.

Have you ever wondered why so many employees complain about having to work in departmental silos—and why, if it is so miserable, their sadistic managers compel them to work in silos? Employees do not complain about working in silos when they can resolve the issues with which they are dealing by using established processes within their departments. But when managers mandate creating a new architecture for a product or a process and then expect their people to achieve this from within the confines of their departmental units, team members become encumbered with functional details before they resolve system-level choices. Their work is overtaken by turf wars, coordinative headaches, and painful compromises that frustrate them, their bosses, and their customers.

❖ INNOVATION AND ORGANIZATIONAL STRUCTURES IN PUBLIC SCHOOLS

The impact that structure has on the ability to innovate lies at the root of many of public schools' struggles to improve. Like most organizations, the structure of public schools mirrors the architecture of their products. High schools are organized in English, science, math, social studies, and foreign language departments because they offer courses in those categories.[4] The faculty members in each department make up functional teams. If the science department introduces a new chemistry lab experiment, it does not need to coordinate the activity across departments. It simply makes the change within the courses it controls. Activities such as these are part of the daily routine in schools. Likewise, teams organized by grades serve as functional teams in elementary schools.

A typical school has a few lightweight teams. In a high school, the department heads often form lightweight teams to coordinate activities across the various subject areas. Similarly, if fourth grade teachers decide to teach long division in a new way, a lightweight coordinative team could identify and agree upon what subsequent changes this would require in the fifth-grade math curriculum.

The problem arises when improvement requires a fundamentally different architecture, and yet administrators and regulators establish committees and task forces to address the job but do not allow the teachers to use heavyweight teams. When the task of rearchitecting is given to teams of teachers who work within their departments, the projects are characterized by endless debates, grudging compromises, and little change.

Heavyweight Teams in Education

How can districts set up heavyweight teams? They can take several forms, but chartered schools and pilot schools—now emerging with a variety of names in districts from Baltimore to New York to Los Angeles—are among the most common.

Chartered schools can constitute heavyweight teams. As we approached the study of education through the lenses of our research on innovation, our instinct was to frame chartered schools as disruptive innovations, but upon reflection that was not correct. Most chartered schools are *sustaining* innovations, in that their intent is to do a better job educating the same students that districts educate. But chartering legislation gives innovative educators the freedom to step outside the departmental structure of the district schools and enroll the faculty of the chartered school as members of a heavyweight team with the flexibility to create new architectures for learning— architectures for learning that *could* be developed in our regular public school districts if *and only if* they were also willing to create heavyweight teams.

We have found it useful to divide the architectural innovations of most successful chartered schools into two categories, which are not mutually exclusive. The first comprises new architectures through which subject matter is learned. The second has focused on integrating beyond the normal school day and curriculum to address the factors that influence the behavior and other needs of particular categories of students.[5]

Academic Architectural Innovations

Integrating online delivery of content in student-centric ways can entail academic architectural change whose implementation can be done effectively only through a heavyweight team. Other academic architectural changes will entail learning some subjects, such as mathematics, in the context of such other subjects as economics, chemistry, and physics. Combining the study of history and literature into a single course in which each discipline is used to examine the other is another example of an academic architectural innovation.

One form of academic architectural change that has gained some traction has been that of using a heavyweight team in education to create project-based learning schools, epitomized by the Metropolitan School (The Met) in Providence, Rhode Island. The Met, which is the original of the Big Picture learning schools, is not organized by subject departments. Rather, the school places students in real-world internships and lets them do projects of their choice. Instead of teachers, the Met employs advisors who help the students learn and integrate in the context of their project all of the math, literacy, and other traditional skills and content required to succeed in their projects. The Met's architecture integrates learning into projects that help the students feel successful while they learn—the key job that the students need to do every day, as noted in Chapter 7.

High Tech High in San Diego is an example of another chartered school whose focus is on an innovative academic architecture through project-based learning. Its use of technology is distinctively *not* layered over traditional practices. Rather, technology, as its chief executive Larry Rosenstock says, is "to allow school to be like the students' real world." He continues, "Sure, technology is all over the place here. But it's for production—not consumption. We actually have kids here who've received patents over the past couple of years."[6]

Rosenstock was careful to assemble a team of teachers interested in stimulating students to assume responsibility for their own learning. The teachers are more like coaches and lecture rarely. They help, guide, and evaluate. Indeed, having decided that there was no reliable correlation between teaching credentials and teaching competence in this context, Rosenstock received permission from California to run a school of education, along with the high school. This has resulted in an approach that is "team taught, group learned, and assessed experientially": If students are building a hovercraft, does it get off the ground?

Learning through video games has been an area that has excited some educators for some time. At one level, video games are nettlesome things about which parents love to complain. Video games, however, if used for good ends, can teach our children so-called twenty-first–century skills like problem solving, decision making, hypothesizing, and strategizing. They can also be used to teach the underlying principles of mathematics or engage students in reading. And what's more, if done properly, children love playing them. A whole literature has arisen about this "serious games" movement, and more and more video game designers and programmers are designing fun games that have educational value. Marc Prensky has written prolifically on this topic. Three of his most recent books are *Digital Game-Based Learning*, *Don't Bother Me Mom—I'm Learning!*, and *Games and Simulations in Online Learning*. James Paul Gee, a professor at Arizona State University, has also written extensively on the topic. His books include *What Video Games Have to Teach Us about Learning and Literacy* and *Good Video Games and Good Learning: Collected Essays*. Gee's research has pioneered some exciting educational game breakthroughs.

There is much to be excited about the convergence of games and learning. But this technology has, for the most part, not been a self-contained, modular, plug-and-play vehicle for improvement. As a result, many educational video games have struggled to gain traction or make meaningful change in schooling. Heavyweight teams that can rethink the curricular architecture will be a necessary tool to enable educational video games to make an entrance and have meaningful impact.

One new school in New York has done just that. Called the Quest to Learn (Q2L) school, its curriculum is based entirely on learning through games, many of which are video games. The research behind Q2L is inspired in part by Gee's research. What is new about the school—which started with 12-year-olds in the 2009–2010 school year and will keep the students until they are 18—is twofold. First, the curriculum is based on games. Second, the curriculum is dramatically different from the traditional one with the familiar English, social studies, math, and so on. Q2L's school day is divided into four 90-minute blocks for the study of domains. These domains include things like Codeworlds (which includes mathematics and English as well as HTML, as they are all code systems with their own distinct logic), Being, Space and Place (English and social studies), The Way Things Work (math and science), Sports for the Mind (game design and media arts), Wellness (socioemotional learning, physical education, health, and nutrition), and Being Me (a social networking space). Students work through missions to master the work; the missions culminate with a two-week examination called a *boss level*—a common phrase in video-game parlance—where the whole school works to solve a particular challenge. A focus of the school's curriculum is on helping students understand systems—from how to take one apart and understand everything from its discrete elements to how those elements interact with one another. Because the school is public, its students will still have to take the normal subject-matter tests, but the staff's ultimate focus is to prepare its students for the complicated world into which they will enter after graduating.[7]

Innovation in Behavioral Architecture

Other chartered schools focus on the architecture of factors that guide student behavior. Just as important as employing student-centric software to tailor learning opportunities for individual students is tailoring the structures that influence student behavior. Public schools tend to be comprehensive and target all students in a given geography, regardless of personal circumstance. But not all students bring from home the same preparation to learn. As the diversity of students has increased markedly in the past 30 years, this need for customization has only grown.

To understand this need, let's revisit the model in Chapter 8 about building good research and theory. Valid models rarely can assert that one size fits all. Rather, researchers must define the set of situations in which leaders might find themselves so that they can make circumstance-contingent "if-then" statements. If you find yourself in this situation, then you should do this. But if you're in *that* situation, don't—it won't work. Do this instead. This enables people in any given circumstance to predict the results of their actions.

The dominant school categorization scheme that society uses today is geographical: All students who live in this neighborhood should attend the nearest local school. Geographical categorization made consummate sense in the early 1900s when automobiles and mass transit systems were rare. To get children to school at all, we needed to assign them to schools within walking distance. Though this constraint is now largely gone, we continue to follow a policy whose implicit assumption is that all children within a given geographic district are best served by one type of school architecture.

When students are in primary schools, sorting them by geography perhaps is logical. One of the basic jobs for which society hires primary schools is to foster democracy by assimilating people into their communities and allowing people from all sorts of backgrounds to mix. There is value in this, not only for society but also for the children themselves.[8] But as students progress in age, geographic categorization makes less sense.[9] Test score gaps suggest that geographic sorting cannot serve the needs of different types of students. Do we really think that just because someone lives a block away from someone else they automatically have the same schooling needs? Geographic categorization suggests that we assume they do.

If school districts were to frame their task as a continuous search for the best architecture for different categories of students, it would recast how they view chartered schools. They could say, in essence, "It's okay if one type of school does not work for all students. We need different types of schools." Districts should see chartered schools as heavyweight research and development laboratories whose charter, in essence, is to help the district match a school typology with students in a given circumstance.

KIPP, Amistad, and North Star chartered schools are examples of a new school architecture that has achieved stunning success with students who come from homes where fundamental behaviors essential to learning have not been instilled. KIPP's architecture includes a system for classroom behavior called "SLANT," which instructs students to "Sit up, Listen, Ask questions, Nod, and Track the speaker with their eyes."[10] KIPP co-founder David Levin contends that most Americans learn these methods for taking in information early on and employ them instinctively. KIPP students, he says, "Need to be taught the methods explicitly." KIPP has longer school days, which are important in its architecture and likely less important in others. KIPP's structure also requires parents to make a pact with the school that entails a certain level of involvement in their child's education. KIPP will not admit children whose parents will not meet this requirement because its architecture is not designed to work for everybody—only students in the specific situation described above. A KIPP school is specifically designed to support students from a particular home background, as it integrates functions not associated with a typical school but that are necessary if the school is to educate successfully the students it serves.[11]

Critics rightly point out that KIPP's architecture is not the answer for many students—but that's the point. It is folly to accept or reject an experimental school's architecture on the basis of whether all students thrive within it. SLANT's methodology would be a waste of time for many students—and a hindrance to their learning.[12] Rather than view them as competitors that are to be isolated, district schools need to monitor the success of chartered schools so that they can define the circumstance for which each different architecture is the superior solution. This will allow administrators to direct students who are in a particular circumstance to a school that is designed to address it.

Chartered schools are only one type of heavyweight team. Districts can set up heavyweight teams within the district structure, as the Boston Public Schools district has done with its pilot schools. Schools within schools can serve this role, too. Indeed more and more districts are now responding to chartered schools not by simply fighting their creation but by creating heavyweight teams themselves. Many cities, including Baltimore, Boston, Chicago, New York, Los Angeles, and Washington, D.C., and states such as Minnesota are creating portfolios of school types under various names.

Capturing the Benefits of Chartered and Pilot Schools Systematically

Although the specifics of how and where heavyweight teams are implemented might differ, the principles that underlie them do not. Team structure is a critical weapon in the arsenal of school reformers. Architectural change cannot be achieved through a lightweight committee structure.

Viewing chartered and pilot schools—mostly aimed at reaching the underserved segment of the market—as experiments rather than competitors leads to a very different view of how to measure the impact that the experimental architecture is having.[13] Measuring school-to-school differences is a fallacious unit of analysis. Contrasting the performance of paired children from similar backgrounds, one educated in a geographically organized school and the other studying in a chartered school employing a different architecture, is the right way to measure.[14]

As school models emerge that appear to have success with certain types of students, we should study and codify what works and how that success is achieved. Charter organizations could do this themselves. Alternatively, state legislators and philanthropic organizations could commission studies so that districts could most efficiently learn from this burgeoning statewide network of R&D laboratories. We suspect that in many instances the superior performance of a chartered school will be found to be attributable simply to the fact that its teachers work harder—and that the school's out-performance recedes to the mean as those teachers burn out. In other instances, however, we suspect that enduring architectural changes will be found at the root of observed improvements.

To foster architectural innovations such as those we've highlighted above, it is absolutely critical that standards be established. *Process* standards—dictating *how* students should be taught—are anathema to innovation. But *capability* standards are critical because they give innovators a common target toward which to improve. Without such standards, the innovative energy of school improvers will dissipate.

The Difference between Heavyweight and Autonomous Teams

Rather than viewing their charge as preserving the public *schools* in their geographical jurisdiction, public school boards and superintendents should view their mission as educating well all the *students* within that area. Unfortunately it is a rare school board that views chartered schools as new vehicles for improvement. Instead, most school district leaders view them as competitive threats whose achievements must be dismissed or explained away. As a consequence, most states have found that funding for charter schools must come directly from state school budgets and cannot be distributed through district budgets—because district leaders are committed to focusing their resources on operating and improving *their* schools, even if that means starving the chartered institutions.

In this arrangement, charter schools have been positioned as competitive *autonomous* teams, in terms of Figure 9.1 above—separated organizationally from the mainstream school organization to minimize the conflicts for funding that one has on the other. As a competitor with a sustaining innovation, the start-up chartered schools have fared just as the theory of disruptive innovation would predict. First, the incumbents—the school districts and their affiliated groups—have fought tooth and nail to protect their franchise for creating and managing schools. Given the power the incumbent has in a battle of sustaining innovation, it is not surprising that the growth of chartered schools has been slow and begrudging, as they have struggled for permission to create new public schools, enroll students, and receive funds, among other legal battles. More recently, as discussed earlier, some districts are beginning to respond with sustaining innovations of their own, as they have moved to create the space for different school types. Indeed, one of the schools mentioned earlier—Quest to Learn—is a New York district school organized as a heavyweight team. As districts create the space for these new schools within their own portfolio, our theories would predict that the incumbents would by and large "win" these battles of sustaining innovation and continue to have the dominant market share. But the competition seems to be working to a limited extent, as the threat of chartered schools has prompted some districts to innovate in ways they previously have not and probably would not have.

❖ THE POLITICAL POWER TO IMPLEMENT ARCHITECTURAL CHANGE

To this point in this chapter we've focused on *what* must be done: New school architectures must be incubated within heavyweight teams such as chartered and pilot schools and "schools within schools." This frees teachers and curriculum designers from the rules and habitual interface standards that are embedded in the departmental boundaries of schools. We have also pointed to the value of considering these teams to be integral elements of our school districts rather than competitors outside of them. But knowing what must be done is just the beginning of the solution. *How* to muster the political clout to convince everyone who needs to cooperate in fact to cooperate in such initiatives is the subject of the final section of this chapter.

Our recommendations for how to accomplish what needs to be done are grounded in another model that has emerged from our research on managing innovation, called *the tools of governance*.[15] This model asserts that although leaders can use a variety of tools to get concerned parties to cooperate—tools like financial incentives, negotiations, vision statements, training, performance metrics, and even litigation—most of these tools of governance don't work most of the time. As a result, leaders often waste their credibility, energy, and resources when implementing change. The efficacy of any tools in eliciting the cooperation needed to march in a new direction depends upon two variables: the extent to which the concerned parties agree on what they want, and the extent of their agreement on how to get it. We have concluded from examining schools through this lens that democracy itself—as practiced in most school boards—is a fundamental barrier that will block implementation of many of the changes recommended in this book unless leaders deal with it correctly.

Charting the Degree of Agreement

The tools of governance model is depicted in Figure 9.2. Its vertical axis measures the extent to which the people involved agree on *what they want*—the results they seek from their participation in the enterprise; what their values and priorities are; and which trade-offs they are willing to make to achieve those results. The extent of agreement can range from none

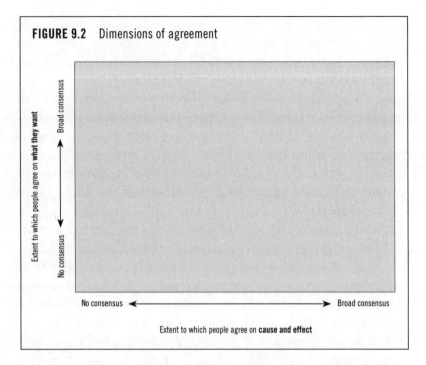

FIGURE 9.2 Dimensions of agreement

Extent to which people agree on **what they want**

Broad consensus

No consensus

No consensus ◄————————————————————► Broad consensus

Extent to which people agree on **cause and effect**

at the bottom to complete agreement at the top. The second dimension is the extent to which they agree on *cause and effect—* which actions will lead to a certain result. Strong agreement on cause and effect implies a shared view of how the world works.

Think of Figure 9.2 as a map of sorts. Leaders might find themselves anywhere on it. In the southwest extreme they are embroiled in deep disagreements among the people involved on what they want and how to get it. In the northeast extreme, all concerned parties share the same goals and similar beliefs about the methods that will yield those results. Leaders can find themselves anywhere on the map. There is no "best" location. The key is to recognize where you are. This model applies to units as small as families; to project teams, business units, and corporations; to school districts; and even to nations. The extent to which members of a group have been successful in doing what they've been chartered to do influences strongly where they are positioned on this map at any given point in time. Many groups start in the lower-left corner. But if their members succeed repeatedly in doing their work, their success tends to build consensus around what the members want and how to get it, and this shifts their position toward the northeast region of the map. As an example, when Singapore was expelled from Malaysia in 1964, the tiny impoverished nation was composed of ethnic Chinese, Indian, and Malays whose cultural traditions, family structures, and religious beliefs shared little common ground. Prime Minister Lee Kuan Yew stepped to the fore in this chaotic environment and dictated autocratically—using power tools—a set of rules by which Singaporeans would live. By following those rules, Singapore has become one of the most prosperous, modern, and safe places on earth to live. As a result, a strong set of beliefs on how to create and maintain a society such as theirs has coalesced among Singaporeans. Those rules are quite different from those that are commonly followed in western democracies, but the success has nonetheless migrated Singapore from the southwest of the diagram to the northeast.

Conversely, when members of a group that historically has been successful find their organization spiraling toward failure, the crisis unwinds consensus on both dimensions. The group begins to fracture as the scarcity of resources and opportunities causes people to begin striving for themselves at the expense of others. How to stem the decline also becomes a matter of contention rather than consensus. General Motors, at the time of the writing of this book, finds itself in this situation. Not long ago it was in the northeast portion of the map. But today there is little consensus among the company's managers, unions, suppliers, and dealers about how to resolve the company's problems.

In sum, success shifts concerned parties to the northern and eastern regions of the map. But if the formula that led to success stops working and the organization drifts into crisis, its position shifts toward the south and west.

Figure 9.3 summarizes the types of governance tools for eliciting cooperation among groups and members of groups that will be effective when wielded in organizations that are in different locations on the map. The boundaries depicted on the map that suggest what will and will not work in a given area are not rigid, but the broad labels can give leaders a sense of which tools are likely to be effective in various situations.

In the southwest region of the map, when there is little shared consensus on either dimension, the only tools that will elicit cooperation in pursuit of a new course of action are "power tools" such as fiat, coercion, threats, punishment, and decapitation—figurative and occasionally literal.

For example, the various ethnic and religious groups in the Balkan Peninsula have been positioned in the lower-left region of the map for centuries. The fighting among these groups has been so intractable and incessant that it has given a new word to the English language: Balkanization. After World War II,

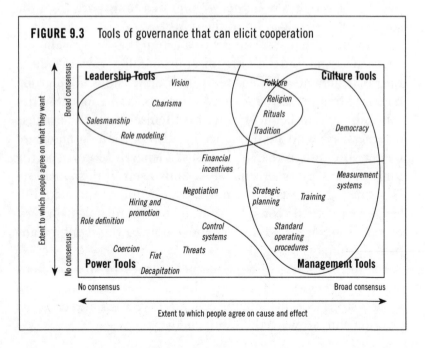

FIGURE 9.3 Tools of governance that can elicit cooperation

Marshal Tito herded these disparate groups into one more or less artificial nation called Yugoslavia and said to its citizens, in effect, "I don't care if you agree with me on what you want out of life or how to get it. I just want you to look into the barrel of this gun, and cooperate with me." It worked in a sense. Tito brought peace to the Balkans, although he did not create the shared success that migrated the country toward the northeast corner of the diagram, as happened in Singapore.

When Tito died, no one emerged with comparable capacity to wield power tools, and once again the groups became embattled in brutal, Balkanized conflict. At the time of the writing of this book, a measure of peace has been brought to the peninsula by world powers that have dismembered Tito's Yugoslavia into individual nations for each ethnic group. *Within* each nation there is substantial consensus on both dimensions of the map, even while disagreement persists across groups. If the nations that now compose the Balkan Peninsula can prosper through peaceful commercial and political interaction with one another, however, the region will shift upward and rightward, into situations where power tools are eschewed. Conflicts will then be resolvable through tools such as negotiation and, ultimately, democracy. The model asserts that the tools of negotiation and democracy could not have worked, however, in the lower-left region of the map.

Now let's employ the model to examine a company, General Electric. When Jack Welch took the helm of GE, the company was a disparate collection of businesses ranging from chemicals to lightbulbs, from jet engines to washing machines, and from financial services to semiconductors. The situation, as these business units battled one another for resources, was Balkanized. The tools that Welch used to turn the ship around were remarkably Tito-esque: He declared that these businesses would be divested if they were not number one or number two in their markets, and he fired about 250,000 people. He was known as "Neutron Jack"—and he had to be. As the company prospered under Welch's heavy hand, its location on the map shifted toward the upper right. As this happened, Welch wisely took his finger off the trigger. To elicit the needed cooperation in the company he began using management tools such as strategic planning, financial incentives, training and performance metrics, and leadership tools such as vision and role modeling.

Although management tools such as training and performance metrics worked when GE had shifted to the right portion of the map, the model suggests that they would not have been effective earlier. You can train people endlessly, for example. But in the absence of trusting agreement that doing the things you're training them to do will yield the needed results, they won't voluntarily do it. Instead you are compelled to use compulsion. Similarly, the tools that are grouped as leadership tools in Figure 9.3 work only in the upper regions of the map. People follow charismatic, visionary role models only when they want what the leader wants. People who want something different would treat the same leader with indifference, defiance, or disdain.

Now back to General Electric. As its new CEO Jeff Immelt faces the need to steer GE into new directions, power tools will not work. The GE culture has become so strong that it would expel Immelt in an instant if he tried to do what Jack Welch did in the 1980s. He faces perhaps a bigger management challenge than Welch did because when widespread agreement on how to become successful is deeply embedded in the culture of an organization, change is *very hard*. The tools of governance that now are at Immelt's disposal—things like tradition, religion, and democracy—are famous for their resistance to change and their persistence with the way things have long been done.[16]

The Tool of Separation

There is a final salient element of this model that is not captured in Figure 9.3. There are instances when there is such fundamental disagreement among the parties from whom you'd like to have cooperative behavior that it is simply impossible to reach consensus on a course of action, and yet no one has amassed the power to coerce cooperation. In such instances there is a trump card to play when all other tools have failed. We call it *separation*: dividing the conflicted parties into separate groups so that they can be in strong agreement with others inside their own group and yet don't need to agree with those in other groups. In the post-Tito Balkans, as mentioned above, no one could amass and wield the requisite power to maintain peace, as Tito had done. So we tried the charisma of Clinton and salesmanship of Blair. We tried democracy and negotiation. We used economic sanctions and incentives. Nothing worked—except separation. Peace came to the Balkans when the need for cooperation across antagonistic ethnic divides was obviated by dividing the peninsula into nations and regions for each ethnic group. The tool of separation underlies our recommendation that heavyweight or autonomous teams are required to achieve architectural innovation in schools.

❖ THE TOOLS OF GOVERNANCE FOR CHANGING SCHOOLS

Now, enough of Tito, Welch, and Immelt. What light does this model shed on schools? For the most part, public school systems are in the lower-left corner of the diagram. Teachers, taxpayers, administrators, parents, students, and politicians have divergent priorities and disagree strongly about how to improve. Recall from Chapter 2 the many jobs that society has assigned to schools—from socializing students to live in a democracy to alleviating poverty. Different stakeholders prioritize each of these differently. And all these constituent groups have different ideas of what will cause schools to improve—from more money to more computers; from better teachers to smaller class sizes; from more autonomy to less autonomy; and many more.

The fact that schools are in the lower-left world of disagreement helps us understand why certain remedies that reformers have experimented with in the past have not worked.

The model asserts, for example, that financial incentives, like pay-for-performance schemes for teachers, will not work. This tool has been used in a variety of formats in various districts over several decades. Most of these schemes have failed because their efficacy is predicated upon a modicum of agreement on what is wanted and how to get there.[17] The board of almost every school district has a vision statement and strategic plan for how to get there. But the boards find that these rarely cause their diverse constituents to line up and cooperate in pursuit of those plans. Instead, they get caught up in the conflict and compromise that are inherent in the lower-left realm of disagreement.

The sobering conclusion about this situation is that democracy—the primary tool that the law allows—is an effective tool of governance only in the upper-right circumstance, when there already is broad, preexisting consensus on what is wanted and how the world works.[18] And like religions and traditions, democracy's nature is to preserve the way things have been done, rather than change them. So is it possible that changing public schools is impossible?

We believe change is possible. We wrote this chapter, however, to warn reformers to be wise and realistic. Over and over people have tried democracy, folklore, charisma, salesmanship, measurement systems, training, negotiation, and financial incentives. All have failed. Separation works. But it takes power to wield the tool of separation.

Political and school leaders who seek fundamental school reform need to become much more comfortable amassing and wielding power because the other tools of governance will yield begrudging cooperation at best. By illustration, the elementary schools of inner-city Chattanooga, Tennessee, were failing. Superintendent Jesse Register turned to power tools and replaced all but one of the schools' principals. He made all the teachers in the school reapply for their jobs and pass a test. And although he could not actually fire the 100 teachers who did not make the cut, he managed to shift them out of the inner-city schools into the suburban Chattanooga schools where the infrastructure offered them more support. The schools turned around dramatically.[19]

School districts typically are governed by elected school boards, whose members decide what to do by majority vote after fractious debates. To gain enough votes for any proposal, however, the proposal must generally be watered down and compromised. This preempts the possibility of significant change. Not surprisingly, few school boards are capable of mounting a decisive change in school architecture and strategy.

Over the past decade or so, an increasing number of mayors, including Michael Bloomberg of New York City, Thomas Menino of Boston, and Adrian Fenty of Washington, D.C., have taken direct control of their school districts. The mayors were able to appoint a superintendent who shared their same vision, and the superintendent did not have to worry about pleasing disparate school board members who have competing visions for reform. One of the factors that has enabled recognized leaders of school reform such as New York's Chancellor Joel Klein to do what he thinks needs to be done is that, in many ways, many of the structures of democracy no longer stand in the way.[20]

❖ THE EDUCATOR'S DILEMMA

Something has to give. The old public utility model of public education struggles more each day with what society increasingly asks it to do. Other options on the outside continue to grow in number, as state laws permit public funding to support a widening variety of schools. Technology is also navigating around the traditional model and is getting more sophisticated and user-friendly.

Will districts answer the call? We see mixed signals certainly, but there are some signs of hope. Many districts are beginning to launch sustaining innovations of their own. Many others are grabbing onto the disruptive innovation of online learning to fashion new learning arrangements in their domains and tap areas of nonconsumption in their midst.

Will the districts that seize onto the online learning use it to truly change how they do business? The picture is much less clear here. If the traditional public schools can see how the circumstances have changed, they could pursue this market in ways they have so far not succeeded in doing. Even the more flexible chartered sector has not seized this option at any scale as yet.

We understand that this is not an easy transition. We look across multiple industries and find few incumbents with the vision, capacity, and will to create the organizational space through which they might succeed in managing their own disruptive innovation. They have to be willing to grant fledgling ventures considerable autonomy. They have to understand that placing a disruptive project squarely in the middle of a traditional operation likely condemns it to failure—or just to sustain what they already do. They will have to commit the right team structure. Senior management—whoever that is—will need to commit serious support. The enterprise will have to be focused on the job to be done rather than on individual educator or even group preferences.

Although better learning is the goal, states and districts cannot "enact" better learning. All they can do is to create the conditions that motivate teachers and students to do whatever it takes to get better results.

While new and different schools scramble to serve students who were never the ideal customers for the traditional public schools, most educators find themselves at an intersection of unprecedented change and necessary choices. It is their dilemma to resolve.

NOTES

1. Tracy Kidder, *The Soul of a New Machine* (New York: Avon, 1981), p. 32.
2. The model of team structure around which this section is structured was developed by Kim Clark and Steve Wheelwright of the Harvard Business

School. See Steven C. Wheelwright and Kim B. Clark, *Revolutionizing Product Development* (New York: The Free Press, 1992).

3. As discussed in Chapter 1, this standardized architecture allows for modular components within a Dell computer, which enables affordable customization.

4. These departmental structures stem from the fact that when school districts first established high schools in the mid-nineteenth century, they modeled these schools upon the small liberal arts colleges that had these same academic departments and recruited teachers trained in separate academic disciplines. Larry Cuban, *Oversold and Underused: Computers in the Classroom* (Cambridge, Massachusetts: Harvard University Press, 2001), p. 160.

5. In the language of our other theories—and as we will explain—these schools have understood the job to be done that society hires them for—educate all students—and from that understood the experiences they needed to offer to nail that job for the circumstance in which they are operating. As a result, they have integrated backward into functions and services not traditionally associated with a school so that they could nail the ultimate job, in much the same way that Henry Ford had to integrate backward and make his own steel if he wanted to be able to build reliable cars, which is discussed in Chapter 1.

6. From Larry Rosenstock remarks to a visiting delegation to High Tech High School in San Diego, California, notes by Curtis W. Johnson (October 17, 2006).

7. This information is compiled from several sources, including an interview with Robert Torres, executive director of research at Q2L and chief research officer at Mission Lab on February 16, 2010. See also http://q2l .org/ (accessed May 5, 2010, 2:50 p.m. PDT) as well as "Teaching Children Hard Stuff with Games," *The Economist* (September 3, 2009), and Jeremy Hsu, "New York Launches Public School Curriculum Based on Playing Games," *Popular Science*, September 16, 2009, http://www.popsci.com/ scitech/article/2009-09/first-public-school-based-games-set-nyc-debut.

8. A problem of course is that people self-segregate into communities with other people of similar backgrounds, so this geographical sorting does not necessarily achieve this purpose.

9. We note that there are still some geographical constraints that are significant. Students in rural areas understandably will still have to be sorted by geography, given that building multiple schools in those communities is impractical. And in urban areas, some geographic constraints remain as well. For example, as discussed in the case study "VOISE Academy: Pioneering a Blended-Learning Model in a Chicago Public High School," for students who lived in the Austin neighborhood in Chicago, Illinois, "attending schools in other neighborhoods was often not the safest or most practical option for Austin students" for cost reasons or because, in this particular case, "traveling to different neighborhoods often involved traversing gang

boundaries, which could be dangerous." See James Sloan and Katherine Mackey, "VOISE Academy: Pioneering a Blended-Learning Model in a Chicago Public High School," Innosight Institute (December 2009).

It is possible, of course, that either small schools housed in the same building or schools powered by online learning, which obviates geographical differences in learning opportunities, that operate in a flexible "community-center model" in which students from different backgrounds can have different nonacademic experiences as well may obviate some of the challenges we discuss in this section and potentially allow geographic categorizations to remain.

10. According to Professor Don Deshler of the University of Kansas, the SLANT routine was developed by Ed Ellis, who is now a professor at the University of Alabama.

11. Paul Tough, "What It Takes to Make a Student," *New York Times Magazine*, November 26, 2006, http://www.nytimes.com/2006/11/26/magazine/26tough.html?ex=1182142800&en=f88b748bf061ed7e&ei=5087.

12. Likewise, Mass2020 and others have done some significant work in illuminating the value of extended learning time for students. It is likely, however, that this is also a circumstance-based theory. Some students may need extra time for learning in school, but for others this might be a negative, because it may prevent them from partaking in enrichment activities to which they would otherwise have access.

13. This is a critical point. Sustaining innovations is vital for underserved portions of any market as opposed to unserved populations, where disruptive innovations are what is needed.

14. In some instances, even this may still be the wrong unit of analysis, since to get closest to causation, one would have to examine a student's individual experience with a class, teaching arrangement, module, or even piece of content.

15. See Clayton M. Christensen, Matt Marx, and Howard H. Stevenson, "The Tools of Cooperation and Change." *Harvard Business Review*. October 2006. For purposes of clarity in this application of the model, we have renamed these as *tools of governance*.

16. We use the term *religion* here consciously because beliefs are so strongly held in successful companies like GE or Apple that they are followed with religious zeal.

17 Richard Murnane and David K. Cohen have documented why most merit pay plans fail and only a few survive in schools in their landmark article on the subject. Their argument for why is remarkably in agreement with the theory we put forward here—that, according to Tyack and Cuban, "Murnane and Cohen argue that merit pay seldom works if its intent is to get teachers to excel, for little agreement exists among administrators and teachers about

just what effective teaching is and how to measure it. In part, the complexity of the teaching act foils merit pay. Internal strife erupts over administrators' judgments when some teachers win "outstanding" marks and others only "average" grades." Murnane and Cohen say that these plans worked only when teachers helped shape the plans and the plans did not judge actual teaching but instead gave teachers extra money for doing school-related work outside of their ordinary teaching duties. R. J. Murnane and D. K. Cohen, "Merit Pay and the Evaluation Problem: Why Most Merit Pay Plans Fail and a Few Survive." *Harvard Educational Review*, 1986. Tyack and Cuban also reference Susan Moore Johnson's work on the subject, which echoes this same theory, as it details why teachers tend to resent and reject these plans. David Tyack and Larry Cuban, *Tinkering toward Utopia* (Cambridge, MA: Harvard University Press, 1999), pp. 130-131.

18. A moment's reflection supports this assertion. Whenever the United States has tried to impose democracy in a country where there wasn't broad consensus in the population about what it wanted or how to get it without first using power tools and then created shared successes, the result has been a widespread breakdown in social order. Just witness what happened in Haiti and Nigeria. The counter examples to this are Japan and West Germany, where the United States used power tools to restore and hold order and then created shared successes that propelled the countries to democracy. In the Philippines, although the United States used power tools, the country did not enjoy the same successes that moved it toward a robust democracy. We still await the outcome of what Iraq will look like when the dust settles, but when the United States was initially hesitant to deploy power tools in the vacuum of the collapse of Saddam Hussein's government, chaos reigned. The imposition of power tools reversed much of this and restored some measure of order, and now, at the time of the writing of this book, it is unclear whether the Iraqis will enjoy enough meaningful shared successes to propel them toward the northeast corner of Figure 9.2.

In addition, the nations where fundamental regulatory changes have been implemented that have enabled rapid economic development in the last 50 years—including South Korea, Taiwan, Singapore, and Chile—were all governed by relatively honest dictators who could wield the tools of power to do what needed to be done. As those countries have prospered, consensus on the two axes increased, and they have moved in the direction of democracy.

19. The *NewsHour*'s special correspondent for education John Merrow reports on efforts to fix a group of trouble elementary schools in Tennessee. Merrow, John. "Chatanooga (sic) Elementary Schools Struggle to Improve Low Test Scores,"*The NewsHour*. June 20, 2006. http://www.pbs.org/newshour/bb/education/jan-june06/chatanooga_06-20.html.

20. Of course, Joel Klein is still responsible to the voters and therefore to democracy to some extent, albeit indirectly. Were Mayor Bloomberg to lose in a reelection bid, for example, it is likely that Klein would lose his post as well.

In addition, we do recognize that there is much value and intentionality in the American democratic process that prevents leaders from plowing through ambitious changes without broad consent from various factions after long and considered—sometimes even tedious—debate. This was the brilliance behind much of what James Madison constructed in the Constitution and what he called the "auxiliary precautions" of American government. This is consistent with the model that asserts that, as Madison knew, these tools and mechanisms of democracy were not well suited for a leader to institute rapid changes that he thought vital when there is little consensus from the associated groups on what they want or how the world works. To manage change in this circumstance, one needs to figure out how to deploy power tools.

Conclusion

Twenty-five years later, Doug Kim, Jr., is one of some 2,000 students at Allston Circle High School in southern California. The school bell now rings at 7:35 a.m. to indicate that the building will open in 10 minutes. The skinny sophomore dawdles in the parking lot. Talking to his band buddies about music class, he pulls out some sheet music and starts explaining parts of the rhythm to one friend. He knows it cold. Although some students will arrive later—depending on the personal schedule they have set for themselves with their learning coaches—this group is excited enough for the day to begin that they actually head in early. Watching them from the blue doorway, Robert James can't help but smile. These gangly teenagers are so far from his own early educational experience that he can hardly believe it, even though he's been teaching for more than a decade.

"Hi, Mr. James!" a voice calls across the parking lot. He turns to see Maria, running toward him as usual.

"Hi, Ms. Solomon," he says.

"Whew! The kids just didn't want to get going this morning," she says.

"The ones here do!" he responds.

They head inside, Maria to her classroom and Rob to his. They work in adjacent rooms, each one equipped with different technologies. Rob's music and art students, including Doug Kim and his entourage, are already starting their computers. In the next room, Maria's students are individually deciding whether to pursue foreign languages or sciences. Through the glass wall dividing their rooms, Rob sees Maria leaning over his own daughter, Sarah, pointing at the screen. This morning, over breakfast, Sarah had said that she was particularly excited about starting her personalized tutorial. Rob remembers when his friend in Japan was grateful for help practicing English. Webcam buddies are standard now, and education has become even more tailored, which has made students more enthusiastic. Like her dad, Sarah learns best through audio methods and repeated practice. Her touch on the screen stops and starts an Arabic movie, which provides grammatical breakdowns when she needs them. Across from her, her twin brother, Sam, repeats words that the program dictates, and then he writes them down.

In Rob's own classroom, Vanessa is showing Tim a program she's found that helps her read music. He'd been having trouble, too, as he repeated the same mistakes over and over again in his trumpet practice. The two had started the year at odds, but now, as the dark-haired girl leans over the football player's keyboard, Rob smiles at the intent look on Tim's face. Vanessa clicks, and the computer plays the line flawlessly. "You can set it to repeat only a certain number of times, so it's an aid instead of a crutch," she says. "You still have to learn to read it. But it'll tell you right away if you're wrong."

Tim sings the line into a microphone hooked up to the program, which duplicates his singing on a treble clef below the actual music. "You're holding the eighth note too long and starting it too late," Vanessa says, pointing.

Rob's own computer has finished booting up while he's been watching them. He navigates his latest find: last night, on the CustomLearning Network, he'd finally found shareware that answered Matt's problem with keeping the beat. If only he'd had this in college himself! Then taking up the drums wouldn't have been so hard.

These days, the "classroom"—or learning room—is kinder than it used to be. The students are together, but are also allowed to stretch themselves. "To each his own," Rob thinks. They haven't made soccer practice virtual yet, but even that might be useful. Maybe he'll run that by assistant coach Doug Kim, Sr.? And to think, he'd nearly failed chemistry.

...

Is this vision of the future far-fetched and impossible? Attempts at education reform throughout the years have yielded only grudging progress. People have tried to reform the public schools directly. Others have sought reform through chartered schools. Many have seen computers as the salvation for schools. The list goes on. And yet we return again and again to the question of why schools don't get the results for students for which we all hope. Why would this time be any different? Should we quit trying?

No. Now is exactly the wrong time to quit. To understand why, let's review the five major messages in this book.

1. Few reforms have addressed the root cause of students' inability to learn. And most attempts have not been guided by an understanding of the root reasons why the system functions as it does or how to predictably introduce innovation into it. Without this guidance, we've been destined to struggle. This also means, however, that we now have an opportunity for great progress.

2. School reformers have repeatedly tried to bash the system and confront it head-on. A major lesson from our studies of innovation is that disruptive innovation does not take root through a direct attack on the existing system. Instead, it must go around and underneath the system. This is how disruption drives affordability, accessibility, capability, and responsiveness.

3. If we acknowledge that all children learn differently, then the way schooling is currently arranged—in a monolithic batch-mode system where all students are taught the same things on the same day in the same way—won't ever allow us to educate children in customized ways. We need a modular system.

4. Some of the places with the highest potential to circumvent the system and create a new, modular education system that facilitates customization are the emerging online facilitated networks—the equivalent of the autonomous business unit we describe in Chapter 9. When the

decision-making process for what is adopted in schools is centralized, as it currently is, there are so many powerful political and other forces at play that change and customization are nearly impossible. But facilitated networks will democratize development and purchase decisions to the end users in the system—students, parents, and teachers. Smart people will do smart things if we just enable them to do so.

5. Finally, to the extent that administrators and school leaders want to implement these changes, they have to use the tools of power and separation. Using these tools is easiest in the chartered and private school sectors. This means that school committees and government officials need to view themselves as not being responsible for the specific schools that exist in their jurisdictions; rather, they are responsible for educating the children in those areas. Systemic reform requires a systemic view—one that includes all schools. If indeed the charter for educators is to eliminate poverty by leaving no child behind, the homes in which children's fundamental learning capacities are forged are critical as well.

There are many actors with divergent interests in the world of public education. They range from administrators and elected officials at the local level to those at state and federal levels; from teachers to parents and students; from philanthropists to reformers and researchers; and from corporate executives to business school professors. With the above understandings in place, what does each of these actors need to do to affect these changes?

To the leaders in the schooling system— elected officials and administrators

Use the right tools to introduce change. Don't think that for some reason you will be exempted from the rules of organizational nature. In this world of deep disagreement among the participants in school systems about what they want and even deeper disagreement about how to get it, negotiation toward radical change simply will not work. The tools of power and separation, though they seem foreign to leaders who have been schooled in consensus, are key pieces of the puzzle of education reform.

As you face budget crises and difficulty finding teachers, don't solve these problems by doing less in the existing system. Solve it by facilitating disruption. And keep the disruption as fully autonomous as possible. This is critical. It is important not to regulate disruptive innovations with the old regulatory scheme, where they won't perform as well and where we risk consigning the disruptive innovations to looking like the old system. Move away from the input-focused regulations that are appropriate for a factory-model system but inappropriate for a student-centric one—from seat time to fixed student-teacher ratios—and toward outcome-based metrics such as tying funding to individual student mastery down to the course level. If we allow time to become a variable in the system, we can hold learning as a constant so that we can pay for performance.

It is the nature of the resource allocation process to preempt resources for new initiatives in order to feed the existing system. This means that each school should have one person—and, over time, an organization reporting to that person—whose sole job is to implement online courses. This person should be different from the chief information officer or information technologies officer for the school or district. She or he should have broad autonomy and report directly to the principal or district superintendent. She or he should not have responsibilities for the rest of the instruction in the school, but instead should be free to take whatever steps are necessary to bring in online courses to help the children in the school have access to and find the classes they need. She or he also should be responsible for capturing the learning from this to make this a more robust process over time. This very well might look like a school within a school, but it will help give schools the organizational space they need to facilitate the disruption and move to student-centric learning.

Furthermore, don't kill the disruption by having online programs strip away funds from districts or compete as whole schools directly *against* the existing system. Don't place artificial limits on what students can take online or what teachers can build online either; if they need access to a class or want to create content and lessons, let them do what they need to do, what they want, and what works best for them.

To philanthropies and foundations

Help fund this disruption and create a market for this innovation. Generous people and institutions have wasted enormous amounts of resources on innovations that well-tested theories of innovation could predict would have little impact. Computers in conventional classrooms; dominant-intelligence software that assumes that all students learn similarly; pay-for-performance schemes for teachers; and descriptive research that correlates the attributes of schools or teachers with their average performance all will do little to improve schools.

Instead, fund research that helps us learn how different people learn, how to identify those differences, and how different students can best educate themselves and each other. Such investments will create inestimable and enduring value because this is the only way that learning will become intrinsically motivating to all those who need to learn. Prosperity, remember, is stripping schools of the extrinsic motivation that has driven so much of our learning in the past. Also, as school models emerge that appear to have success with certain types of students, fund studies that codify what works *and for whom* as well as how it is achieved so that districts can learn efficiently from the burgeoning statewide network of R&D laboratories known as chartered schools. Understanding the circumstances of when one school architecture works rather than another is sorely needed.

To entrepreneurs

Investing in technological platforms that will enable children to create tutorial tools for each other, help parents to create tools for their children and others' children, and make it easy for teachers to create tools for their students and for other teachers will have extraordinary impact. This is because we learn most deeply when we teach others. Funding the development of these platforms and the facilitated networks within which these learning tools can be exchanged will be financially rewarding for investors and socially rewarding for philanthropists. Remember that students, parents, and teachers are desperate to be able to diagnose and resolve their own learning problems and teaching deficiencies. These are highly motivated people who in the past have been trapped in interdependent systems that stymie custom solutions at every turn.

To teacher training colleges

Continuing to train teachers to perform in a world of monolithic, teacher-led content delivery, where the key skills are in holding students' attention to subjects that are being taught to the dominant type of learner in each subject, trains teachers for the past. Future teachers will need the skills to work one on one with different types of learners as they study in a student-centric way. The tools that teachers build and distribute in the facilitated networks of the future will play a key role in making learning student-centric. The next generation of teachers needs to learn how to build these tools for different types of learners and operate in these new environments.

To graduate schools of education

Move beyond doing descriptive research that seeks average tendencies. Study the anomalies and outliers; that is where the richest insight can be found. Only by doing so can researchers see where we don't yet understand the causal mechanism, and where we have not categorized the world by circumstance to understand why an action worked one time but not another.

Over time, what will emerge are circumstance-based statements that will help us make much better progress in the years ahead as we learn what each individual student needs, not what works on average for students in a school.

To teachers, parents, and students

When there are no courses available for a student at your school, seek them online and demand that your school accept them for credit. When a student is struggling with a concept, seek the facilitated networks that entrepreneurs are building to help locate a tutor or content online that can help that student. And when possible, create these tools yourself; don't be afraid to share them with the world. Parents should seek for their children at an early age exploration opportunities that they can do with their children at home and that are fun but that would also identify students' interests and learning interests and allow for the celebration of their uniqueness.

There is power in our communities to effect change. By disrupting the classroom as we now know it, we can break apart the fundamental obstacles with which educators, parents, and students have struggled for so many years. These technologies and organizational innovations are not threats. They are exciting opportunities to make learning intrinsically motivating, to make teaching professionally rewarding, and to transform our schools from being economic and political liabilities to sources of solutions and strength.

Index